IMAGES
of America

LANDO

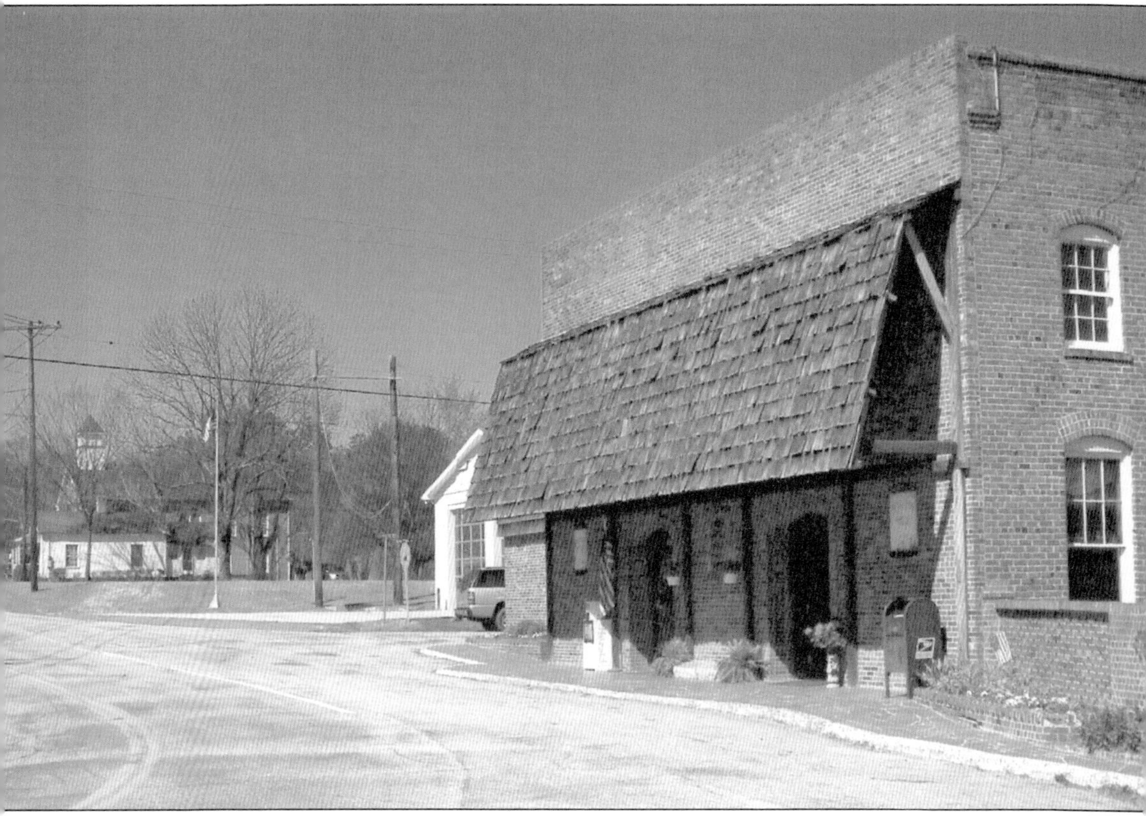

LANDO ROAD. Since 1762, people have traveled this path to do business or return home. The Manetta Mills office building, Lando Fire Department, and a mill house are at the heart of the community. (Lando–Manetta Mills History Center.)

ON THE COVER: A group of young ladies from Lando, South Carolina, enjoy the beautiful countryside along the banks of Fishing Creek. (Lando–Manetta Mills History Center.)

IMAGES
of America

LANDO

Paul Scott Williams and the
Lando–Manetta Mills History Center

ARCADIA
PUBLISHING

ISBN 978-0-7385-5268-2

Published by Arcadia Publishing
Charleston SC, Chicago IL, Portsmouth NH, San Francisco CA

Printed in the United States of America

Library of Congress Catalog Card Number: 2007926902

For all general information contact Arcadia Publishing at:
Telephone 843-853-2070
Fax 843-853-0044
E-mail sales@arcadiapublishing.com
For customer service and orders:
Toll-Free 1-888-313-2665

Visit us on the Internet at www.arcadiapublishing.com

To my family

Contents

Acknowledgments		6
Introduction		7
1.	The Land of Revolutions	9
2.	Textile Revolution	17
3.	Transportation Revolution	31
4.	Cultural Revolution	43
5.	Economic Revolution	53
6.	Mill Workers	63
7.	Lando Days	77
8.	Time Goes On	99
9.	Landmarks	113
10.	21st-Century Revolution	121

ACKNOWLEDGMENTS

This book is the combined efforts of a multitude of people. My first recognition has to go to the people that introduced me to Lando, Ollie and Bud Hefner. Ollie and Bud told me my first stories of Lando, and Bud walked with me around the community, showing me where buildings once stood and events happened. It was the permission of property owners Joe and Gayle Lanford and Lando Properties, LLC, that allowed me to deepen my research. All of my research pointed me in the direction of a Lando native, Joe Polk. Joe Polk was able to retain items from Manetta Mills and Lando because of his relationship with Allen Heath, the last president of Manetta Mills. These two gentlemen had the foresight to preserve the records and artifacts within Manetta Mills.

The creation of the Lando–Manetta Mills History Center in the former Manetta Mills office building became the center of research, documentation, and preservation of photographs, names, places, and events that centered on or occurred in Lando and Manetta Mills. The officers of the History Center, Joe Polk, Susan Murphy, Roxann James, and Bruce Coggins have been graciously helpful in the gathering and sorting of pictures and facts. John Coker, James Coker, Harold Tadlock, Marian Tomberlin, Louise Hyatt, Arthur Stewart, and Wayne Alley have provided stories and confirmation of events. All the images in this book are courtesy of the Lando–Manetta Mills History Center unless otherwise noted.

There are dozens of volunteers at the Lando–Manetta Mills History Center who have given their time, pictures, stories, and items to help create the History Center. Sylvia Jennings has been a strong supporter of the History Center, and Charles Black and Crawford Whitaker have added hours of labor and input to the book and the center. Charles Inabinet and his publication, *The Old Mill Stream*, have been valuable resources. Louise Pettus, Lindsey Pettus, and Michael Scoggins have been mentors and resources in the research process.

The strongest acknowledgments go to Joe and Gayle Lanford and Lando Properties, LLC, for their support of the Lando–Manetta Mills History Center; the board members of the Lando–Manetta Mills History Center; Allen Heath for his consistent assistance; and Ollie and Bud Hefner for introducing me to a community that now comprises my friends.

INTRODUCTION

When a person becomes a historian, they find a topic of interest and significance and start researching to validate the facts about the topic. Soon the research and topic become a passion to the historian. Michael Scoggins from the Cultural and Heritage Museums of York County has a passion for the South Carolina backcountry militia during the American Revolution. Scoggins is an expert on this topic and has created the most accurate record of the events in the South Carolina backcountry in the summer of 1780.

To become a professional historian like Michael Scoggins is an honor that few people can enjoy. I studied history at the University of North Carolina at Charlotte with a concentration on the southern United States in the 20th century. I grew up in Cabarrus County, North Carolina, with Roberta Mills in my backyard and Cannon Mills just over the hill. It was the goal of many of my friends to get a job in the mills after high school. No one could imagine Cannon Mills not being there for the people of Cabarrus and Rowan Counties.

While I was working in Chester County, South Carolina, in 2000 and doing documentation on Rosenwald Schools, Jimmy Langley in Edgemoor told me that I needed to go see the Lando School. I had driven past Lando hundreds of times knowing that a textile mill was there, but I had never driven through the community.

When I finally drove into Lando, a sense of anxiety came over me. The streets were lined with empty mill houses. Trash littered the yards and streets. In the center of the community was a post office. The door was open, so I went inside—and that is where I met Ollie and Bud Hefner.

I told them of my interest in the schoolhouse, and they pointed me in the right direction. When I turned on School House Road, I was facing an abandoned three-story schoolhouse constructed of three colors of brick, round windows on the third floor, and boarded-up 6-foot windows on the ground floor. I cautiously walked around and fell in love with the design and age of the structure.

I returned to Ollie and Bud to express my interest in documenting the school and learning the history of the building. When I said this, the stories started coming. Bud took me outside and pointed down the road to what remained of Manetta Mills. He told me of the gristmill, the Cornwallis house, Fishing Creek Manufacturing Company, the Heath family, Lando Days, Lando Beach, brick making, the freshwater spring, the "Quarters," the trestles, the old cemetery, the Edgemoor and Manetta Railway (E&M), Dr. John Gaston, and the floods. The stories went on and on. It was Ollie who told me that a couple from Rock Hill, Joe and Gayle Lanford, along with a group of investors, now owned the property known as Lando.

I called the Lanfords and told them of my historical interest in the property and asked if it was OK to try to validate some of the stories that Bud Hefner told me. They granted me permission to look around but said that they were not liable for any accidents because there are a lot of dangerous areas in the community. There are about 100 abandoned houses, an abandoned church, and 20 acres of what was once Manetta Mills.

When I learned that part of Manetta Mills still standing dated back to 1870, I had to go look inside. The supervisor's tower from Fishing Creek Manufacturing was still intact. With Bud Hefner as my resource, I started to learn more and more about Lando and Manetta Mills. I also learned where Joe Polk, a longtime resident of Lando, lived. When I visited Joe and told him what I was doing, he said, "Come see this." He showed me the B and J's Country Store, which was in his backyard and contained everything from Lando and Manetta Mills that was worth saving when it closed in 1991.

Joe and his grandson Brandon built the store to display his antiques and to create a Lando–Manetta Mills museum. Joe and Brandon had many photographs and articles that were beneficial to my research. The key item to help learn about Lando was Charles Inabinet's two-edition publication titled *The Old Mill Stream*. He and his family collected pictures and oral histories around 1975 and published their findings in *The Old Mill Stream*. The publications contained information from 1890 to 1975, but they were incomplete on anything prior to 1890.

I was able to locate the foundation of the 1780 gristmill, and with the help of Michael Scoggins, I validated the significance of Lando in the American Revolution. I was able to confirm that Cornwallis's route after the Battle of Charlotte brought him through Lando. All the stories that Bud Hefner had told me were true.

It was Bud Hefner's desire to see Lando cleaned up and rebuilt before he died. In the summer of 2005, those dreams started becoming reality. Joe and Gayle Lanford contracted to have Lando cleaned up. With environmental studies and landfill permits in hand, Lando underwent a major cleanup. The Lando–Manetta Mills History Center, a nonprofit organization, was formed, and with permission from the Lanfords, Joe Polk's collection of Lando artifacts was moved to the former Manetta Mills company office.

One day, Bud Hefner walked me down to Fishing Creek and told me stories of him and his dad and the times they had on the creek. I grew up on Rocky River in Harrisburg, North Carolina, and know how much fun it was being part of a community and having a close-knit family. Fishing Creek in Lando has become one of my favorite places to visit. The creek, the people, the history, and the future of Lando are exciting and beautiful. I am very grateful that I have had the opportunity to become part of this community, and I thank everyone who has helped me find my passion.

One

The Land of Revolutions

The banks of Fishing Creek in Chester County, South Carolina, have been attracting people to the natural resources of the area for thousands of years. The Catawba Nation used the areas around Fishing Creek to hunt and fish for generations. In 1492, their land and communities experienced a social revolution with the migration of Europeans to their lands.

The strong current and abundant water was the perfect environment for a gristmill to operate. Yeoman Philip Walker established the first gristmill in 1762. He could harvest enough water power to turn a stone wheel for grinding grains and corn without having to build a dam. The gristmill was a foundation in the development of a community.

The waterpower from Fishing Creek, along with the plentiful hardwood trees and fertile soil of the flood plains, made this the perfect area to establish a homestead and plantation. It is these environmental resources that made the land now known as Lando a profitable place to establish a trade. A sawmill, gristmill, and farms remained active in the area until the 20th century.

The community of Lando has experienced many revolutions since Europeans occupied the land in the mid-18th century. The area played an important part in the American Revolution in the summer of 1780. The Industrial Revolution found the waters of Fishing Creek the perfect power source for a large textile mill. Since 1776, America and Lando have been a land of revolutions.

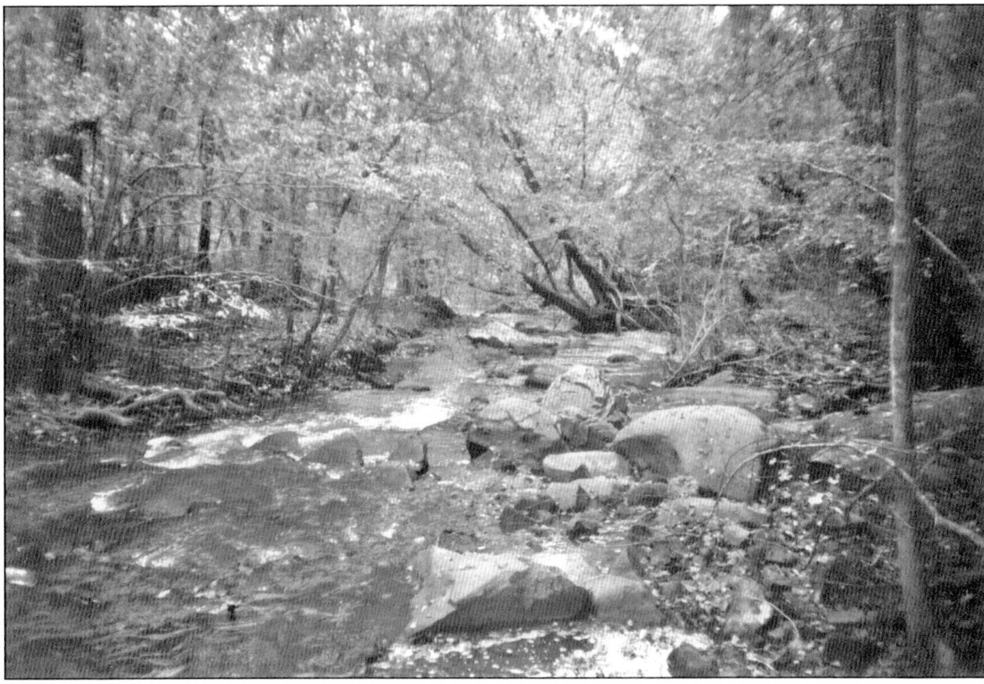

FISHING CREEK. Phillip Walker owned property that is now known as Lando on Fishing Creek in Craven (Chester) County, South Carolina, in the mid- to late 18th century. Walker was a well-known miller and attracted many local farmers to his mill to grind their grains into flour, grits, and feed.

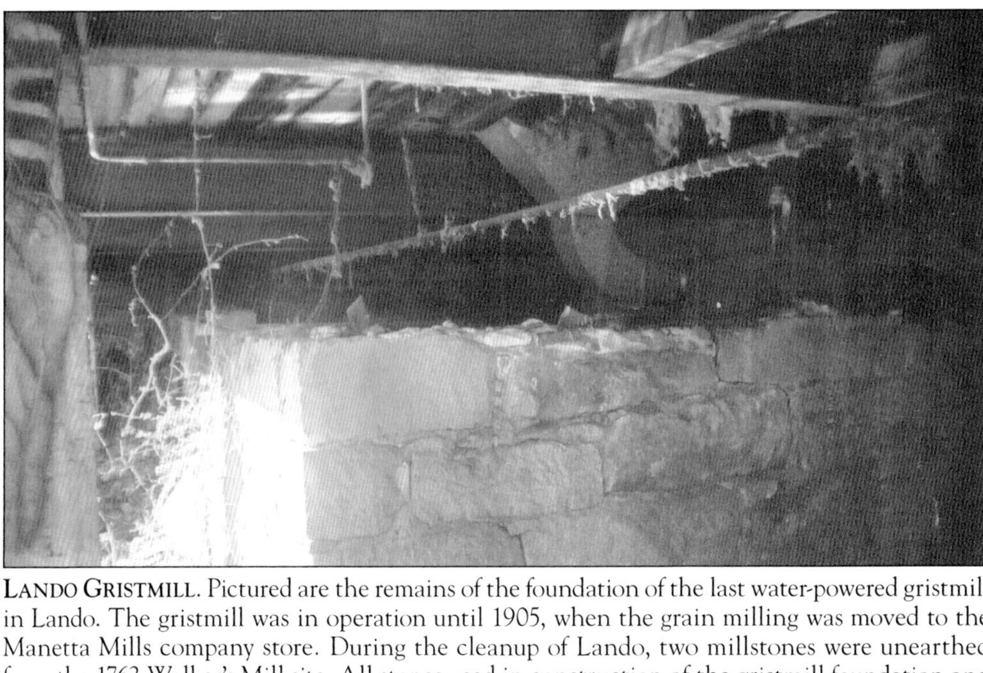

LANDO GRISTMILL. Pictured are the remains of the foundation of the last water-powered gristmill in Lando. The gristmill was in operation until 1905, when the grain milling was moved to the Manetta Mills company store. During the cleanup of Lando, two millstones were unearthed from the 1762 Walker's Mill site. All stones used in construction of the gristmill foundation and millstones were cut and formed in Lando.

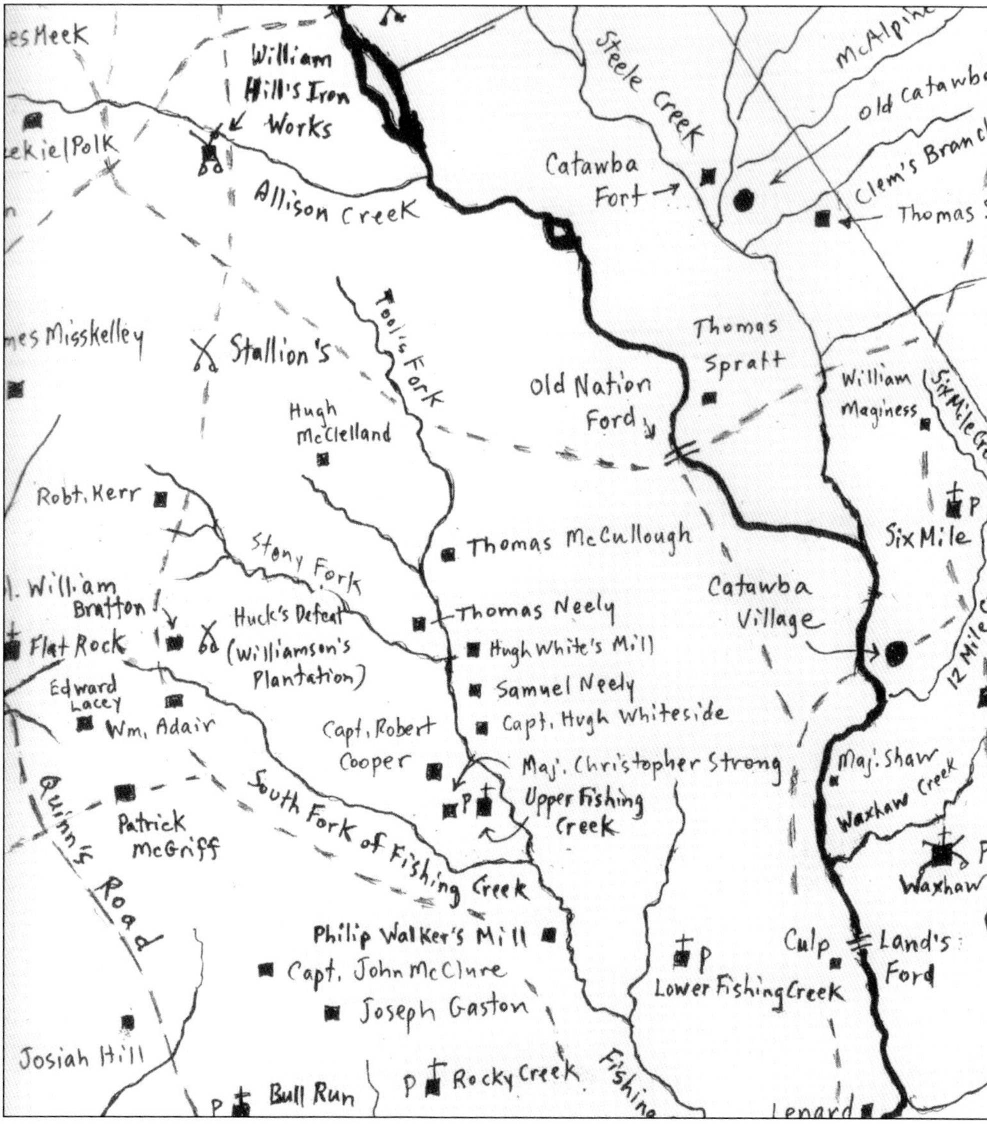

AMERICAN REVOLUTION. This is a map of the central Carolina Piedmont c. 1780. It is documented that Capt. Christian Huck, Lt. Col. Banastre Tarleton, and Lt. Gen. Charles Lord Cornwallis passed through and or camped at Walker's Mill in Lando in the summer of 1780. Huck camped at or near Walker's Mill before attacks on William Hill's Iron Works and Upper Fishing Creek Church. Huck later was killed at Williamson's Plantation. (Map drawn by Michael C. Scoggins, © 2002; courtesy of Culture and Heritage Museums of York County.)

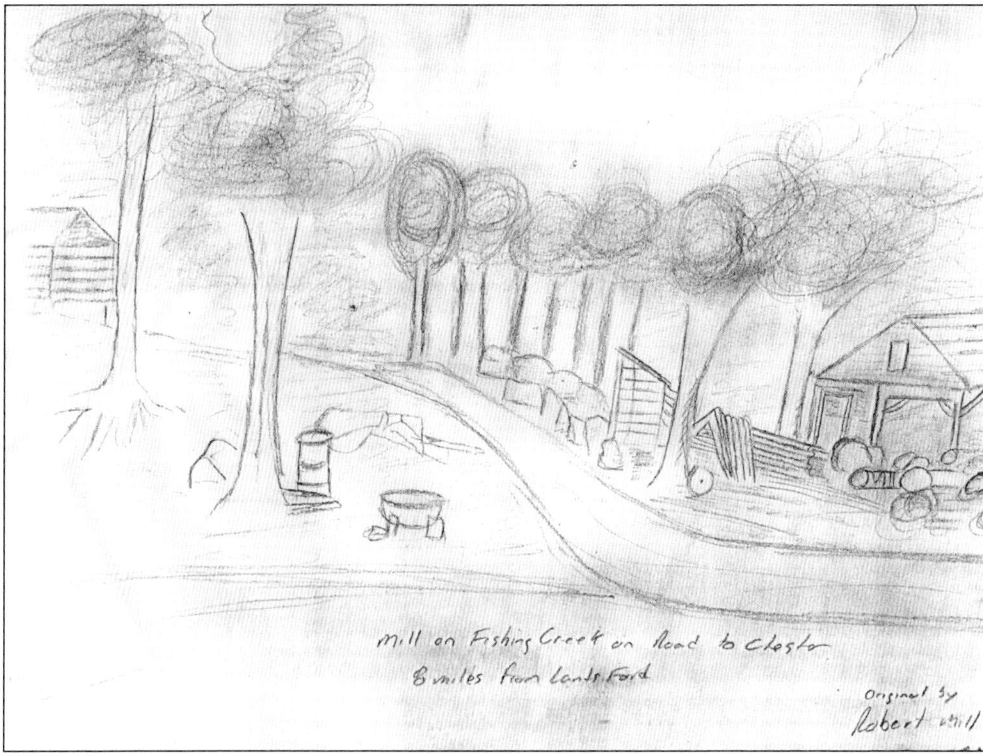

ON THE ROAD TO CHESTER. In 1784, Philip Walker sold his property in Lando to Hugh White of York County. White was a well-known miller and also had a gristmill on Fishing Creek, several miles upstream in York County. In 1801, Hugh White died, and his son, Thomas White, took ownership of the property. The deed from the transfer documents the land, including a gristmill, sawmill, and a fulling mill. Pictured here is a redrawing of Robert Mills's sketch c. 1818, when Mills was working on his cartography of South Carolina. The sketch reads "Mill on Fishing Creek on Road to Chester 8 miles from Landsford." (Interpretation by Paul Williams of Robert Mills's sketch; courtesy of Tulane University.)

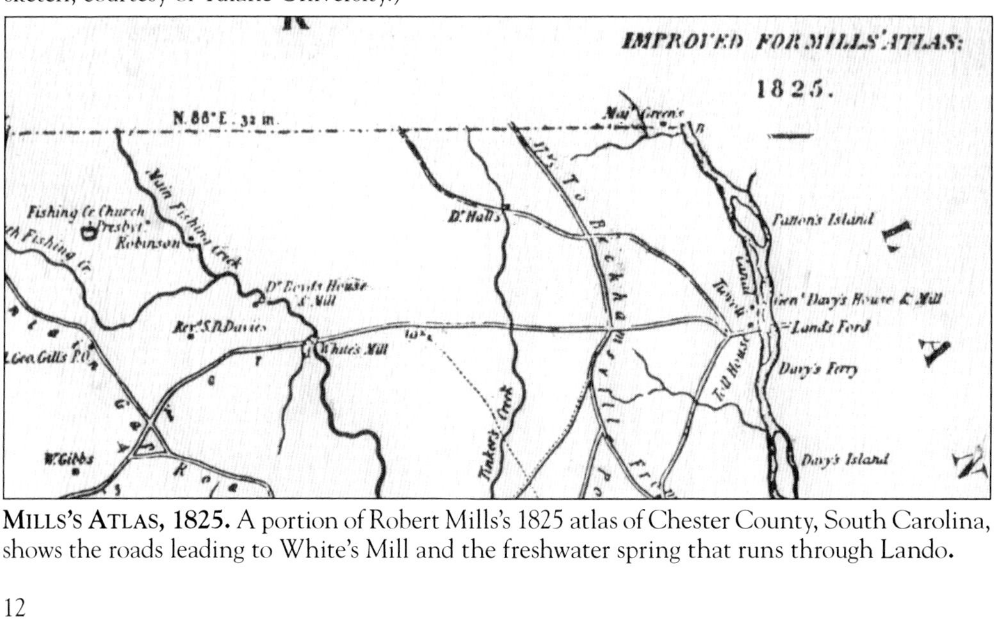

MILLS'S ATLAS, 1825. A portion of Robert Mills's 1825 atlas of Chester County, South Carolina, shows the roads leading to White's Mill and the freshwater spring that runs through Lando.

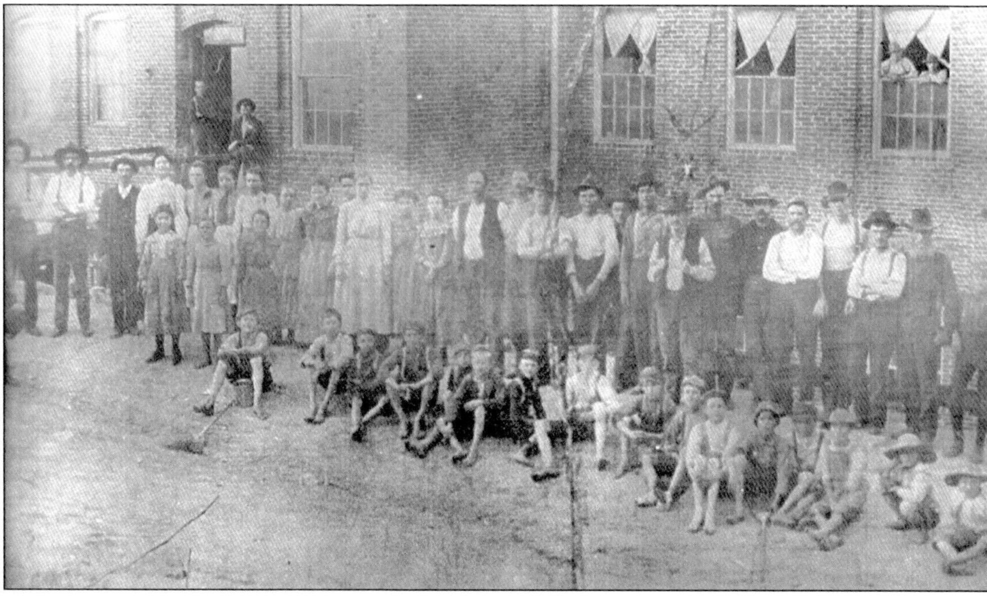

FISHING CREEK MANUFACTURING COMPANY. In 1884, Chester, South Carolina, native Ferguson Barber owned the property and formed Fishing Creek Manufacturing Company along with a group of investors. The company went bankrupt after a few years, and Barber renamed the mill Lewisville Cotton Mill. The cotton mills used waterpower to operate the equipment inside. Some of the early operators in the mill were the Lybrand brothers: Martin, George, John Robert, Will, and Pete.

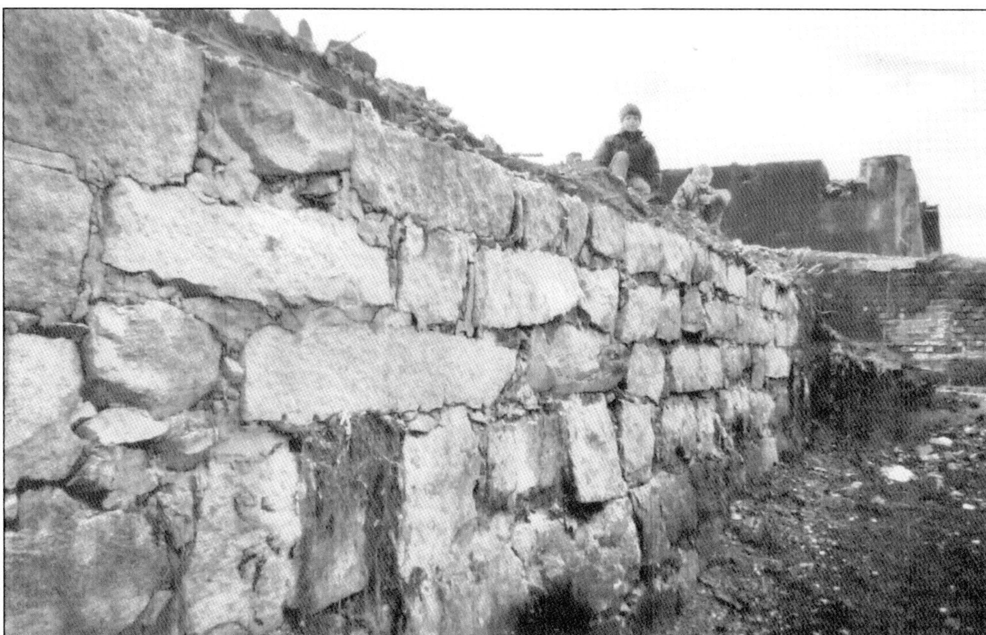

LANDO. The sawmill, gristmill, warehouse, cotton mill, blacksmith shop, and brick kilns existed on the flood plains of Fishing Creek. By 1884, people were migrating to Lando to work in this growing mill community. Daniel (left) and Dillon Williams sit on the retaining wall with the brick kilns in the background. Both items were built around 1870.

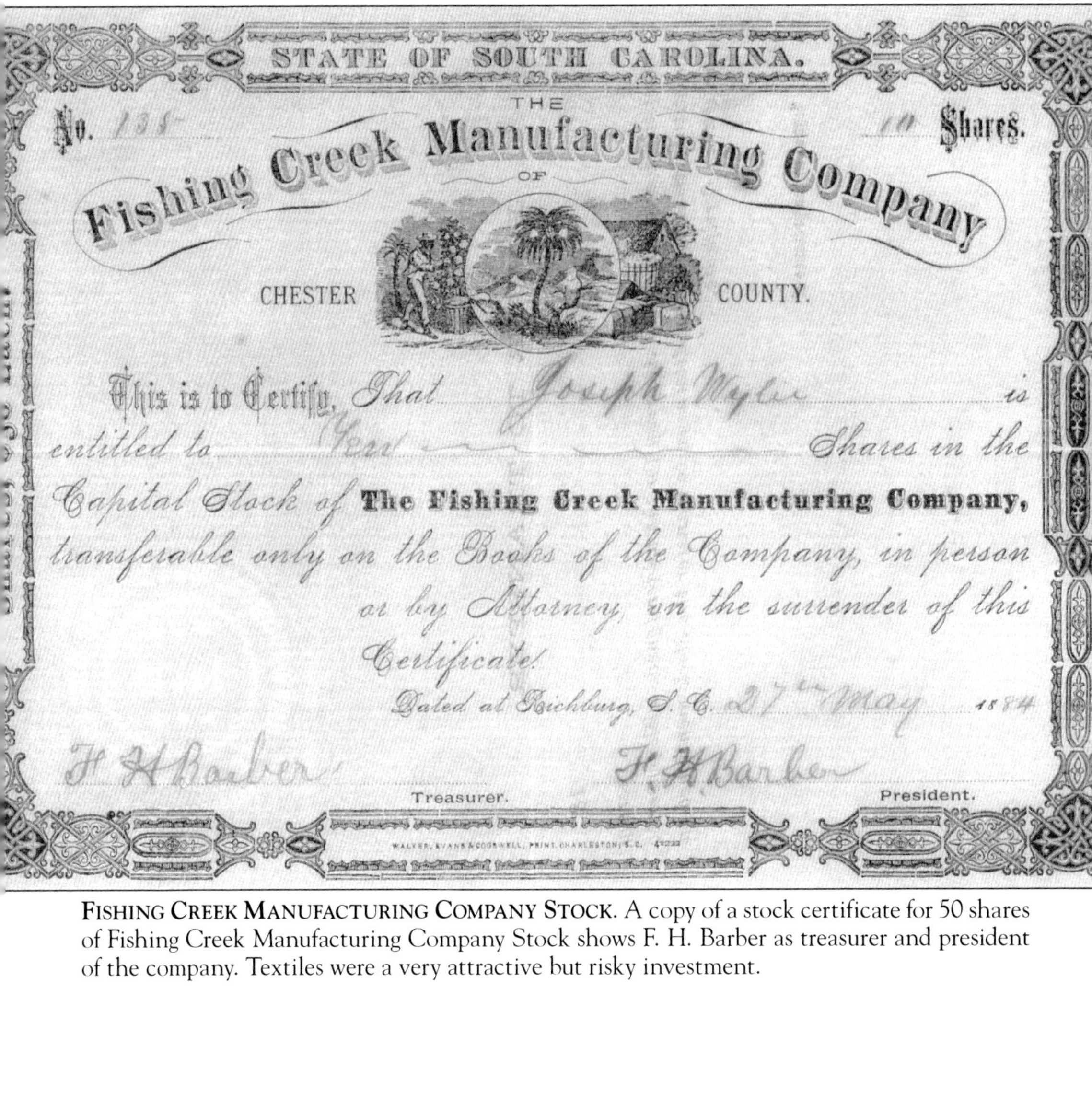

STATE OF SOUTH CAROLINA.

No. 135 — 10 Shares.

THE

Fishing Creek Manufacturing Company

OF

CHESTER COUNTY.

This is to Certify, That Joseph Wyl[illegible] is entitled to Ten Shares in the Capital Stock of The Fishing Creek Manufacturing Company, transferable only on the Books of the Company, in person or by Attorney, on the surrender of this Certificate.

Dated at Richburg, S. C. 27th May 1884

F. H. Barber, Treasurer. F. H. Barber, President.

FISHING CREEK MANUFACTURING COMPANY STOCK. A copy of a stock certificate for 50 shares of Fishing Creek Manufacturing Company Stock shows F. H. Barber as treasurer and president of the company. Textiles were a very attractive but risky investment.

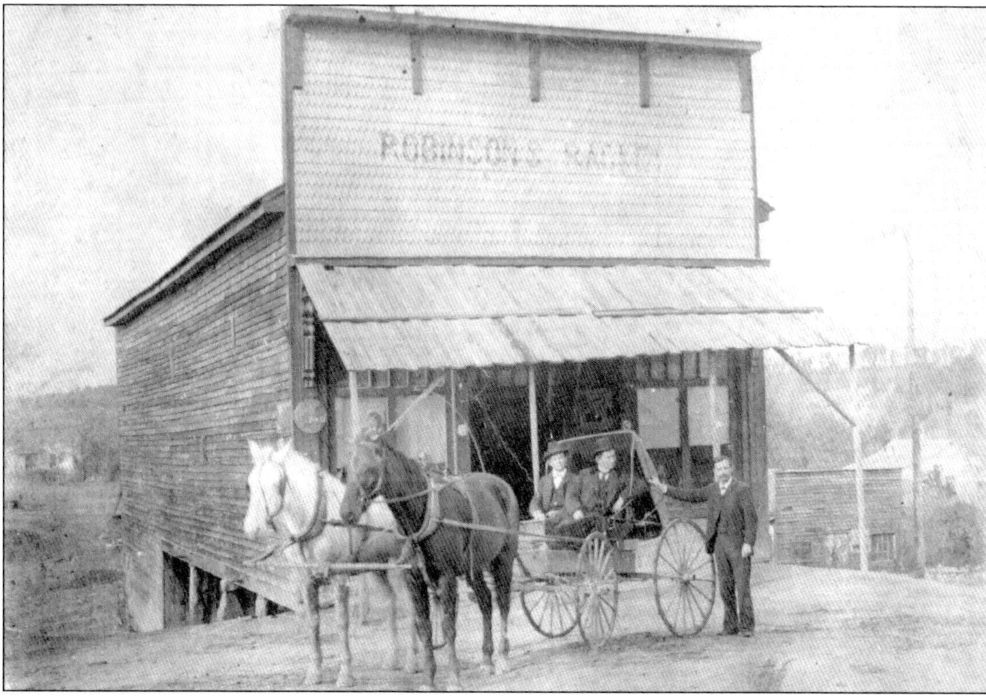

ROBINSON'S STORE. The Robinson's Racket, seen here *c.* 1895, was the community store, which housed the post office and was the gathering place for many people. The hills above Lewisville Cotton Mills were home to many people. The mill village was supported by Ferguson Barber and Lewisville Cotton Mills.

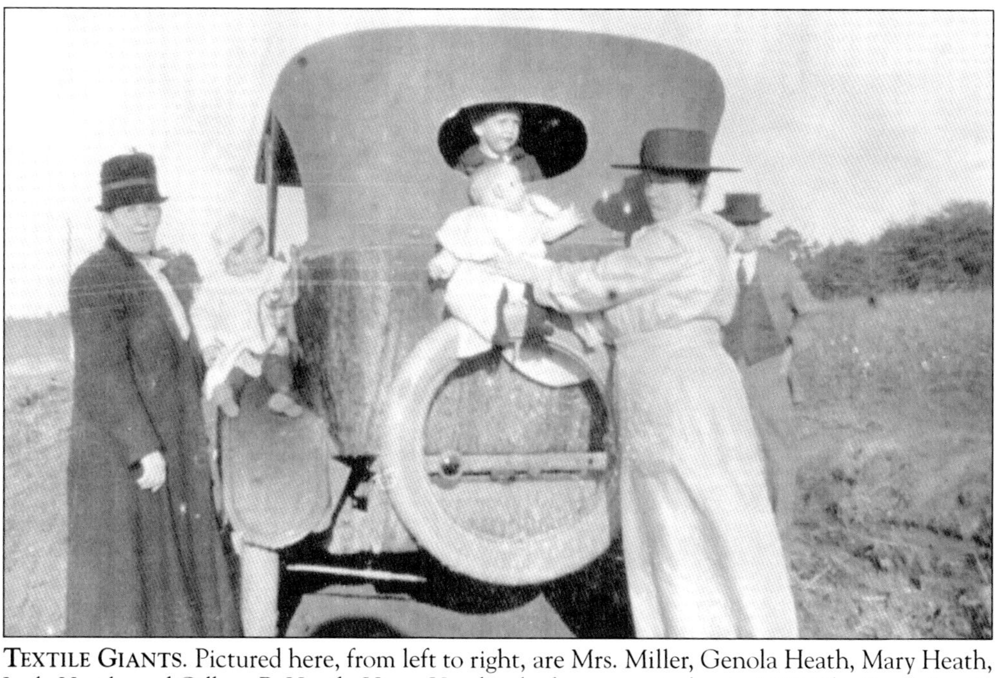

TEXTILE GIANTS. Pictured here, from left to right, are Mrs. Miller, Genola Heath, Mary Heath, Leila Heath, and Gilbert B. Heath. Harry Heath is looking out window in 1918. The Heath family helped establish many textile mills in both North and South Carolina.

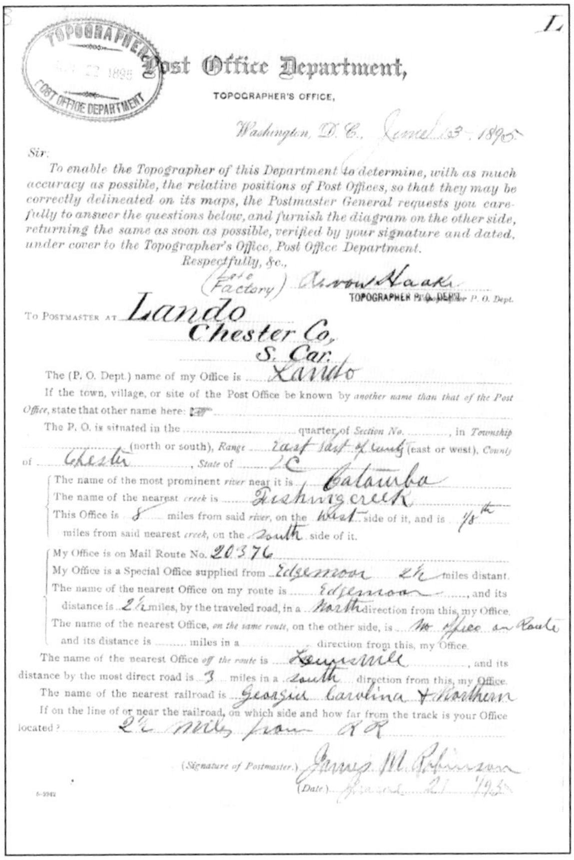

TOPOGRAPHER'S OFFICE POST OFFICE DEPARTMENT JUN 22 1895

Post Office Department,

TOPOGRAPHER'S OFFICE,

Washington, D. C., June 13 - 1895

Sir:

To enable the Topographer of this Department to determine, with as much accuracy as possible, the relative positions of Post Offices, so that they may be correctly delineated on its maps, the Postmaster General requests you carefully to answer the questions below, and furnish the diagram on the other side, returning the same as soon as possible, verified by your signature and dated, under cover to the Topographer's Office, Post Office Department.

Respectfully, &c.,

(Factory) Arrow Haak

TOPOGRAPHER P. O. DEPT.

To Postmaster at Lando Chester Co, S. Car.

The (P. O. Dept.) name of my Office is Lando

If the town, village, or site of the Post Office be known by *another name than that of the Post Office*, state that other name here:

The P. O. is situated in the .... quarter of *Section No.* ...., in *Township* .... (north or south), *Range* East Part of County (east or west), *County* of Chester, *State of* SC

The name of the most prominent *river* near it is Catawba

The name of the nearest *creek* is Fishing creek

This Office is 8 miles from said *river*, on the West side of it, and is 1/8th miles from said nearest *creek*, on the South side of it.

My Office is on Mail Route No. 20376

My Office is a Special Office supplied from Edgemoor 2½ miles distant.

The name of the nearest Office on my route is Edgemoor, and its distance is 2½ miles, by the traveled road, in a North direction from this, my Office.

The name of the nearest Office, *on the same route*, on the other side, is No Office on Route and its distance is .... miles in a .... direction from this, my Office.

The name of the nearest Office *off the route* is Lewisville, and its distance by the most direct road is 3 miles in a South direction from this, my Office.

The name of the nearest railroad is Georgia Carolina & Northern

If on the line of or near the railroad, on which side and how far from the track is your Office located? 2½ miles from RR

(*Signature of Postmaster.*) James M. Robinson

(*Date.*) June 21 '95

Amy Barber Story. James M. Robinson was the first postmaster at the community post office established by Ferguson Barber. In 1895, the community had no name, and the residents of the community had their mail addressed to "Factory." Amy Barber, niece of F. H. Barber, did not like having her mail addressed this way, so she and James Robinson searched the directory of post office names for a new name for her community. She liked the name Lansdowne, but it was already taken. So she shortened the name to Lando. A copy of the Post Office Department's form changing the name from Factory to Lando shows the official birthday of Lando as June 22, 1895. This is one of two theories on the origin of the name *Lando*.

U.S. Atlas, 1895. This map shows Factory existing between Edgemoor and Richburg. Factory had railroads running within three miles of Lewisville Manufacturing but no direct link to the Seaboard Air Line.

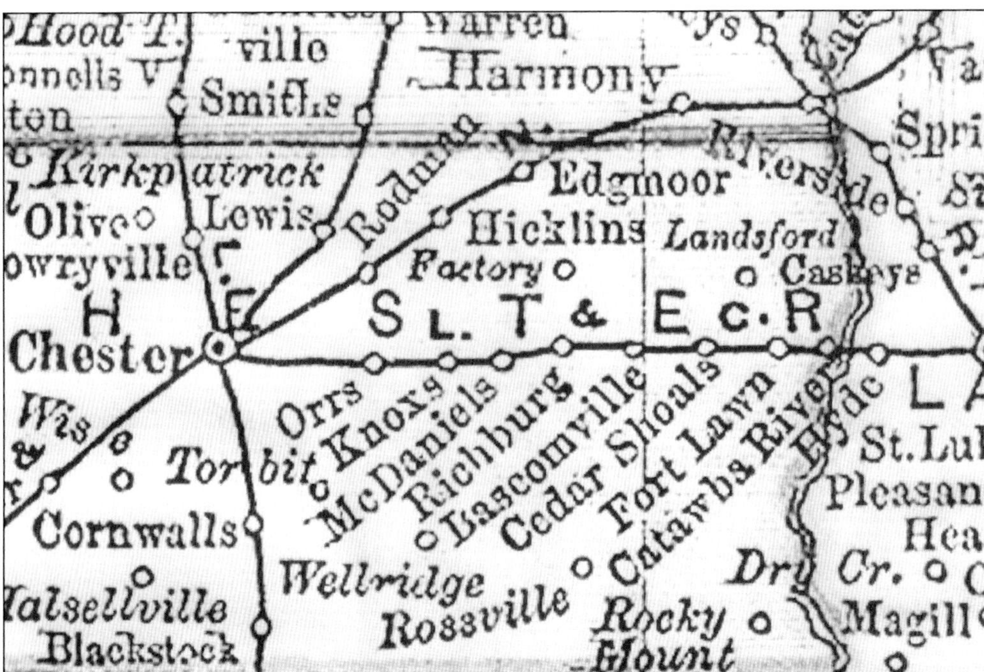

Two

Textile Revolution

The manufacturing of textiles was first introduced in Lando by Hugh White in the late 18th century. It was noted on the deed transfer to his son in 1801 that the property contained a fulling mill. Fulling is the process of making yarn. The area existed quietly through most of the 19th century, until Ferguson Barber's ventures starting in 1880. It was Benjamin Dawson Heath and the Heath family that made the textile revolution "revolutionary" in Lando.

The Heath family used their knowledge of textiles and business to make Lando into one of the largest blanket manufactures in the world. B. D. Heath created Manetta Mills after he acquired Barber's Lewisville Cotton Mills on April 13, 1896. After several years of planning, a major renovation and additions came to Manetta Mills in 1904.

With the additions came the expansion of the mill village now known as Lando. A school, church, and houses were built and roads improved. It was the planning of the Heaths that allowed Lando to develop into a prosperous community. Many families from both Carolinas moved to Lando to learn the trade of making blankets.

In the 1920s, new looms traveled into Lando on the E&M Railway, creating a state-of-the-art manufacturing facility. In 1921, Manetta Mills acquired Jackson Mills in Monroe, North Carolina, doubling its production capacity. The Heath family—Gilbert, Harry, Allen, and Billy—continued to run and manage Manetta Mills and see their communities grow until the late 20th century.

The textile industry provided a way of life for millions of people throughout the South. For more than 90 years, Lando and many mill communities prospered with the textile jobs that the mills provided. It was during the golden years of textiles that Lando was an oasis of prosperity in eastern Chester County.

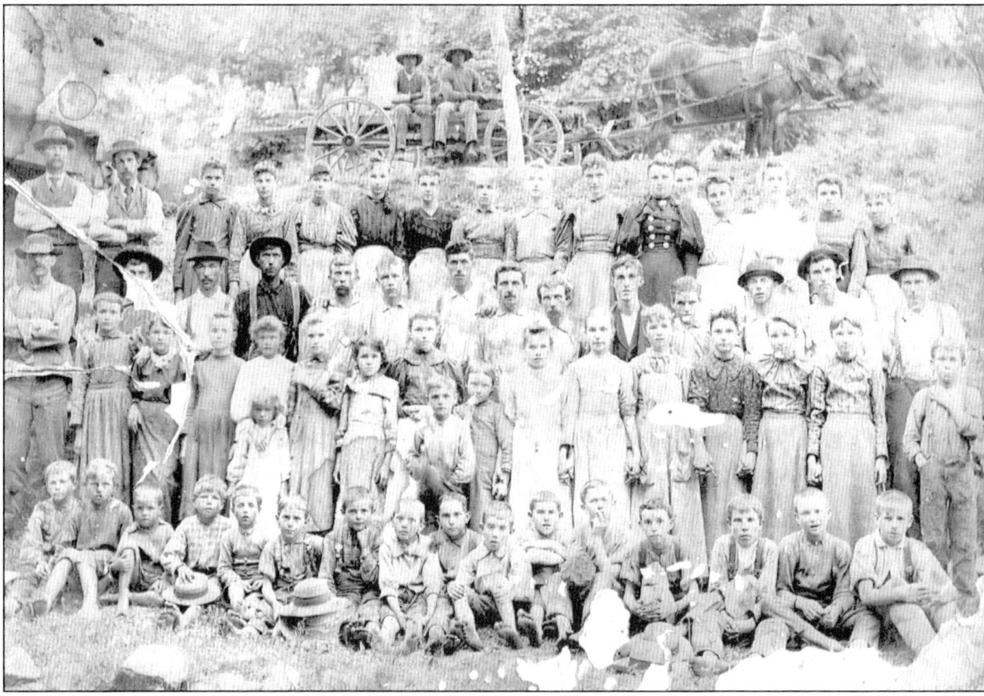

MANETTA MILLS' WORKERS. On April 13, 1896, Benjamin Dawson Heath purchased the bankrupt Lewisville Cotton Mill. In one of the earliest pictures of employees of Manetta Mills (*c.* 1900), they gather on the hillside of the flood plains of Fishing Creek.

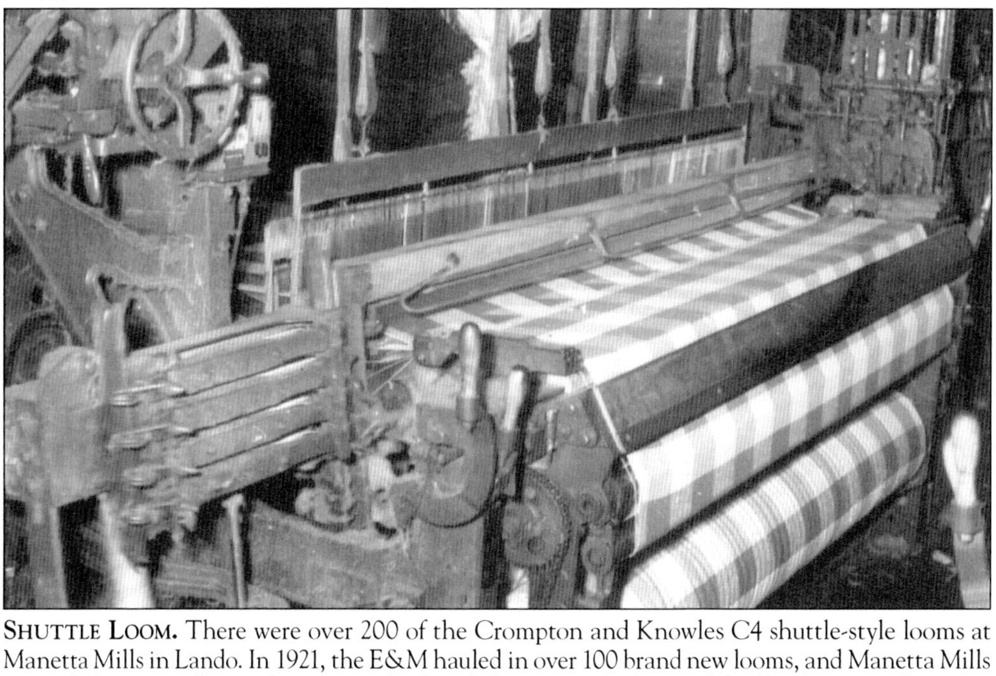

SHUTTLE LOOM. There were over 200 of the Crompton and Knowles C4 shuttle-style looms at Manetta Mills in Lando. In 1921, the E&M hauled in over 100 brand new looms, and Manetta Mills expanded into wool manufacturing. The shuttle loom was the heart of the blanket-manufacturing process. Hundreds of threads of yarn are attached to the loom, and the shuttle carries another thread back and forth across the loom.

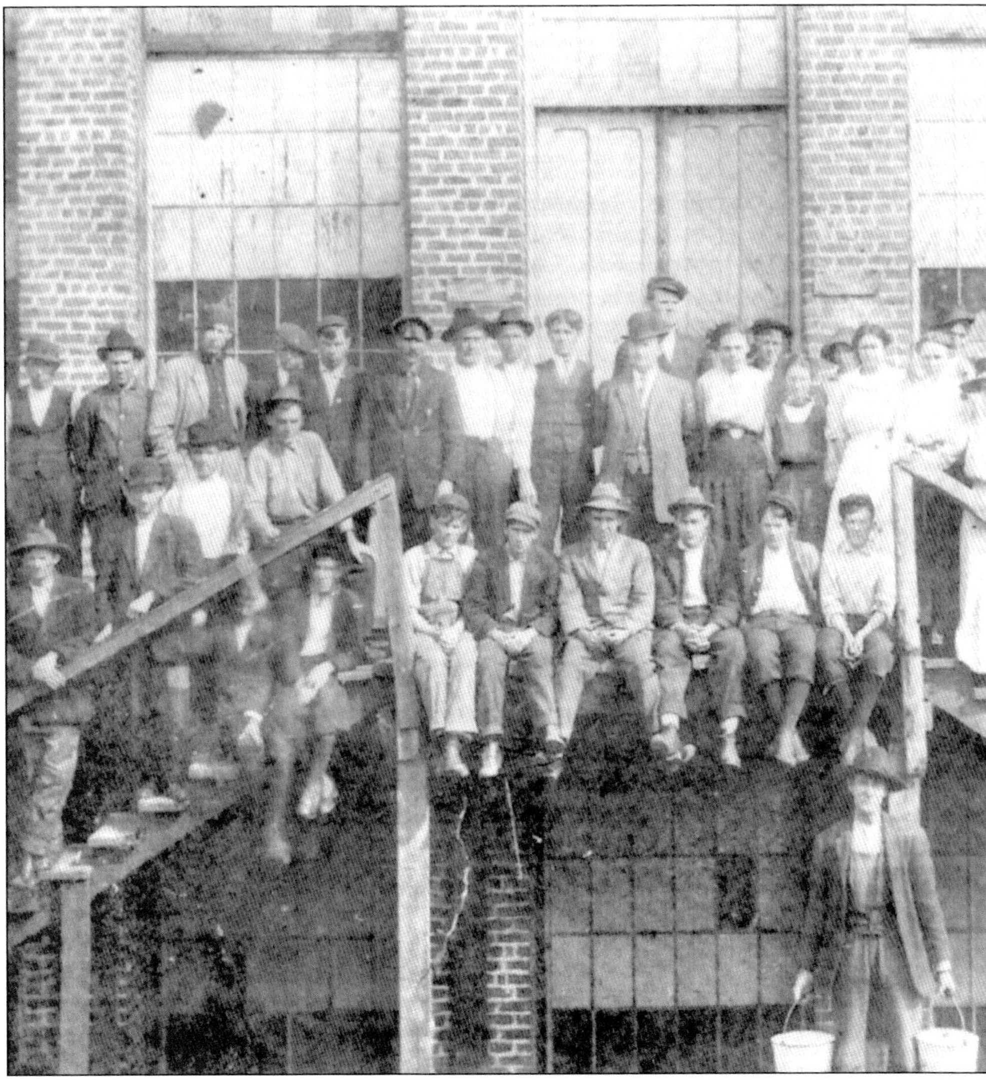

MANETTA MILLS 1906. Manetta Mills' workers pose *c.* 1906 in front of the new buildings constructed in 1904. At the beginning of the 20th century, textiles were a very lucrative business to invest in. The Heath family—being wise investors—knew the key to their success was in their product, the people, and the community. When the Heaths made the commitment to Manetta Mills and Lando, they invested the time and money to make it work. Lando was located in the heart of the "cotton belt" and rail system, which provided great resources for production and distribution. The Heaths built the school, extended the dam for greater waterpower, created the Edgemoor and Manetta Railway, built houses, and bought new equipment for the mill. Manetta Mills provided all the means for a person to start a family and raise children.

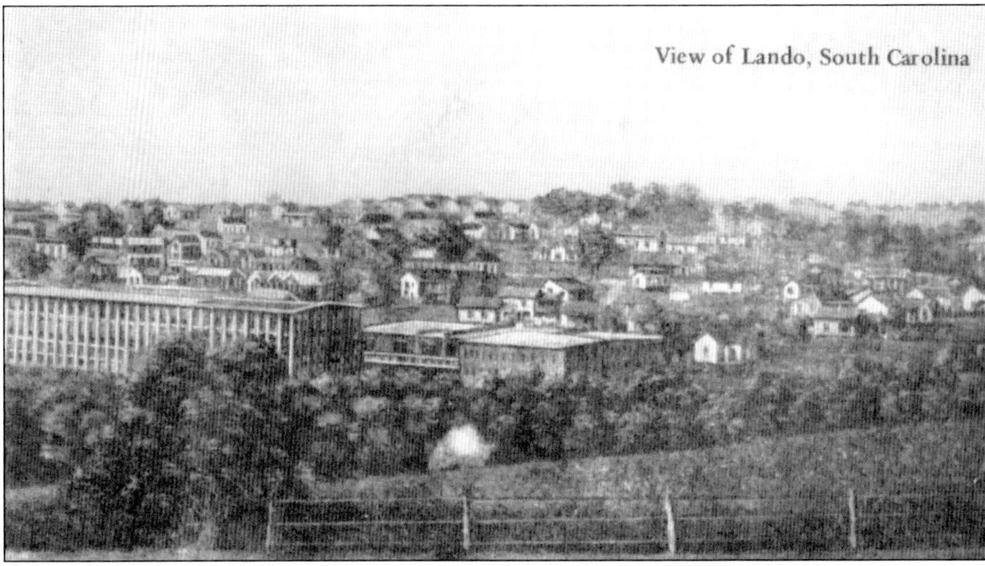

VIEW OF LANDO POSTCARD. This is an unknown artist's view of Lando in the 1930s, when Manetta Mills was at full capacity. With over 800 employees and 176 houses in the mill village, the Heath family was able to provide a good living for many families.

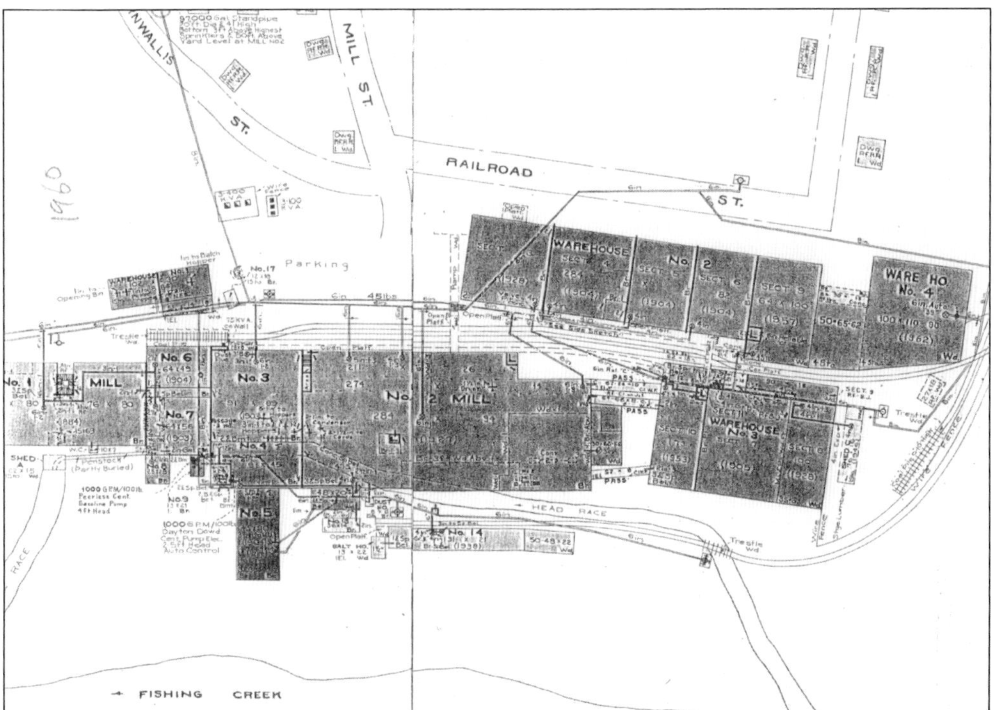

SANBORN MAP. This 1960 Sanborn map shows the age of each building and the layout of Manetta Mills. Sanborn maps are used for fire protection and insurance evaluation.

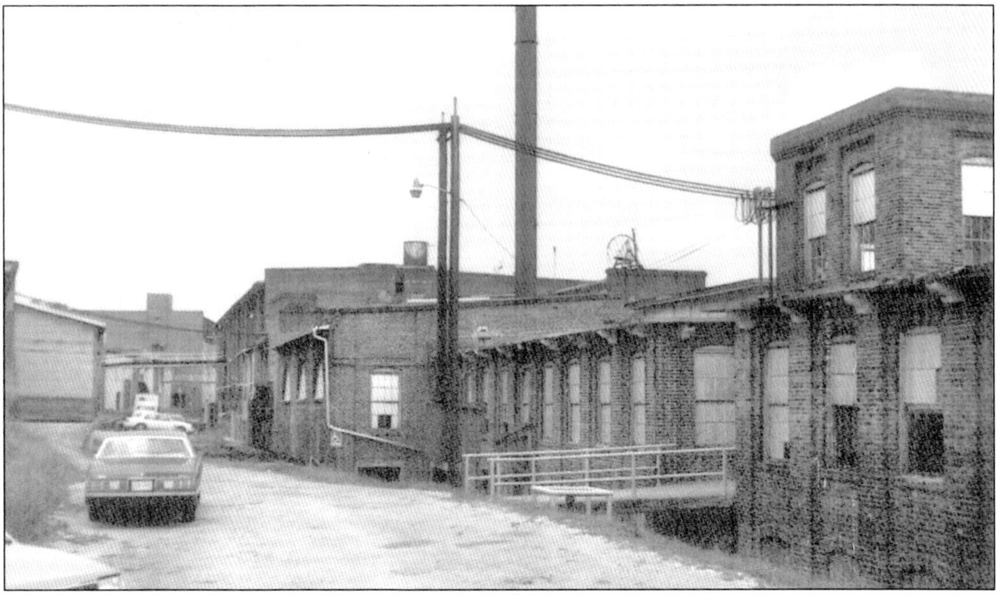

MANETTA MILLS, 1981. B. D. Heath created Manetta Mills and named it after his two wives, Mary and Nettie. By 1904, he had more than doubled the size of the mill. All the bricks used to make the additions were made in the flood plains of Fishing Creek, and all the lumber used was cut at the Lando sawmill. The original section of Fishing Creek Manufacturing Company is on right, and the breakfast bell is on top of the newer mill section.

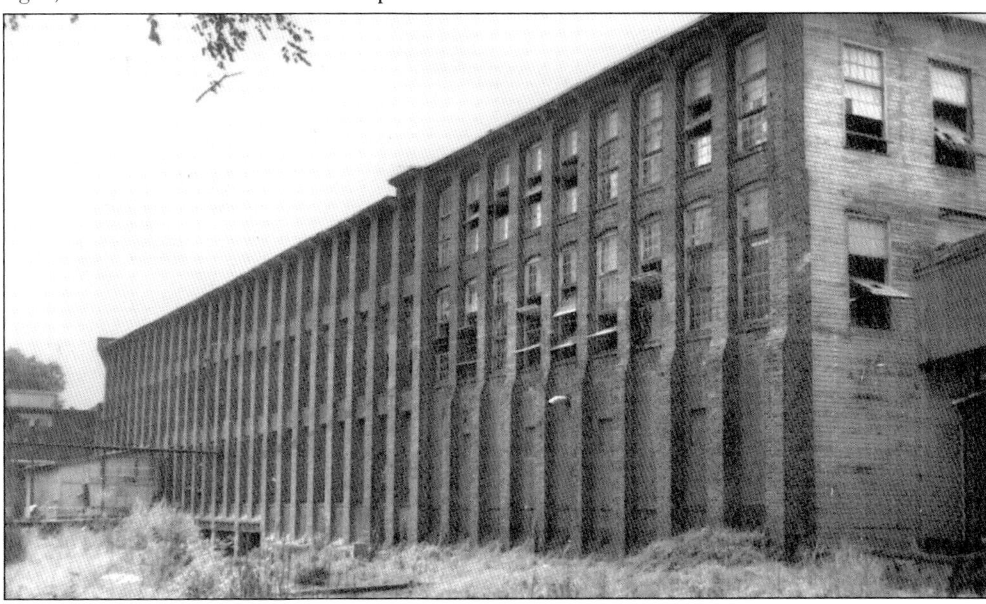

SECTION OF MANETTA MILLS, 1904. The brick-making process involved flooding a small section of Fishing Creek and using a mule-driven auger to churn up mud. The mud was gathered and then formed into bricks and dried in temporary kilns built on the flood plain of Fishing Creek. The millrace (a diverted flow of water from Fishing Creek used to turn turbines that powered equipment in Manetta Mills) goes under the middle section of the mill. Helen Mosley, a longtime Manetta Mills employee, tells of how employees would fish out of the mill windows in the millrace during their breaks.

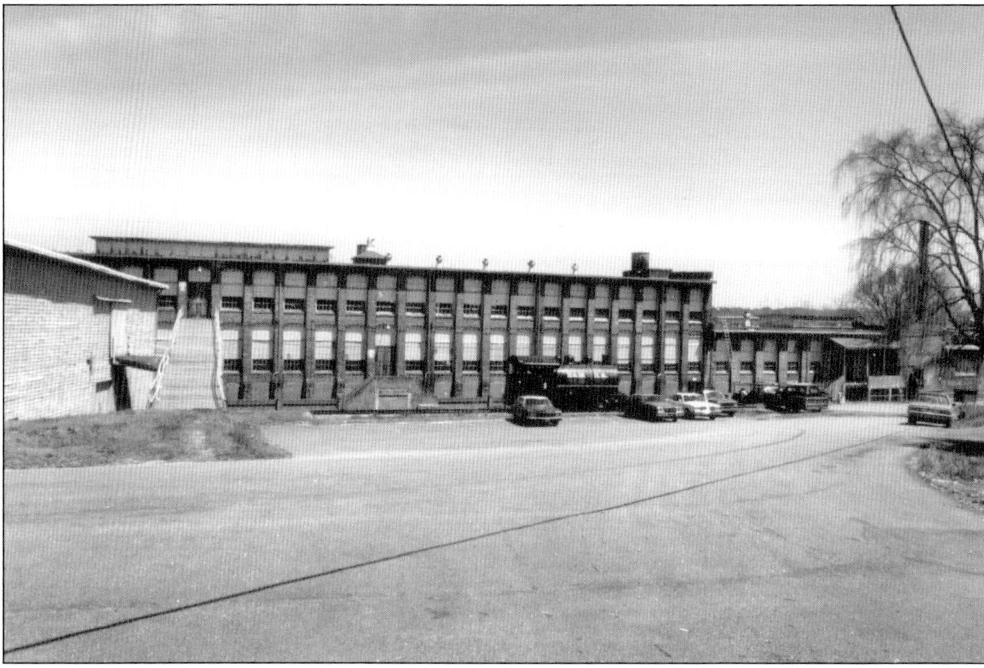

MANETTA MILLS LANDO, 1982. A view of Manetta Mills' Lando Plant on the road in front of the mill office shows the main entrance to the plant. Manetta Mills owned and operated two mill sites. The headquarters was in Lando, South Carolina, and a finishing plant was in Monroe, North Carolina.

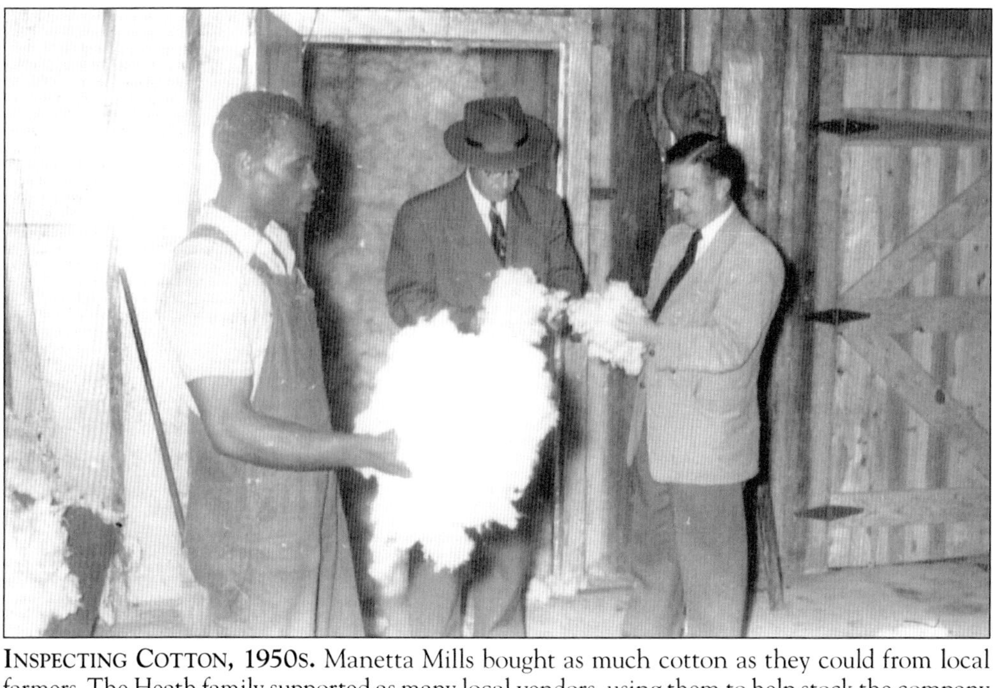

INSPECTING COTTON, 1950S. Manetta Mills bought as much cotton as they could from local farmers. The Heath family supported as many local vendors, using them to help stock the company store, office, and mill. Tun Crockett (on left) has his cotton inspected by Charlie DeBruhal (center) and Harry Heath (right).

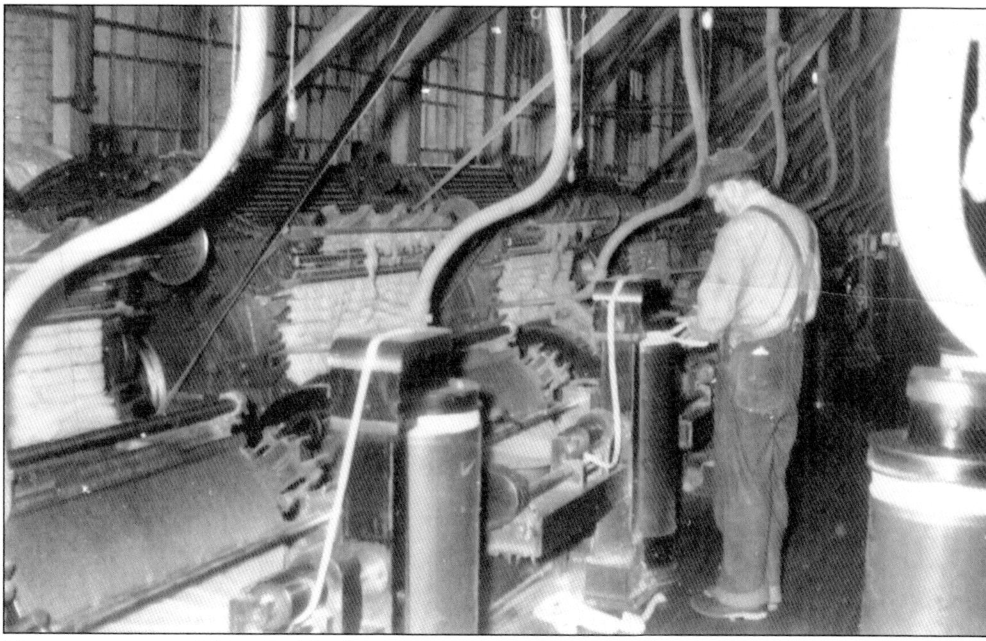

Maintenance, 1950s. Cad Bailey maintains equipment in the card room. The canisters he is attending are spring-loaded and are top-filled. A card machine combs a web of cotton into a rope form, and then it is fed into canisters.

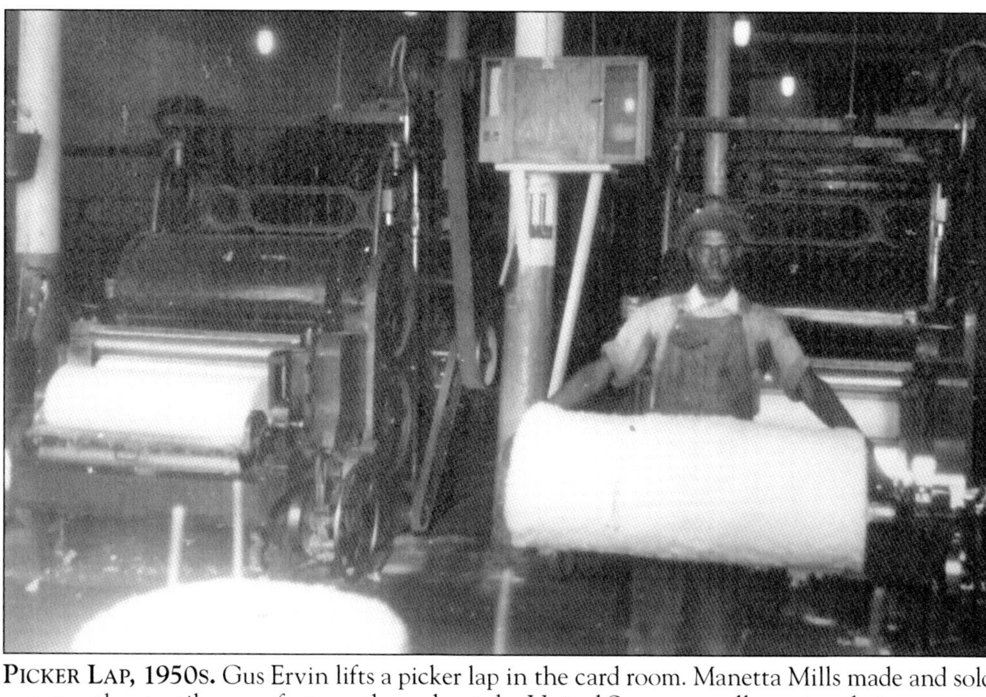

Picker Lap, 1950s. Gus Ervin lifts a picker lap in the card room. Manetta Mills made and sold yarn to other textile manufactures throughout the United States, as well as using their own yarn for blanket production.

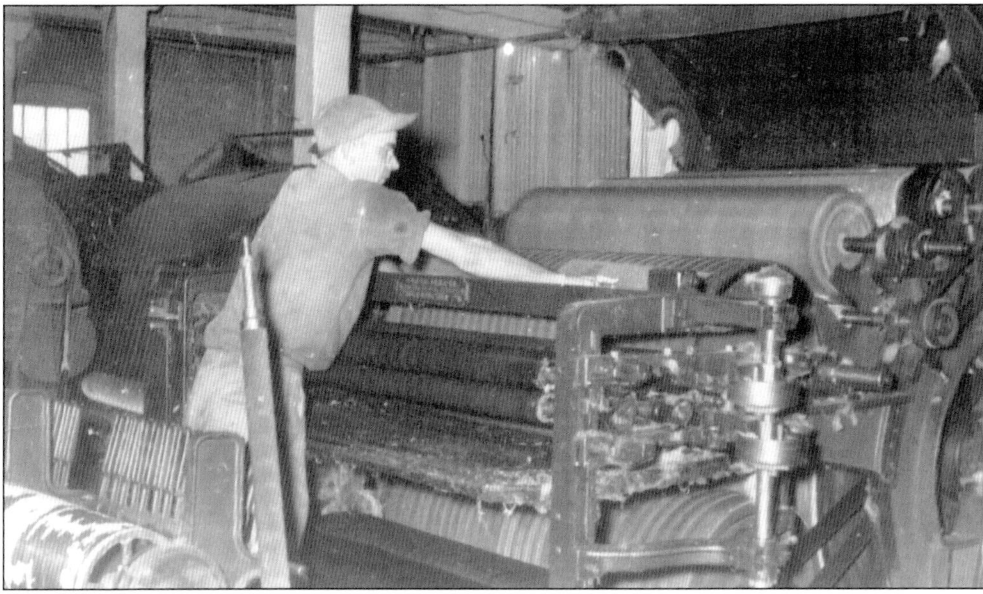

Woolen Card Room, 1950s. Willis Ratteree maintains a piece of equipment in the card room. Maintenance crews were always on call. If a loom or spinning machine was not working, people were not able to work. Manetta Mills provided tools and training for the maintenance crews. Maintenance crews were expected to fix everything from looms to brooms to warping machines and windows.

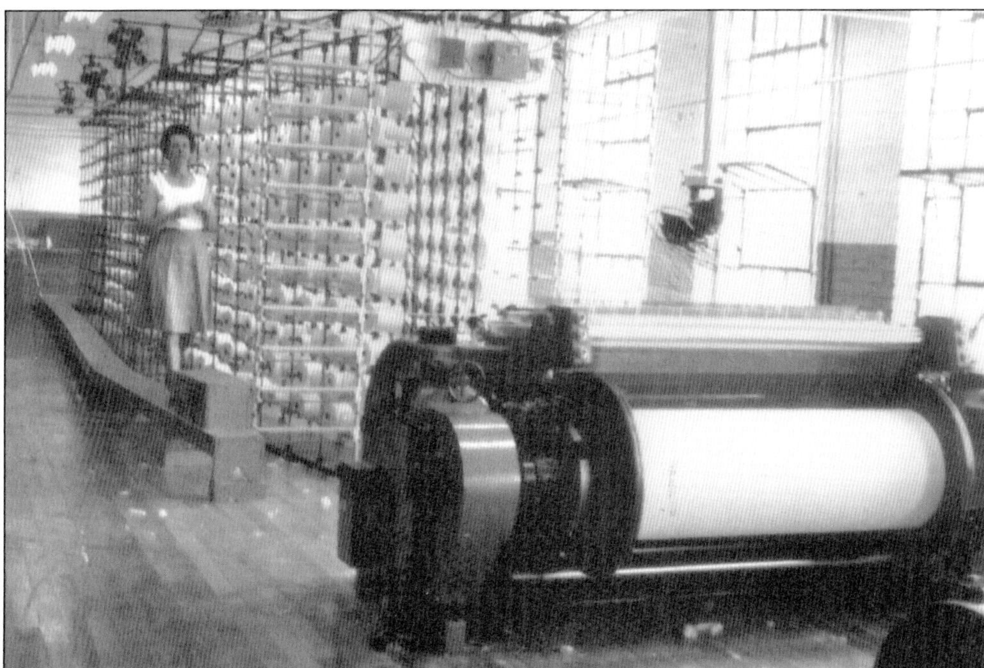

Warping Room, 1950s. Louise Miller is working in the warping room, in which hundreds of spools of yarn are combined in a large roll that is used to feed a loom to create a woven fabric. A non-woven fabric is a fabric created from sheets of cotton that are sewn together and thus does not contain individual yarns. Manetta Mills created blankets from woven and non-woven fabrics.

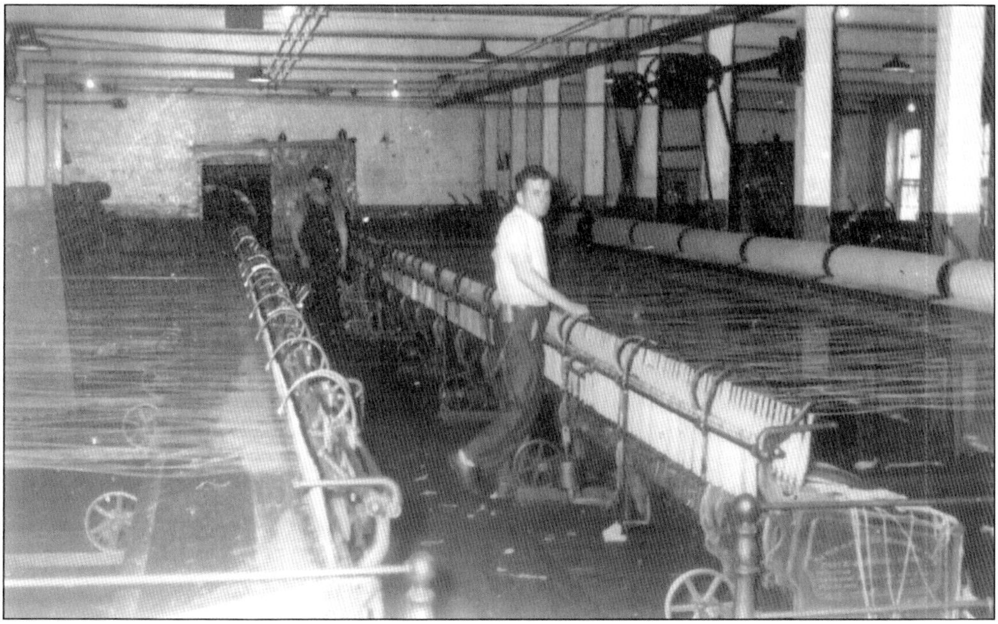

MULE SPINNING, 1950S. Robert Paul Coker is working with the equipment in the mule spinning room. The spinning process takes rolls from the card room and makes individual spools of yarn. Mule spinning was replaced by jack spinning. The difference between mule and jack spinning is the type of equipment used in the process of spinning spools of yarn.

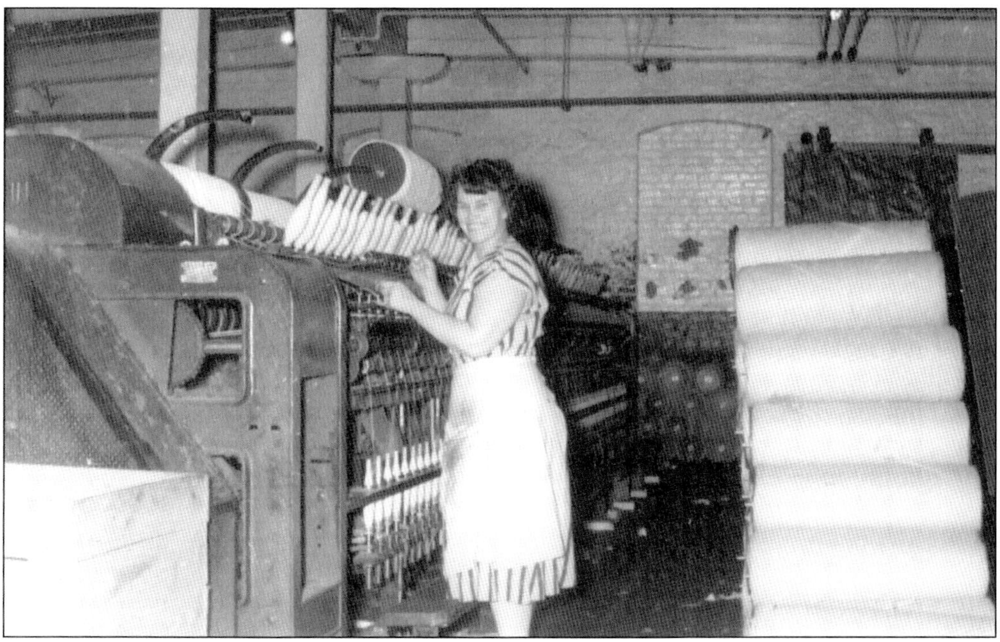

JACK SPINNING, 1950S. Marie Hargrove is paying attention to spools of yarn in the (jack) spinning room. The water pipes above the bricked-up windows would introduce moisture into the air to help prevent the yarn from breaking.

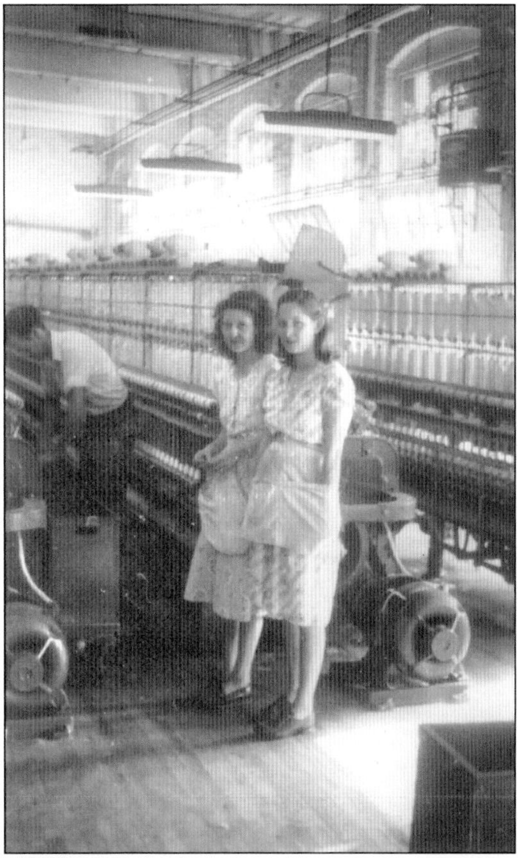

WORKING IN THE SPINNING ROOM, 1950S. Ardrey Robinson (left) and Tiny Ernandez wait while Jess Coker doffs a spinning frame.

WORKING TOGETHER, 1950S. Cecil Polk (left) and Lonzio Simpson are seen here working in the spinning room. Many coworkers were neighbors and friends.

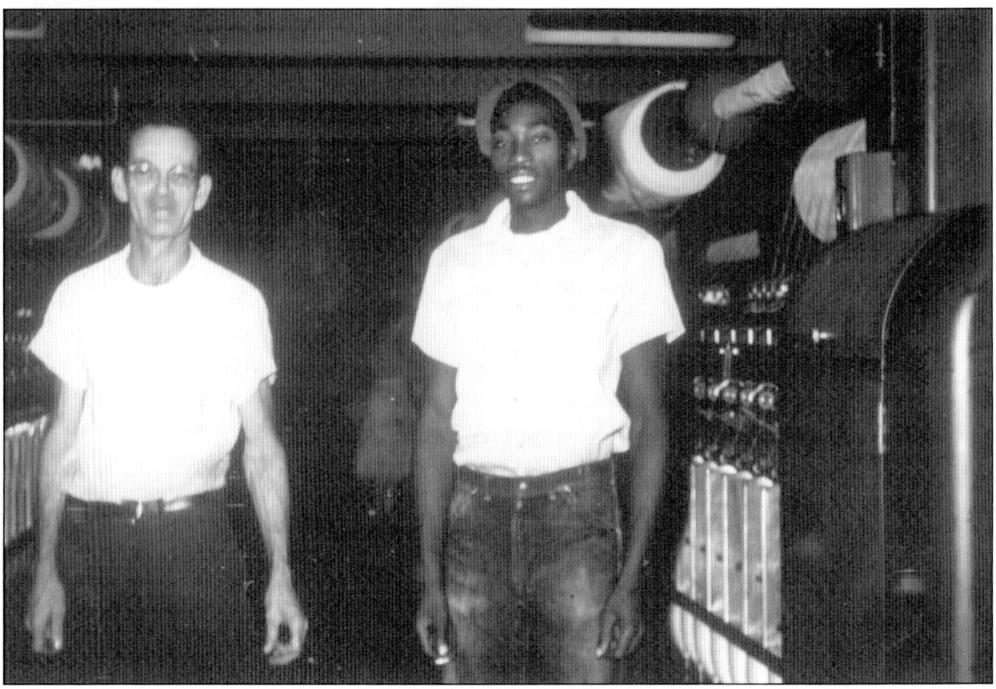

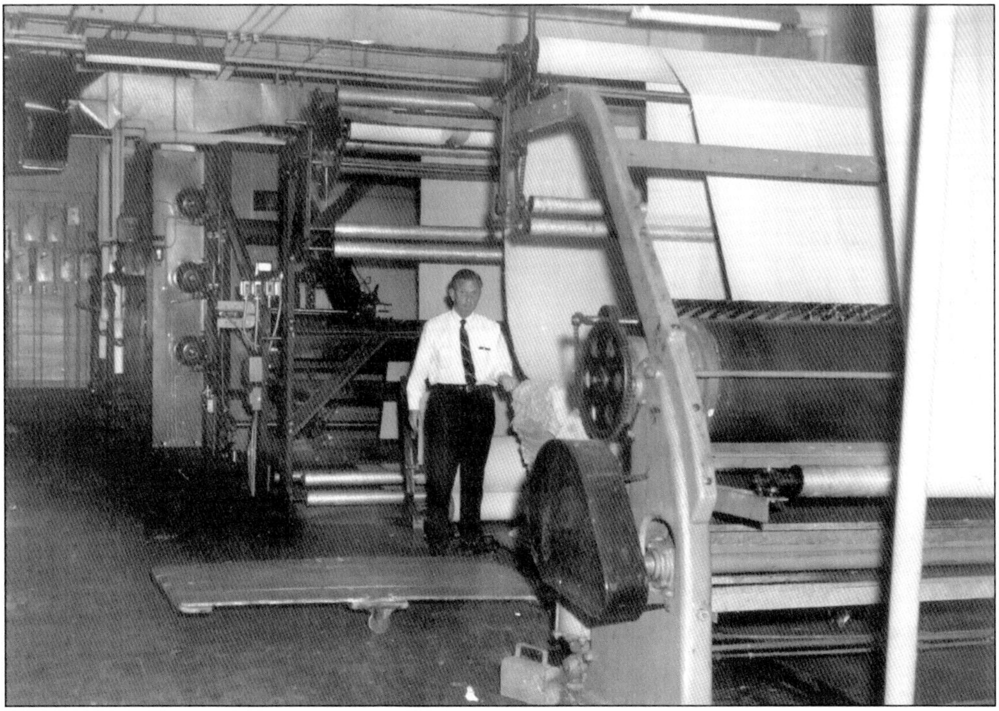

INSPECTING THE EQUIPMENT, 1950S. Harry Heath stands in the modern cloth room. The Heaths were always looking for new ways to improve the blankets that Manetta Mills produced.

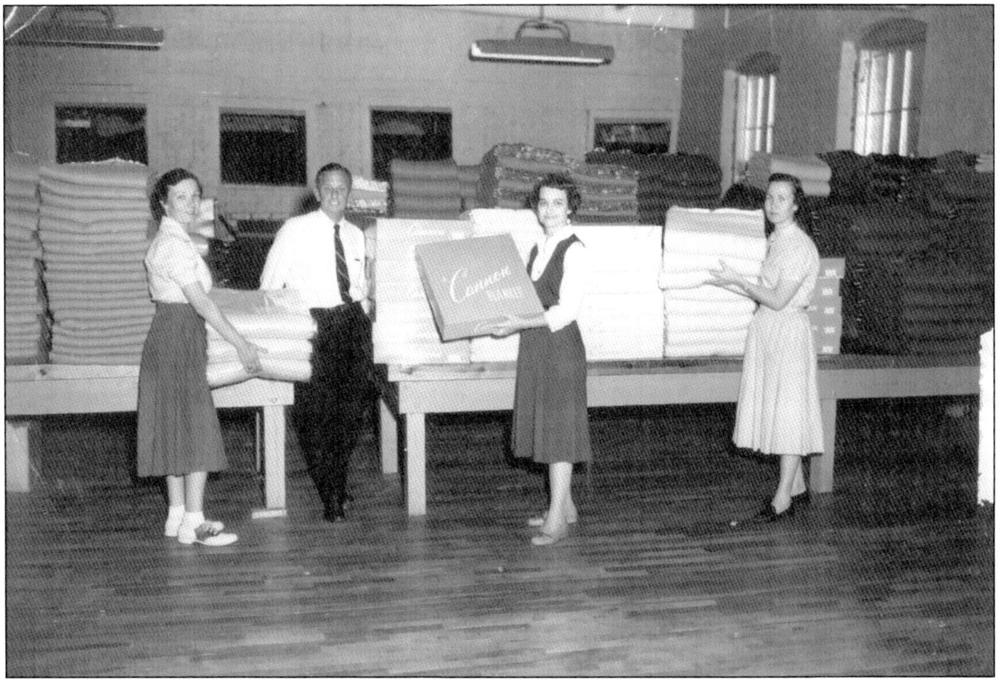

THE PRIDE OF MANETTA MILLS, 1950S. From left to right, Lucille Guinn, Harry Heath, Plummie Ernandez, and Ollie Hough Hefner pose for a Cannon publicity photograph. The Cannon blankets were shipped to retail stores all over the United States.

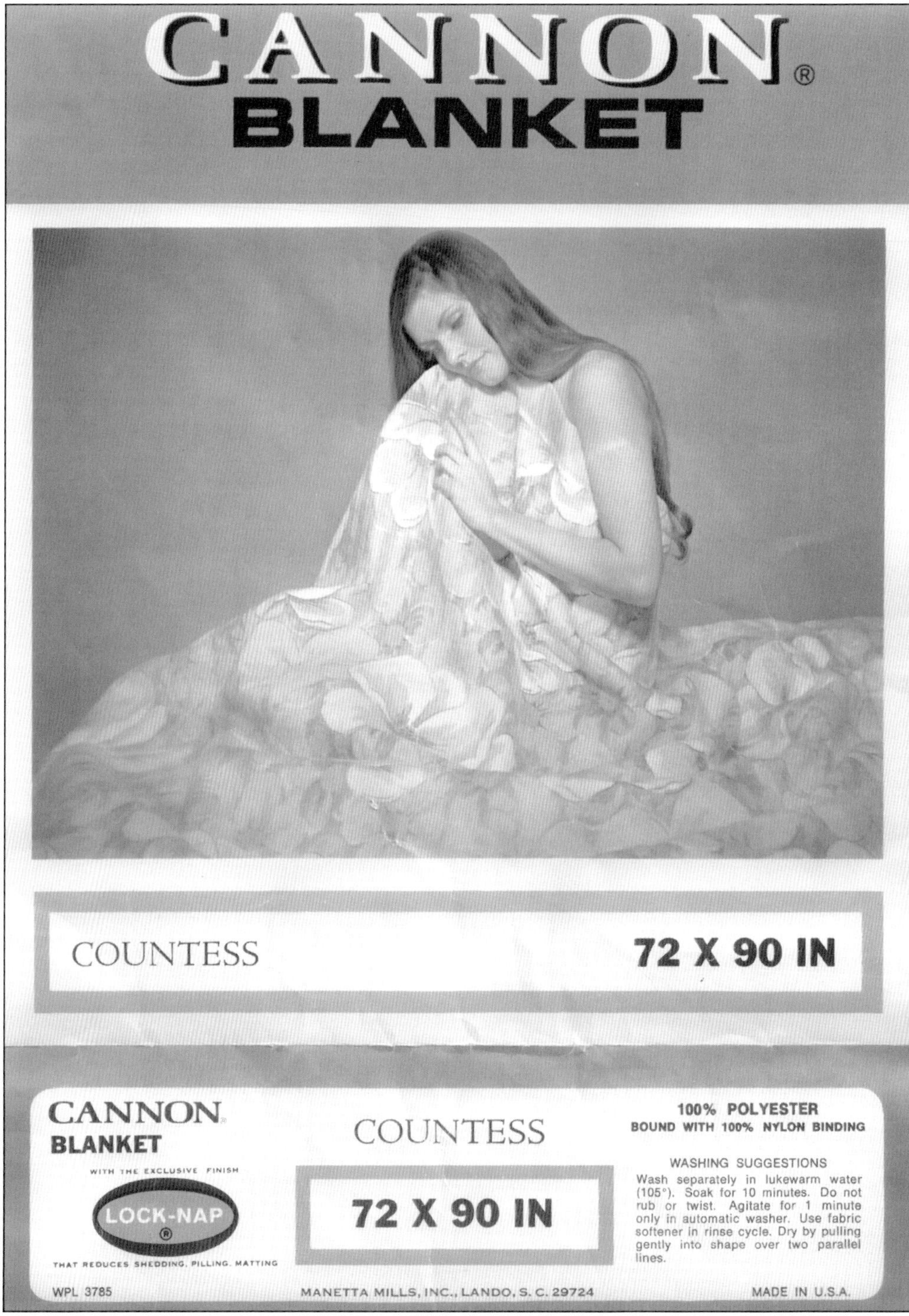

CANNON BLANKET. The Cannon blanket was one of several blankets that Manetta Mills manufactured. This blanket featured "Lock-Nap." Cloth was sent to the nap room, where the cloth was napped or picked to give the cloth a warmer, fuzzy feeling. Lock-Nap blankets were then treated with a chemical to hold the nap in place.

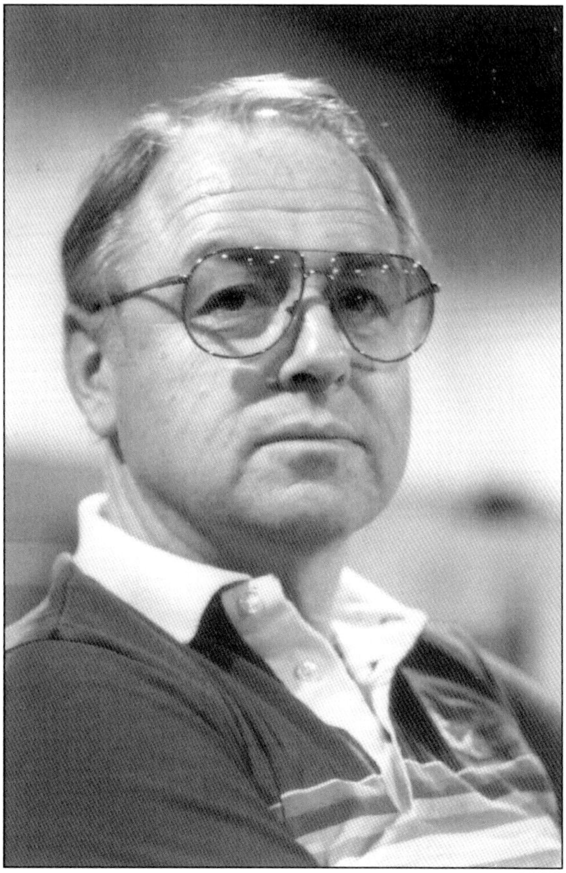

Billy Heath. William "Billy" White Heath was manager of the Monroe, North Carolina, Manetta Mills plant, as well as president of the Edgemoor and Manetta Railway. Just like his brother Allen, Billy was required by his father, Harry Heath, to work in the mill to learn all aspects of the business.

Manetta Home Fashions, Inc., 2006. The marquee still faintly reads "Manetta Home Fashions, Inc.," in Monroe, North Carolina. The current owner, Mark Nettles, plans to renovate the buildings on the site for light industrial use. This building is part of the original 1890 Monroe Cotton Mill facility.

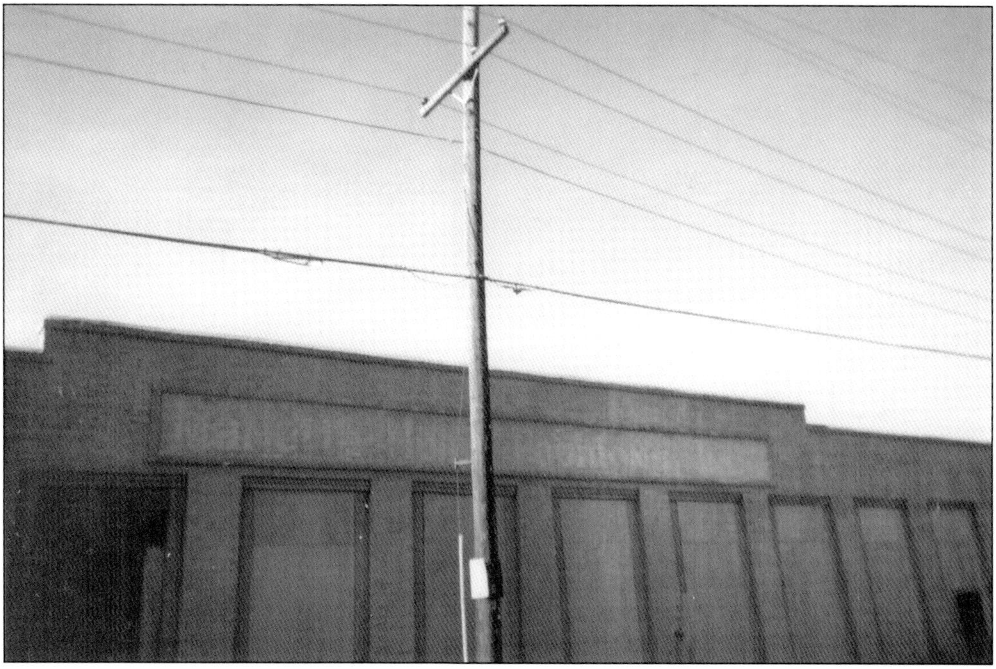

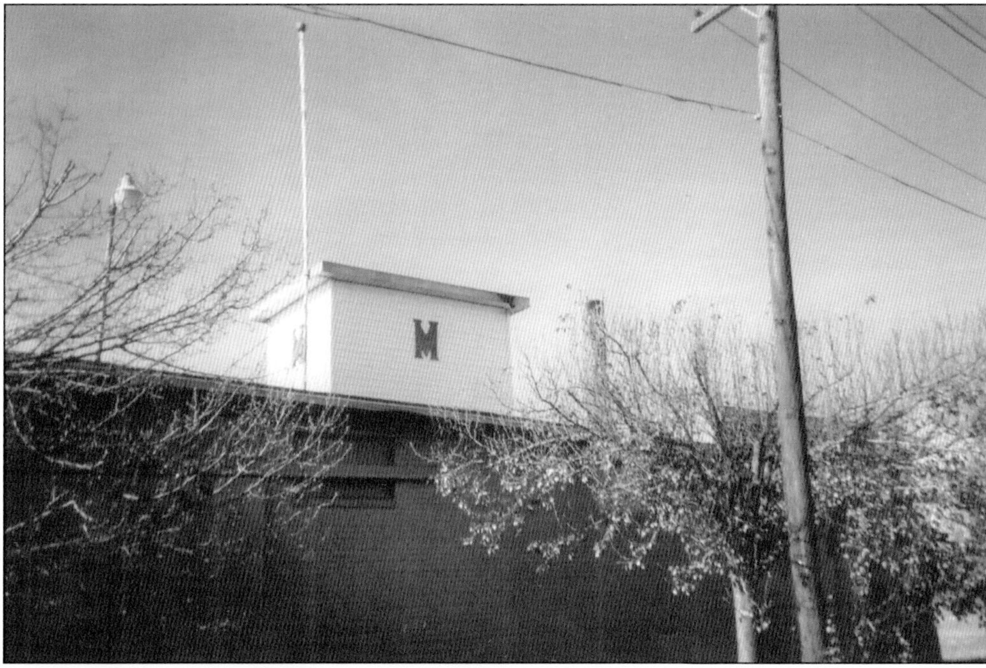

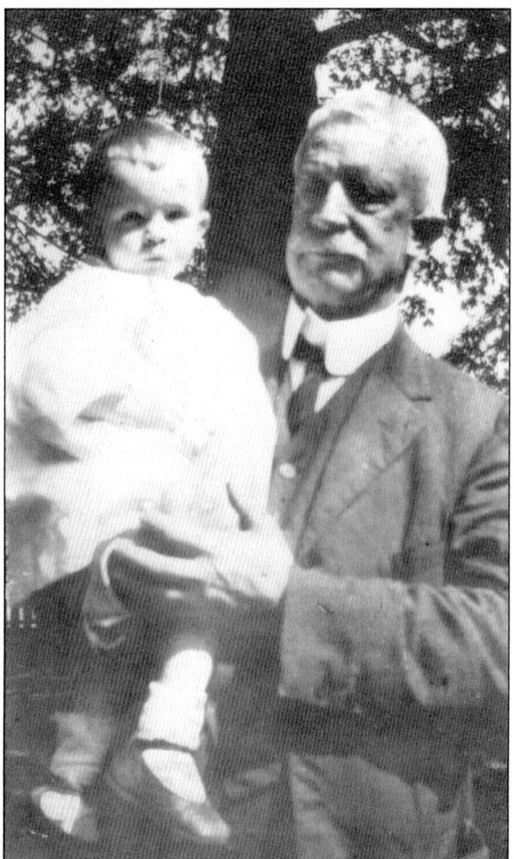

MANETTA MILLS, MONROE, 2006. A black "M" for Manetta was still attached to the Monroe plant in 2006. The Monroe plant is located on the corner of Miller and Heath Streets. The Heath family was well known throughout the Carolinas and influential in the startup of many textile mills throughout the Carolinas. The town of Heath Springs, South Carolina, was a joint venture between the Heath family and the Springs family. Today Springs Global US, Inc., is still a leading textile manufacturer.

CAROLINA HEATHS. The Heath family was deeply involved in textiles and trades in the early 20th century. Maj. William C. Heath, along with B. D. Heath, started Heath Hardware Company in Monroe, North Carolina. W. C. Heath became involved with Jackson Cotton Mills and Textile Mill Supply Company in Charlotte, North Carolina. Osgood Pierce Heath was also active in Carolina textiles but was greatly involved in cotton brokerage.

Three

TRANSPORTATION REVOLUTION

With the prosperity of Manetta Mills and Lando came many new luxuries to the residents of Lando. One of the new luxuries that people experienced was mobility. Many folks traveled from Chester to Edgemoor on the train and then took a horse and buggy to Lando. In 1903, folks traveling from Monroe, North Carolina, or Chester, South Carolina, could take the train to Edgemoor and then take the Edgemoor and Manetta Railway into Lando. The railroad connected Lando and Manetta Mills directly to the rest of the world.

Residents of Lando were also introduced to the automobile. Using their wages from Manetta Mills, many folks purchased their first automobile from Rock Hill or Chester while living and working in Lando. The automobile allowed folks to travel to the bigger cities. As the automobile became more available, more and more folks were able to purchase one. The automobile became the pride of many folks, and it was a symbol of success for many.

In a small local community like Lando, not every family needed or wanted a car. The use of a bicycle allowed those families on the edge of town to get to work on time without having to walk. The bicycle was used by many folks for going to work but mainly by children going to play at a neighbor's house. The rolling hills along the Fishing Creek valley provided excellent downhill speeds.

In the 1950s, the Carolina Stage, a bus from Rock Hill, would come to Lando on Saturdays and take folks to Rock Hill and then return to Lando in the afternoon. Mass transportation was used by many folks from Lando. Even with all the many ways to become mobile, most folks returned to Lando—the place they called home.

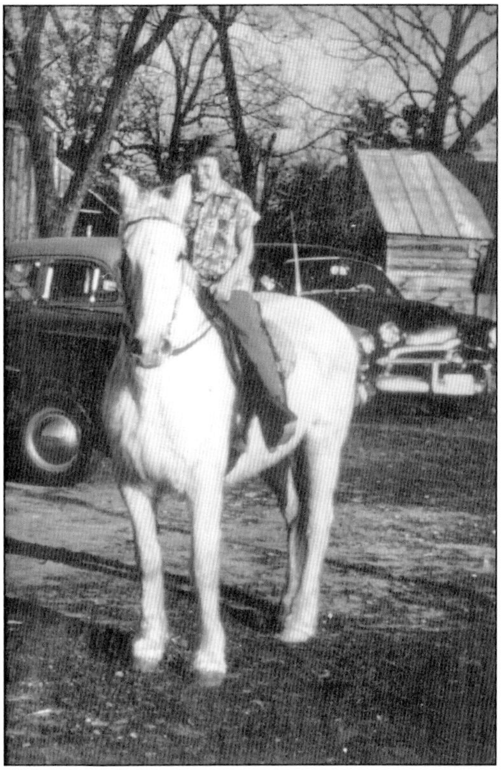

LADY. Sarah Ernandez rides Lady—a horse that belonged to her brother, Hugh Gray Ernandez—to and from Lando in the early 1950s. Lady was a favorite part of Lando for many children.

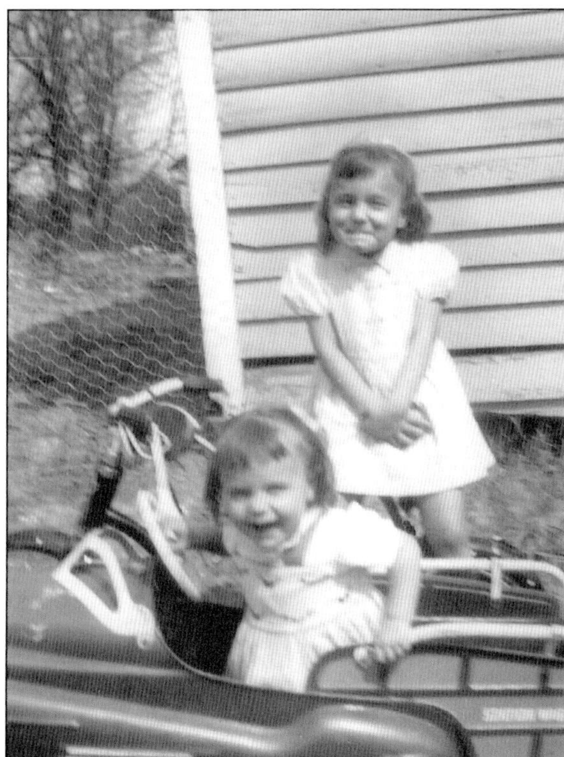

TOY CAR. Ann (standing) and Dale Evans smile as they get caught playing with their toys in their good dresses in the early 1950s.

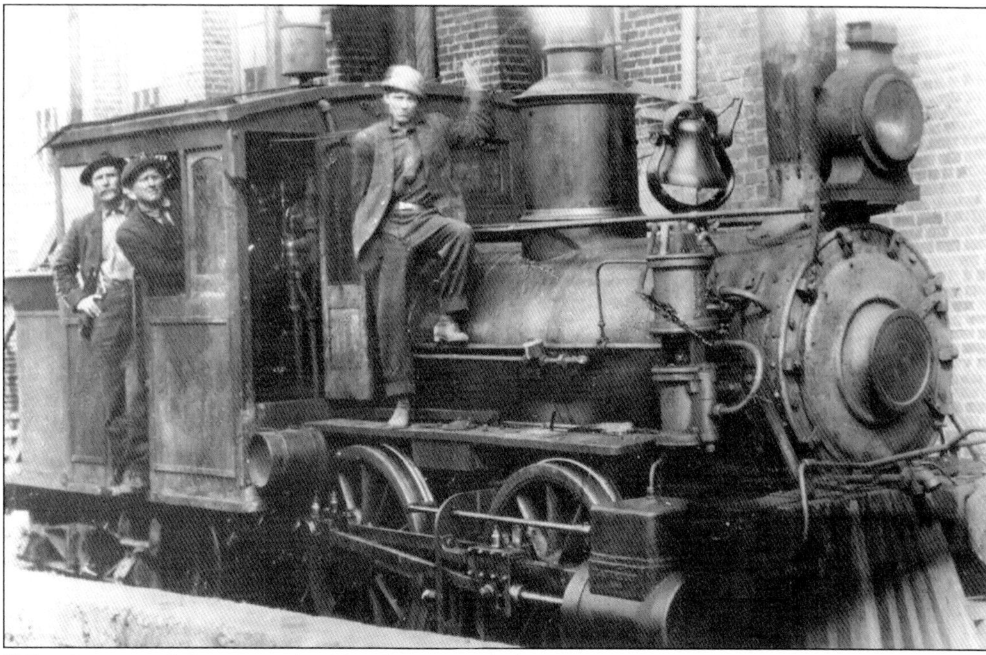

"THE DINKEY." In 1902, the Heaths created the E&M Railway, which ran 2.3 miles from Edgemoor to Lando. Folks often traveled from Monroe, North Carolina, on the Seaboard Air Line Railway to Edgemoor and then caught the E&M to Lando. Here the original engine, called "the Dinkey," which was a Manhattan Railway 0-4-4T built by Baldwin in 1881, is delivered on February 2, 1902.

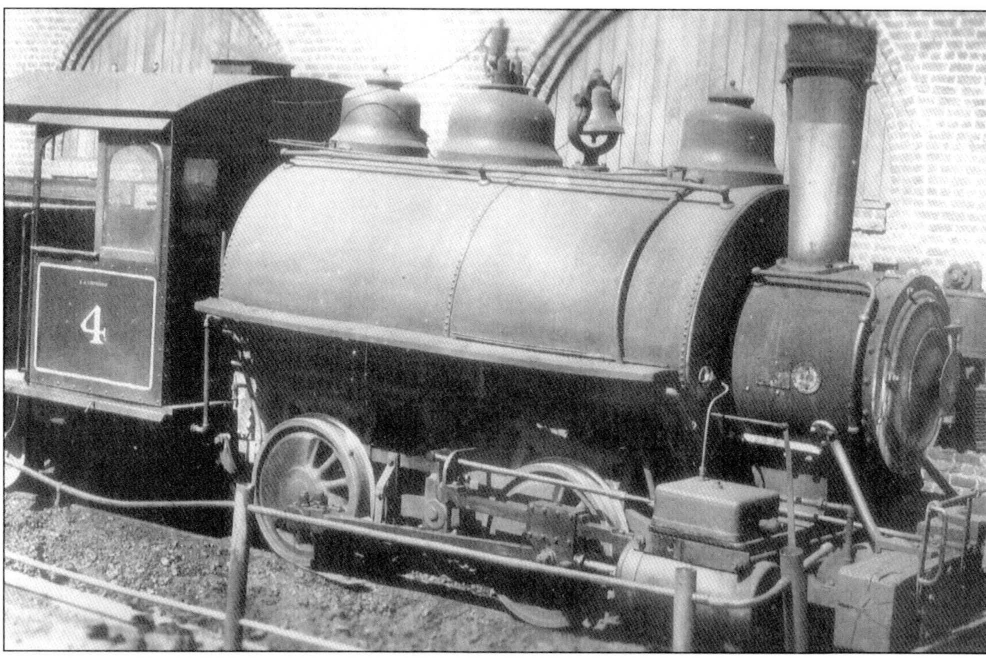

ENGINE NO. 4. The second engine No. 4, a Vulcan No. 1108, 4-1907 0-4-2T, was a backup engine to the Dinkey. The No. 5, nicknamed "the Dummy," replaced the No. 4 and was in operation until the short-line railroad ceased operations in 1975.

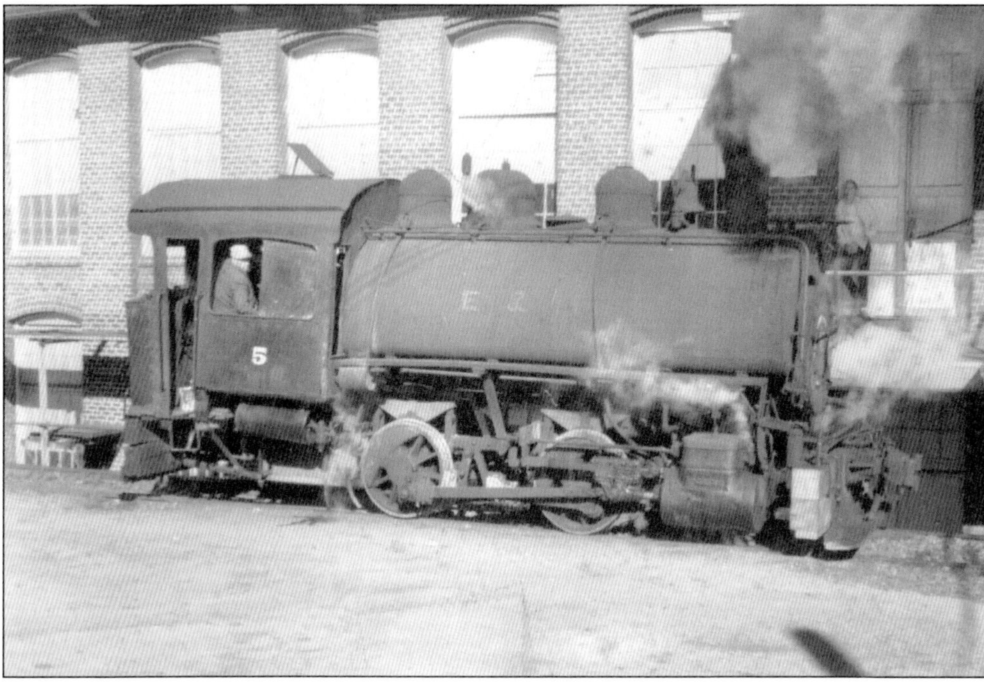

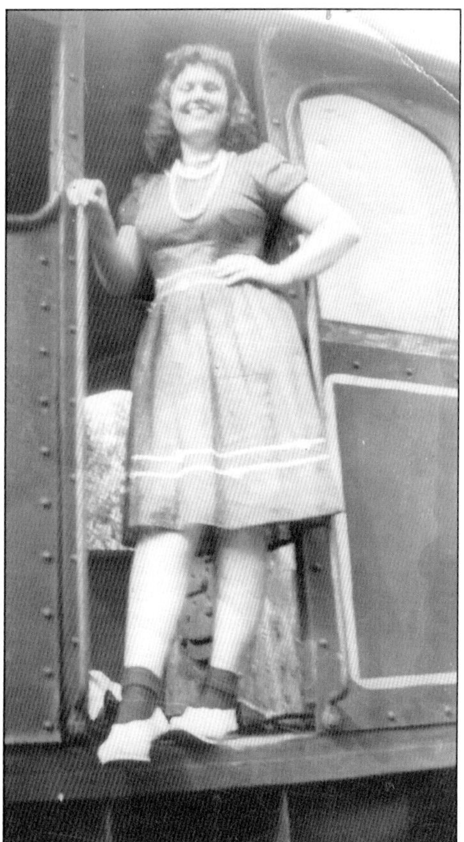

HARD AT WORK. The Dummy, a 1917 Plymouth 0-4-0T No. 5980 that was purchased in 1942, ran twice daily to and from Edgemoor. R. A. Willis was traffic manager for the E&M, and folks could buy tickets for a ride to and from Edgemoor. The Dummy remained in front of Manetta Mills even after tractors and trailers began hauling blankets from Lando.

ALL ABOARD. Kathleen Hough Crocker has her picture taken on the Dummy. People could buy a set of round-trip tickets on the Edgemoor and Manetta Railway between Edgemoor and Lando. The E&M stopped carrying passengers in the early 1920s. R. A. Willis was traffic manager for the E&M until the early 1940s.

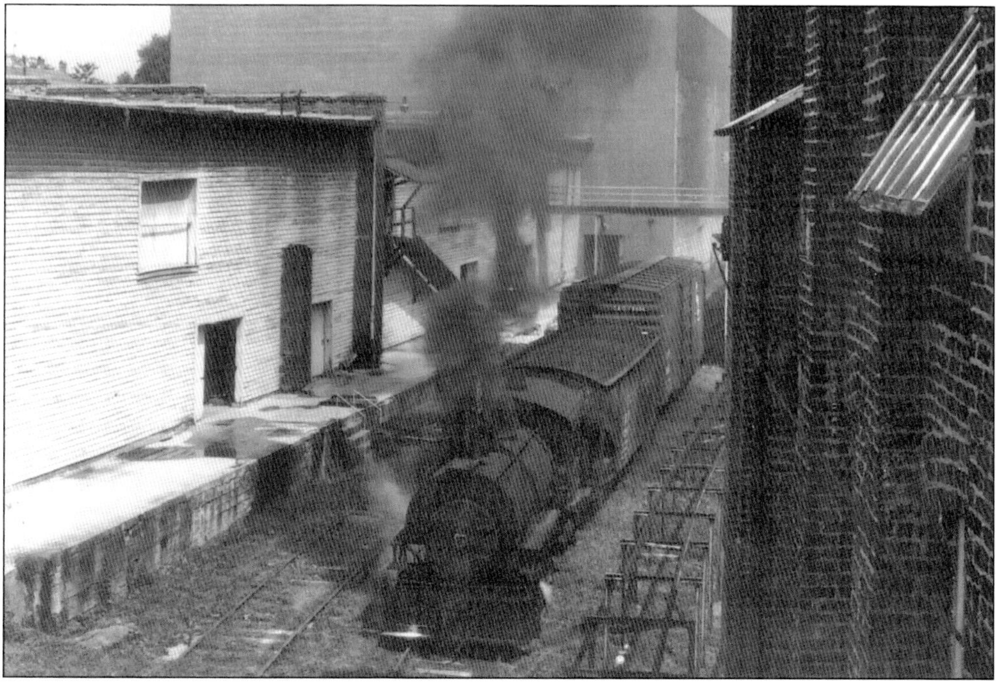

The Golden Age of Locomotives. The Dummy and Tom Buckson worked hard from Edgemoor to Manetta Mills five days a week.

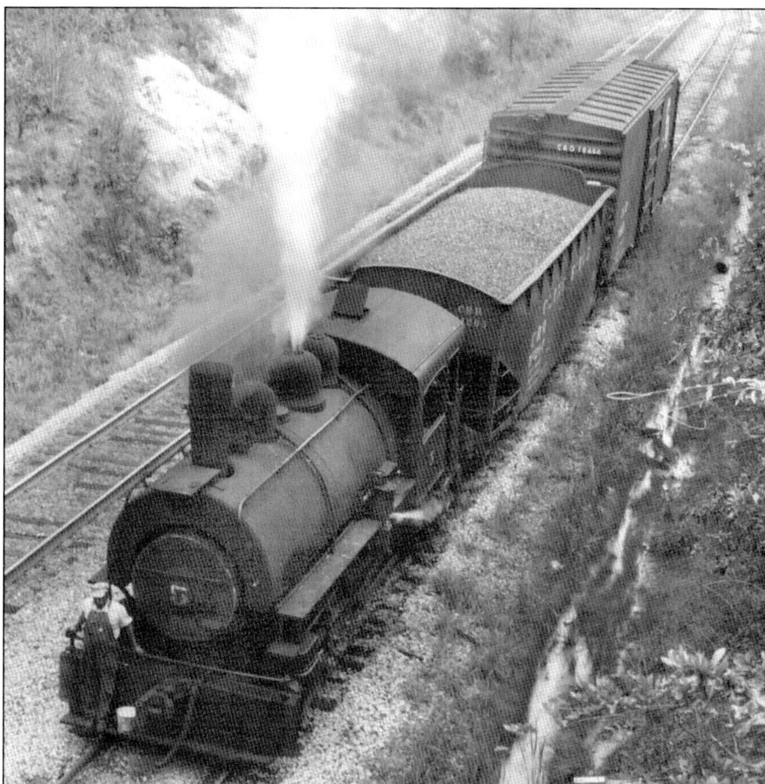

Lane and Dodson. Some folks credit the name Lando to the Seaboard Air Line Railway. It is believed that the last names of two employees of the Seaboard Air Line, Captain Lane and John A. Dodson, were combined to create Lando.

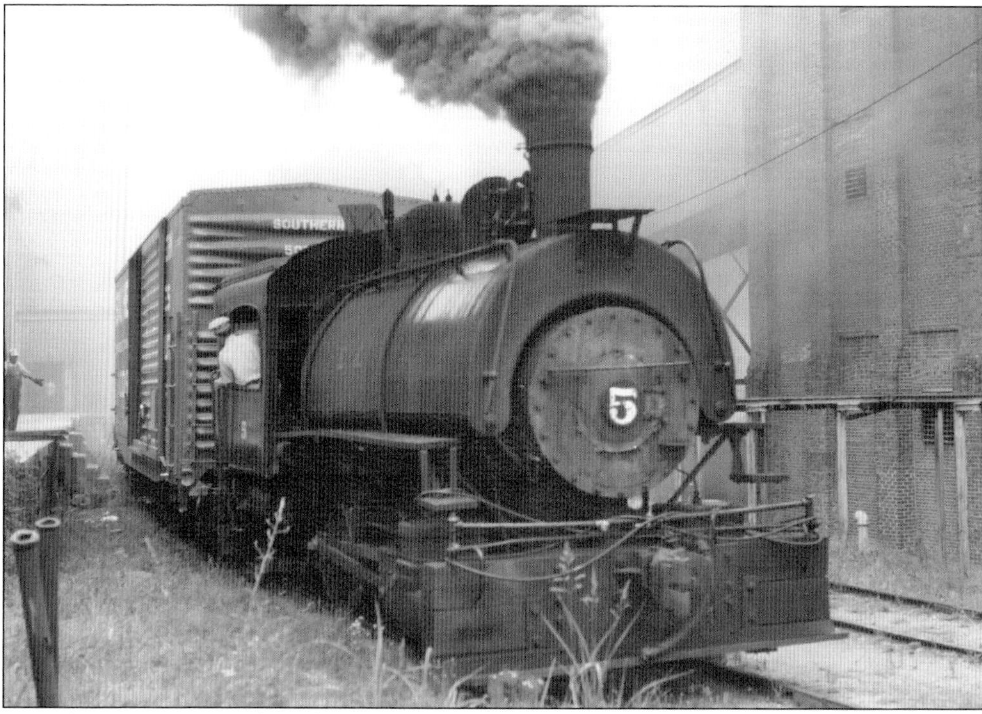

LAST STEAM ENGINE. The Edgemoor and Manetta Railway is credited as the last commercial short steam line that operated in the United States.

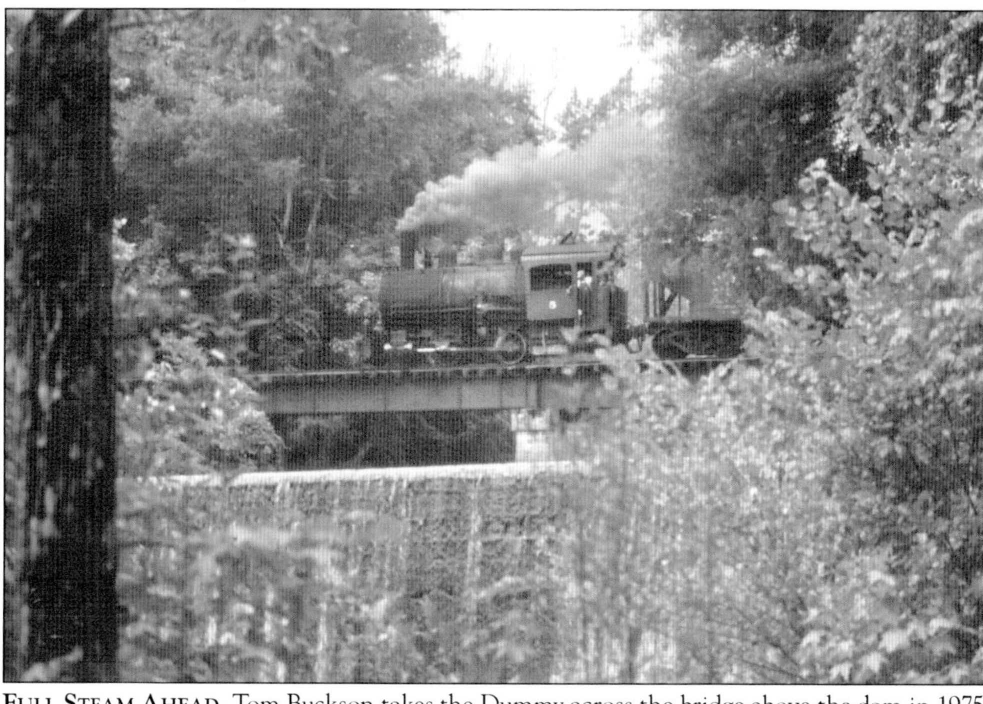

FULL STEAM AHEAD. Tom Buckson takes the Dummy across the bridge above the dam in 1975. Willie Starnes was the engineer/conductor in 1975, and his father-in-law, Jeff Stevenson, worked on the E&M for 47 years.

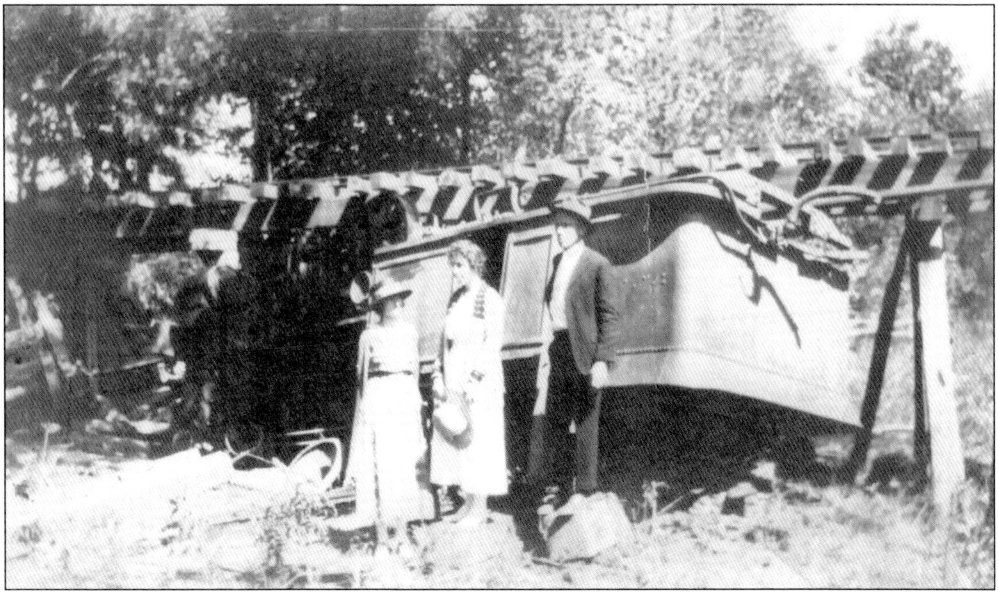

ACCIDENTS HAPPEN. Even a short-line railroad has dangers. In 1919, a coal car derailed, and in December 1972, the bridge gave way as Tom Buckson and Willie Starnes were taking the E&M across it. Again a car loaded with coal fell from the tracks.

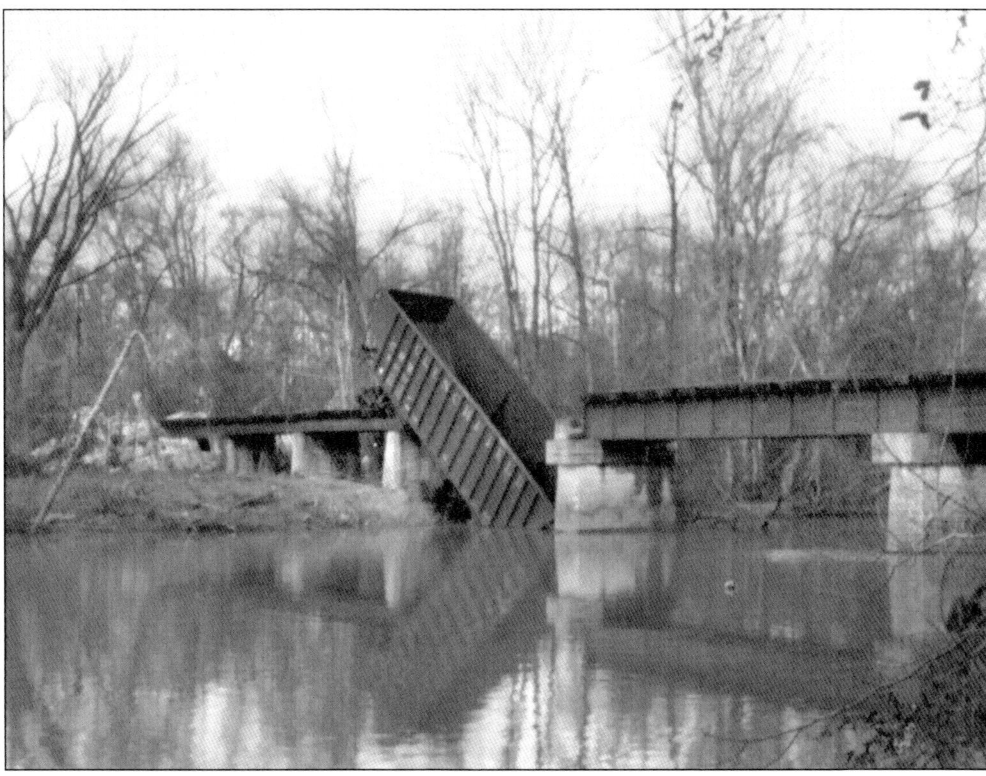

NEEDING REPAIR. Jimmy "Chubby" Long was the maintenance and repair professional for the Dummy. The engine was required to have monthly inspections, and it was Long's duty to make sure the Dummy stayed in working order.

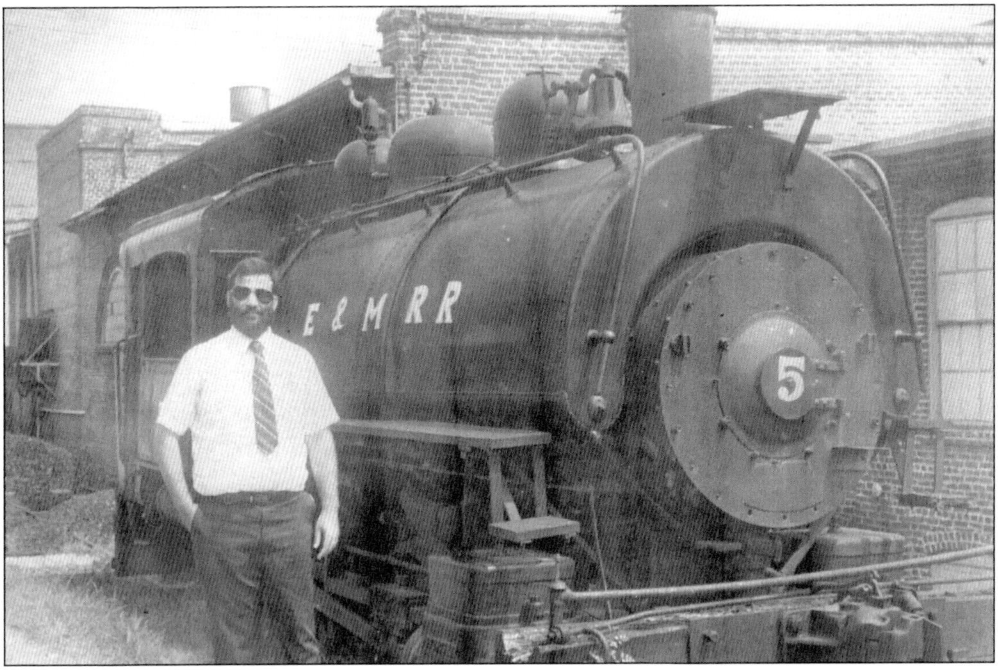

PHOTO OPPORTUNITY. Joe Cale Watson has his photograph taken in front of the Dummy. Watson was pastor at Heath Memorial Methodist Church from 1982 to 1984 and also helped implement the first Lando Days festivals.

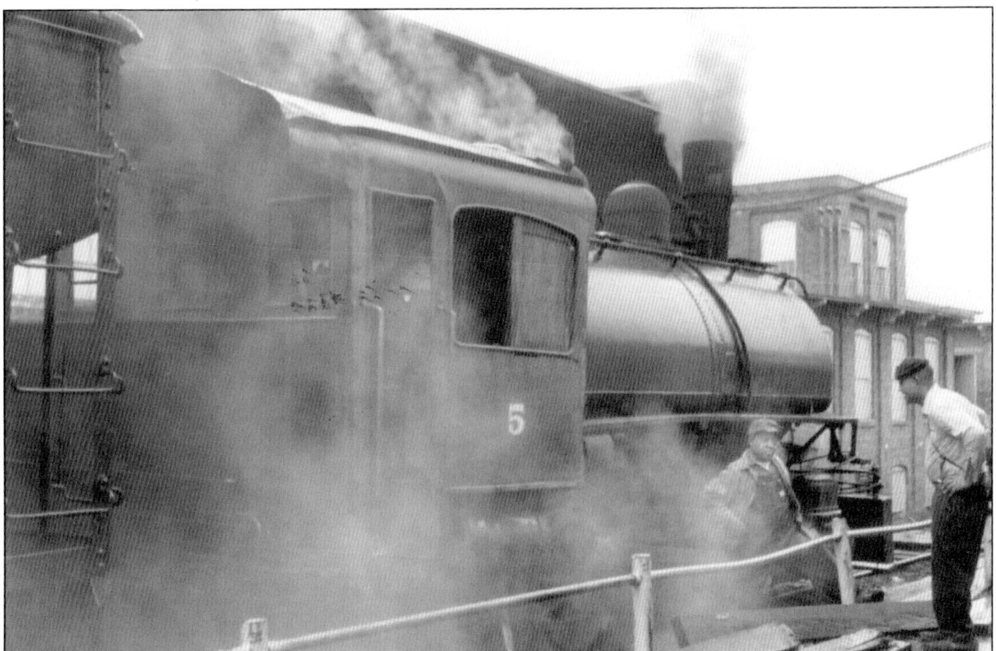

WATCHING FOR SPARKS. Tom Buckson and Sam Basse stand watch near the Dummy in the early 1970s at the coal dump next to the boiler room. A fire broke out from a spark from the engine. Volunteer firefighters employed at Manetta Mills were able to quickly extinguish the fire before it spread to the mill.

POSING WITH THEIR CAR. Ruth Mosley (left) and Linda ? sit on their car as they prepare to drive to Rock Hill in the 1930s.

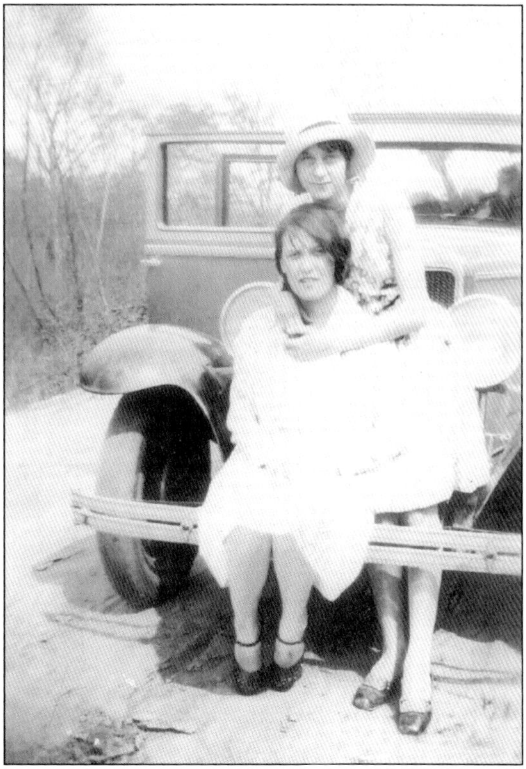

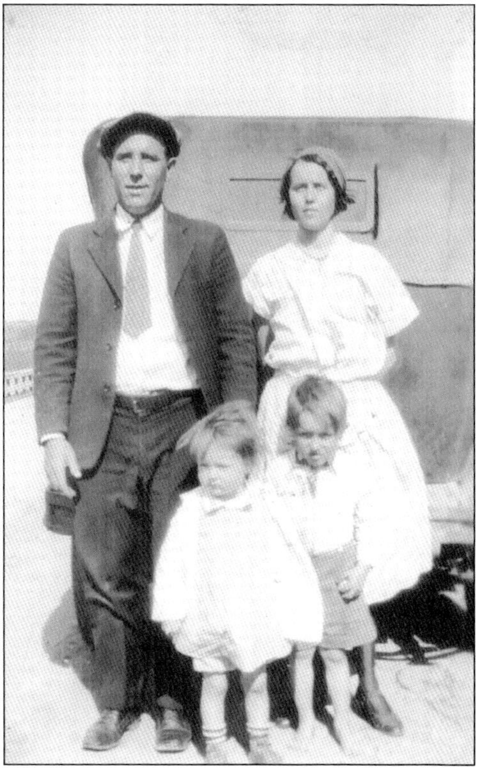

FAMILY CAR. In the 1920s, Mary and Jack Vinson have their picture taken with their children, J. C. (left) and Perry, on the Highway 901 bridge over Fishing Creek.

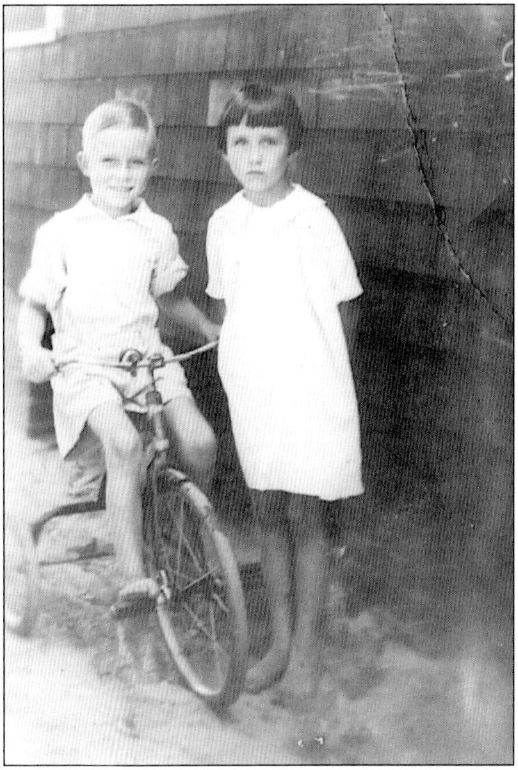

Watch Your Toes. Theodore Hinson smiles in the 1930s as he has mastered the art of riding his tricycle. His sister Joyce Hinson (Ernandez) stands cautiously trying to protect her toes.

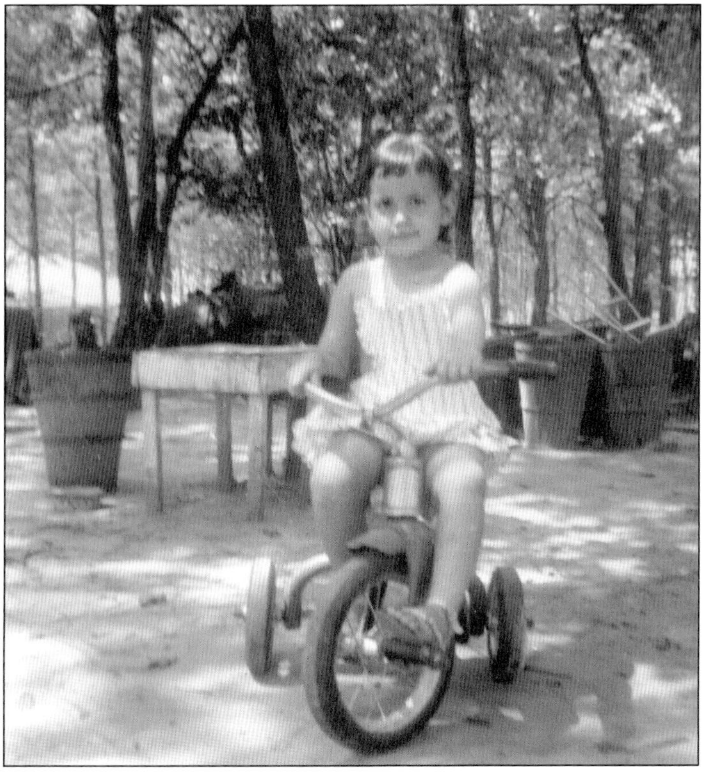

Bicycles. Not everyone in Lando decided to buy an automobile. Many folks enjoyed a ride on a bicycle. Many were able to travel to and from work at Manetta Mills from their homes in Lando. Iris Vinson rides her tricycle on the edge of Happy Holler in the mid-1930s.

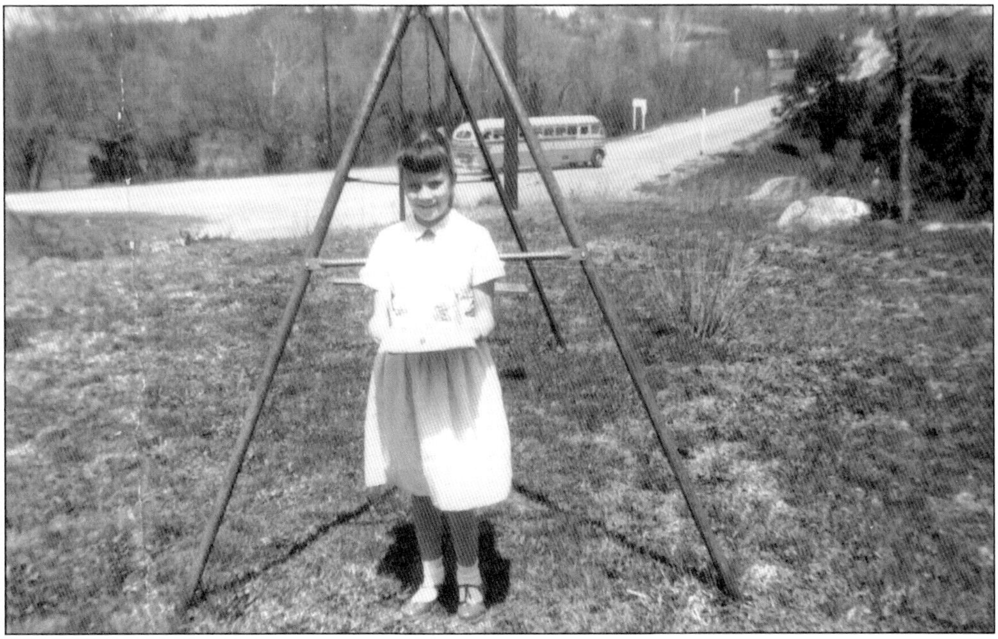

THE CAROLINA STAGE. Mary Francis Rockholt stands near Highway 901 in the 1940s as the Carolina Stage goes by. The Carolina Stage was a Saturday bus that came down to Lando from Rock Hill. Many folks remember riding the stage to Rock Hill with 50¢ in their pocket and being able to go to the movies, buy a snack, and maybe get a treat for a girl- or boyfriend—and still have a few cents left over. John Coker, a longtime Manetta Mills employee and Lando resident, tells young folks how he could buy two pieces of candy in the company store for only one penny.

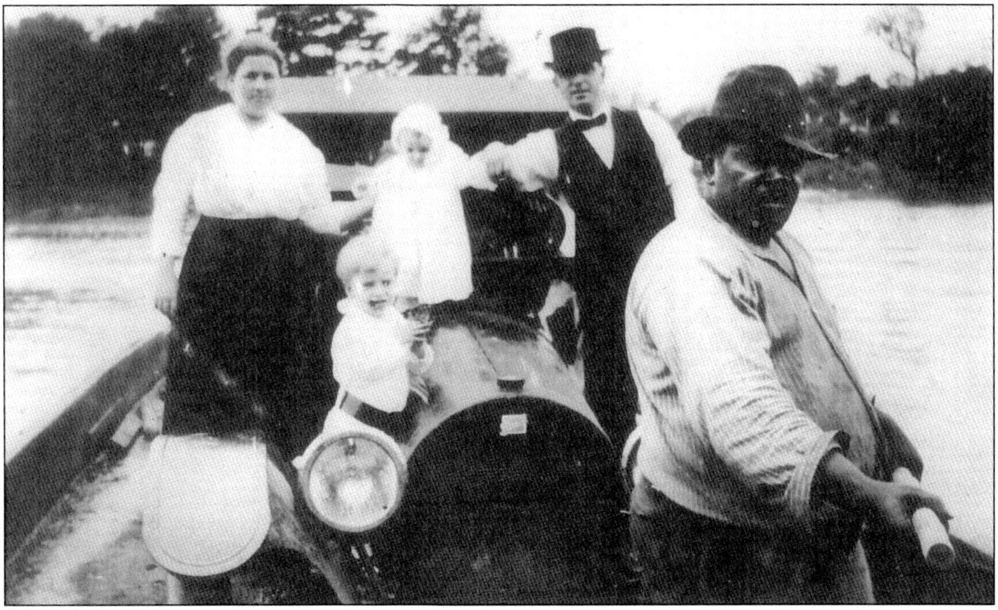

FERRY RIDE. All roads to Lando from Monroe and Charlotte, North Carolina, had to cross the Catawba River. The ferry system at Ashe's Ferry on the Catawba River was active until late 1959. From left to right, Lela, Harry, Genola, and Gilbert Heath, along with the ferryman, cross the Catawba River in 1920.

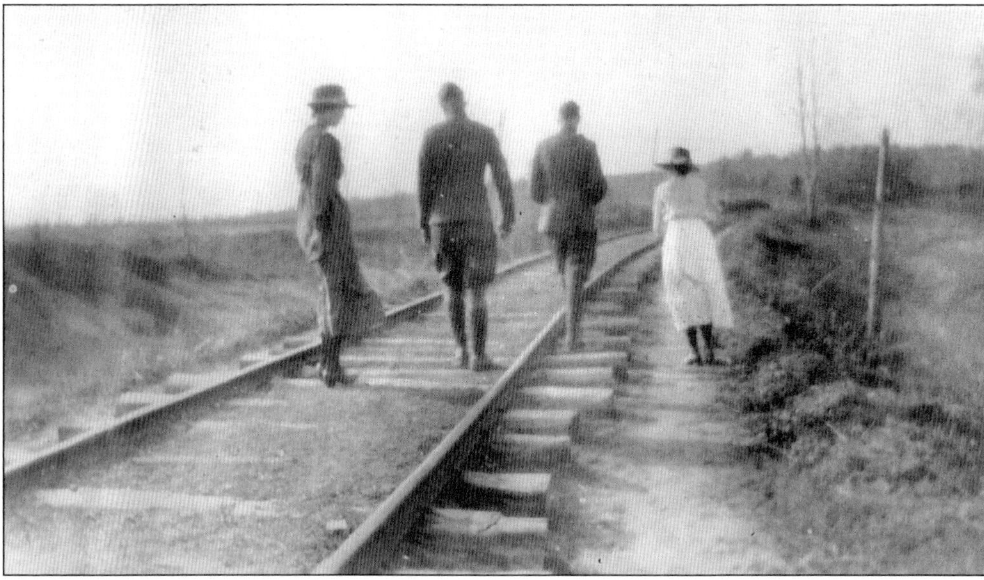

WALKING ALONG THE TRACKS. Sometimes the best transportation is a good pair of shoes. Many residents of Lando talk about lazy days and peaceful evenings. Nothing is more relaxing in the 1920s than a walk along the E&M line.

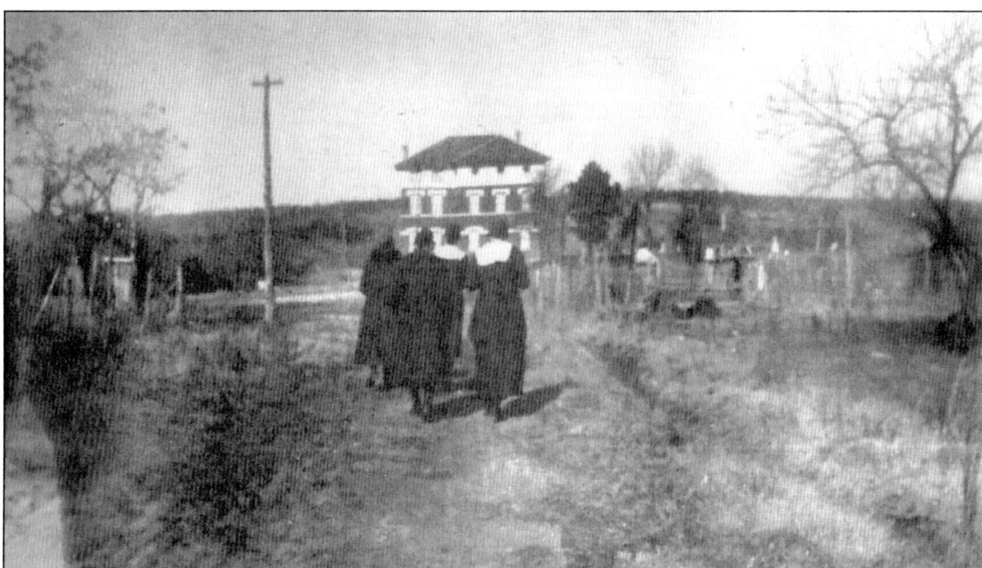

WALKING TO SCHOOL. There was no waiting at the bus stop for students of the Lando School in the 1920s. All children walked to school, and in the winter, they had to go by the mill for a bucket of coal before coming to class.

Four

Cultural Revolution

Many folks came to Lando and Manetta Mills from the rural communities in the Carolinas. Being mostly farmers, these people had to learn the ways of a manufacturing community. This was a culture shock for many folks.

Manetta Mills and the Heath family exposed families to many forms of art, recreation, and education. Education was very important to the Heath family, so during their expansion in 1904, the Lando School was built. The State of South Carolina paid the wages for the four teachers who worked in the school, but the Heath family provided the material and facilities.

The Lando School still stands as a majestic structure—the pride of the community. The multicolor bricks and round windows were unique for a mill school. The Heaths knew the value of education and wanted every child in Lando to have the opportunity to learn. The three-story building has five classrooms on the bottom two floors, and the third floor has a performing stage and a balcony. Music and arts were an important part of the curriculum at the Lando School.

Billy Haggerty lived in Lando all his life, and just about every picture of him shows him playing music. The Fourth of July festivals always had music at the bandstand. Lando also had a brass band and an orchestra. Music was a part of life for many folks in Lando. Many folks would play a harmonica or guitar on the front porch to relax after 12 hours in the mill.

Playing sports was also a part of the "cultural revolution" in Lando. Folks young and old could play organized team sports. Baseball and volleyball were favorite school sports. Manetta Mills supported the Lando baseball team, known as the "Blanketeers," which fielded local legend Grady Bolton, who went on to play minor-league baseball.

The move from a rural agrarian lifestyle to the industrial setting in Lando changed the life of many people. These folks were now exposed to many luxuries, such as a good education and appreciation for the arts.

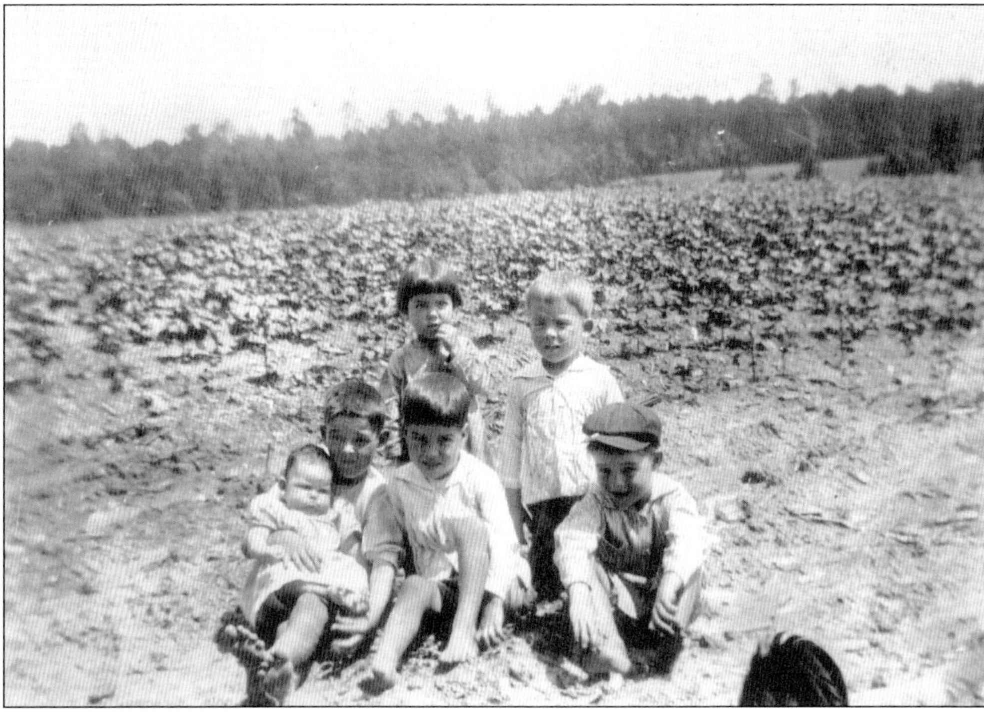

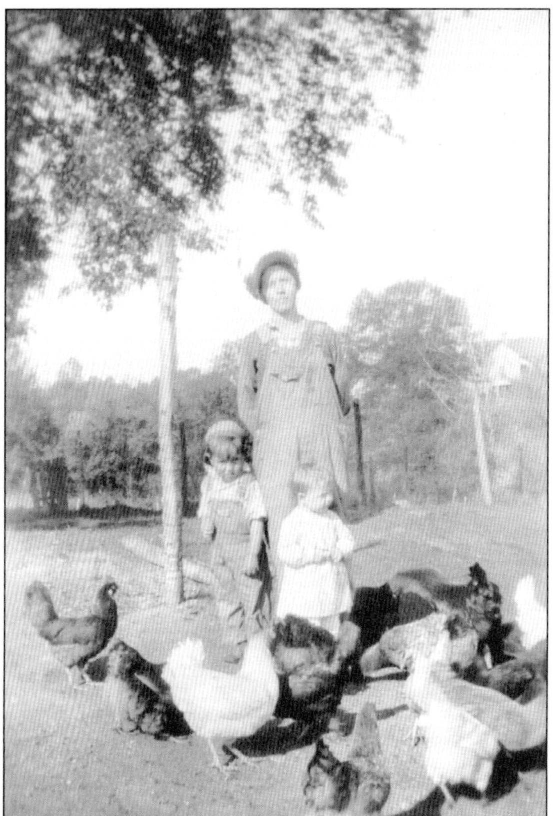

A FIELD FULL OF DREAMS. From left to right, Cecil Polk, Wade Helms, Douglas Polk, R. D. Helm, Tootsie Helms, and Minnie Helms enjoy playing in a plowed field in the early 1920s. The fields were largely worked by mules. Machine-powered equipment did not come around until several years later.

PULLING DOUBLE DUTY, 1920S. Many of the people living in Lando came from rural farming communities. They were able to use the knowledge of farming in the mill village. Mary Vinson (left) and Jack Vinson Jr. (right) feed the chickens at their home in Lando.

ERNANDEZ. Madge Laney Ernandez and her children tend the goats in the 1920s. Ernandez was a popular name in Lando. Many Ernandez children were born in Lando and grew up to work in Manetta Mills.

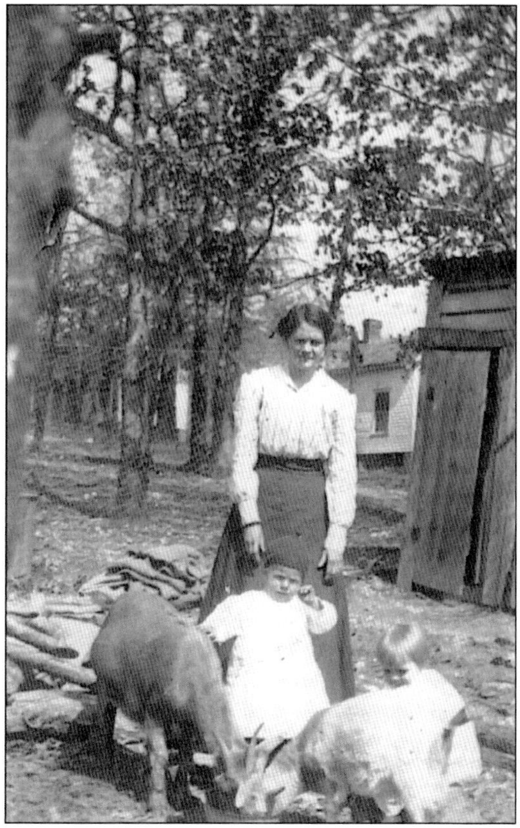

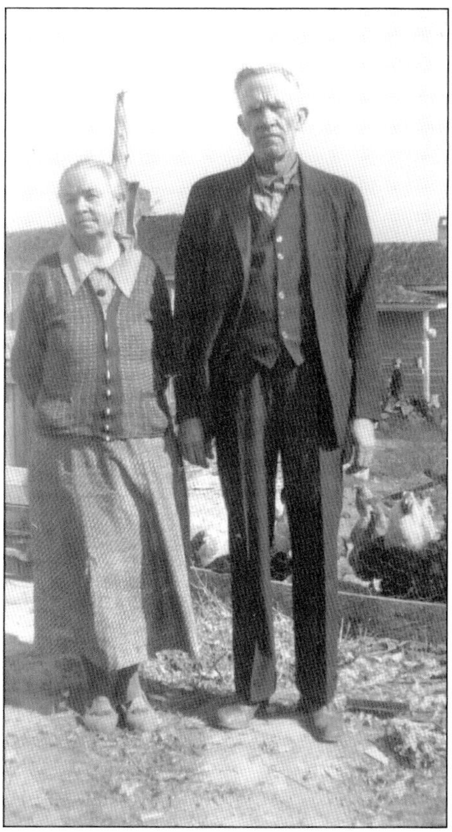

BACKYARD GARDEN. The flood plains along Fishing Creek provide excellent soil for growing corn and other vegetables. The countryside near Lando supported many large farms. Cotton was king, but many local farmers still grew grains and vegetables to sell in nearby cities. Fred and Leila Hefner stand near their chickens behind their Lando home in the 1950s.

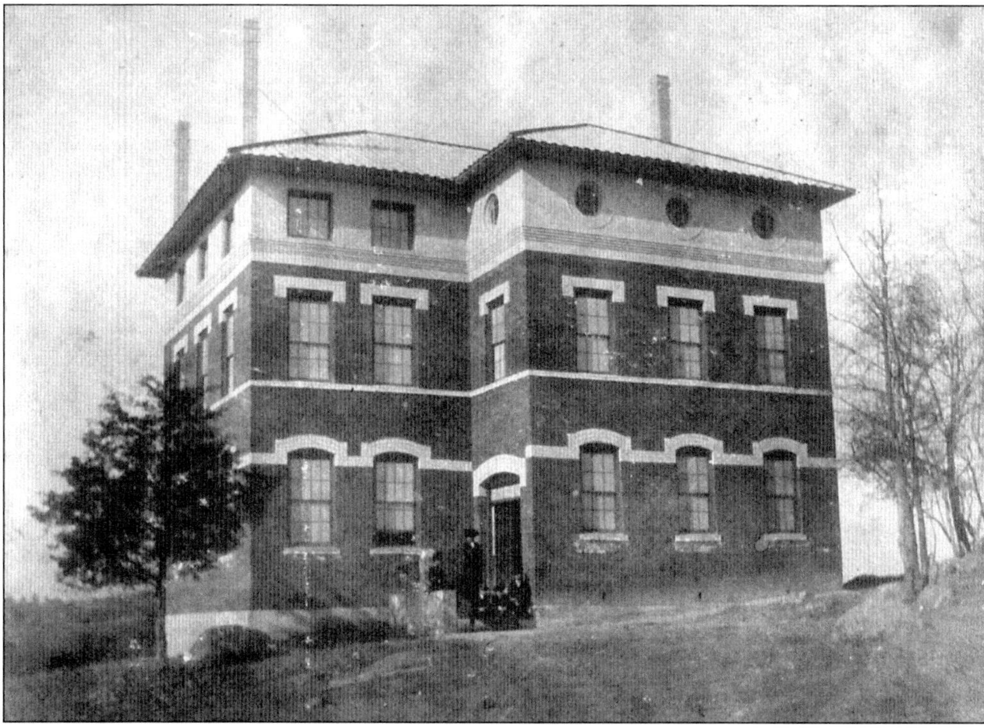

A GOOD EDUCATION CAN TURN YOUR LIFE AROUND. Education was very important to the Heaths, so during their expansion in 1904, the Lando School was built in a majestic style to showcase the importance of education.

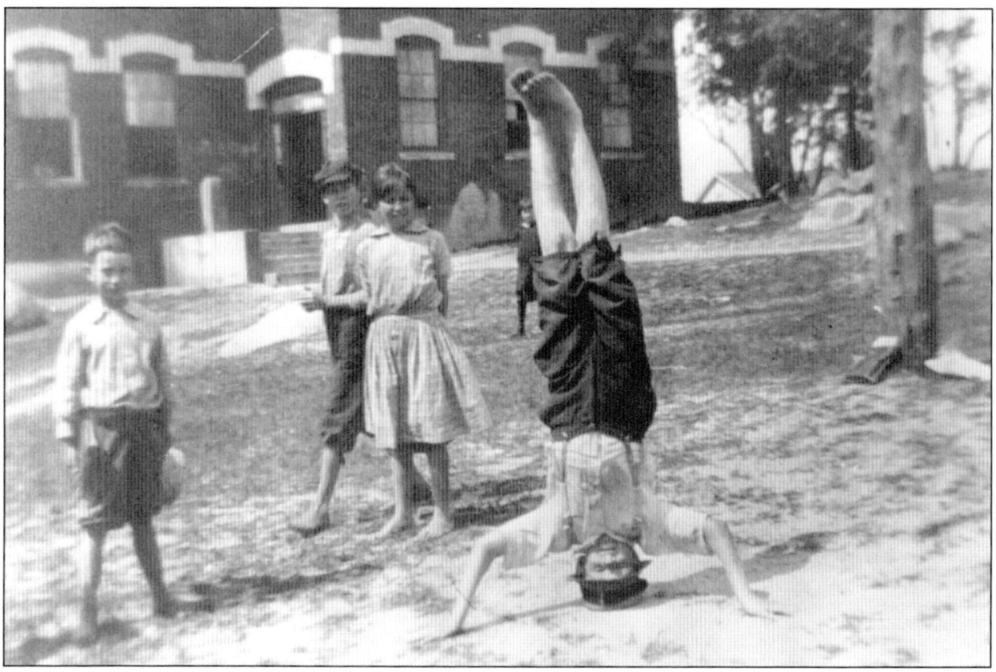

HAND STAND. A Lando School student tries to impress the young ladies by standing on his head. Hats were in fashion at the time of this 1920s photograph, but shoes were still optional.

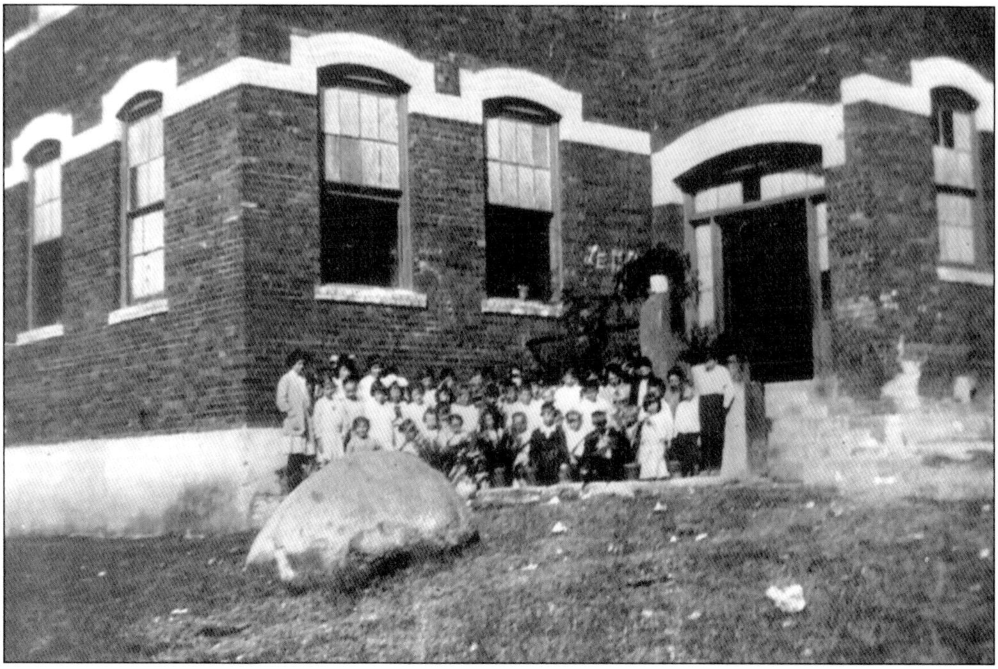

ROCK SOLID EDUCATION. The five-room schoolhouse taught all grade levels in the 1920s. The second floor was an auditorium with a balcony and a stage. The arts were an important part of the curriculum in the Lando School.

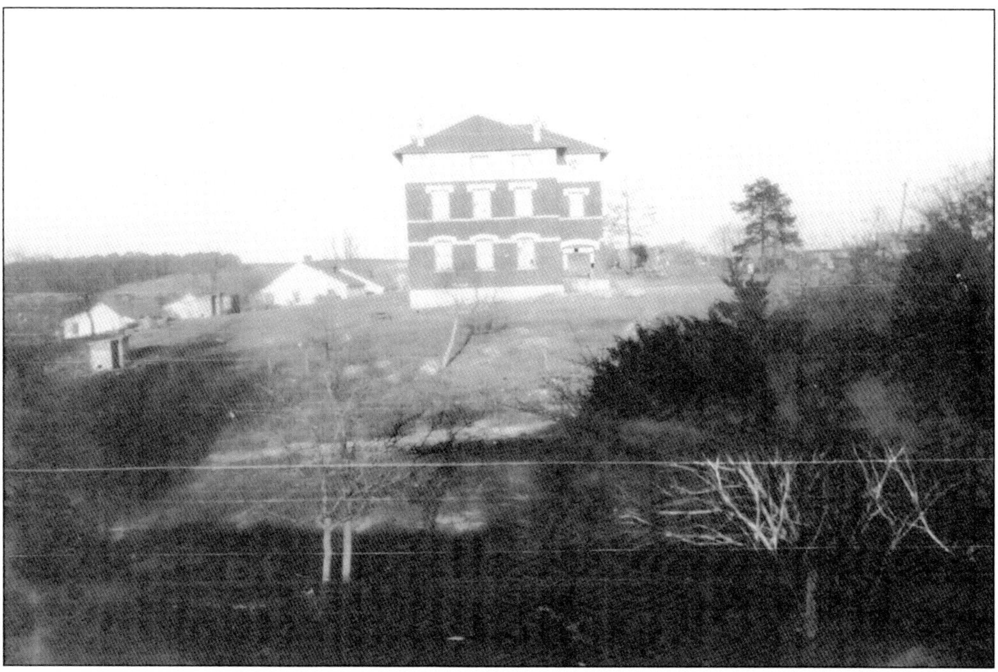

STANDING TALL. The Lando School is the tallest structure outside the mill itself. In 1905, the school could be seen from nearly every house in Lando. There was also a schoolhouse in the "Quarters" section of Lando, the area of town where African American families lived. In the days before integration, African American children had to attend their own school.

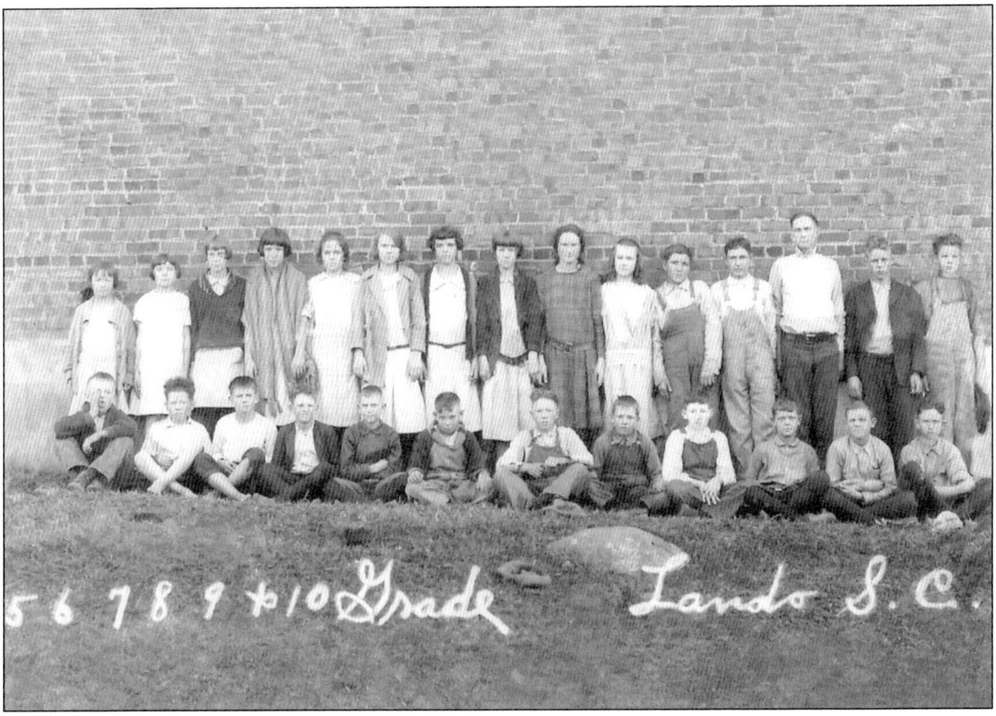

CLASS PHOTOGRAPH. The Lando School taught grades 1 through 11 with only five teachers. Grades 1 through 4 were on the first floor, and grades 5 through 11 were on the second floor.

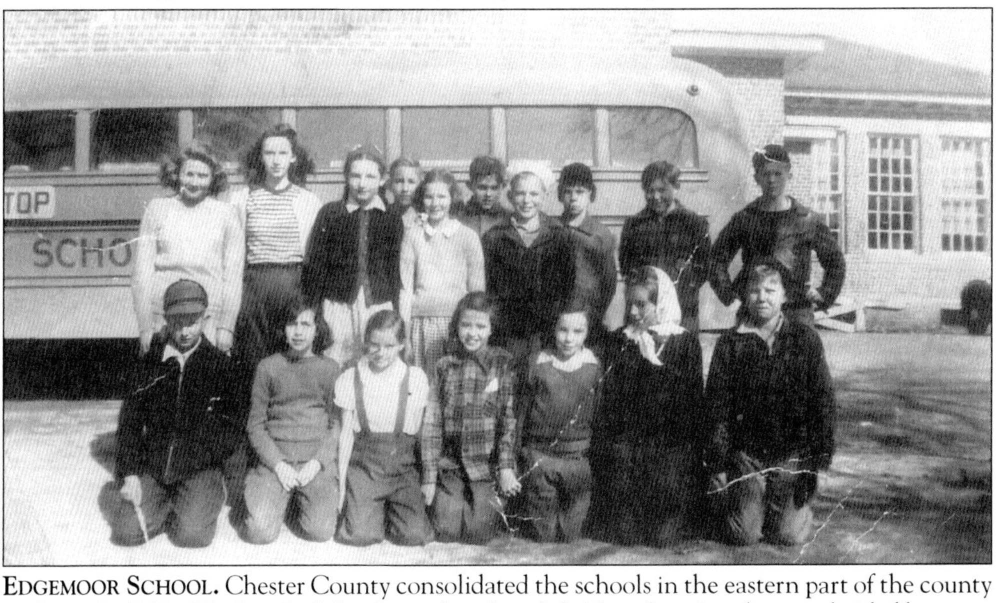

EDGEMOOR SCHOOL. Chester County consolidated the schools in the eastern part of the county in the early 1950s. The Lando School was closed, and children from Lando were divided between Oakley Hall in Rodman and the Edgemoor School. African American children still attended their own school located in the Quarters. Pictured from left to right are the following: (first row) unidentified, Ruby ?, Mildred Glass, Ruth Rison, Jerry Adkins, Betty ?, and unidentified; (second row) unidentified, Janie Belle Gladales, Elenor Reid, two unidentified, Buddy Hinnant, unidentified, Alwin Gibson, Paul Simpson, and unidentified.

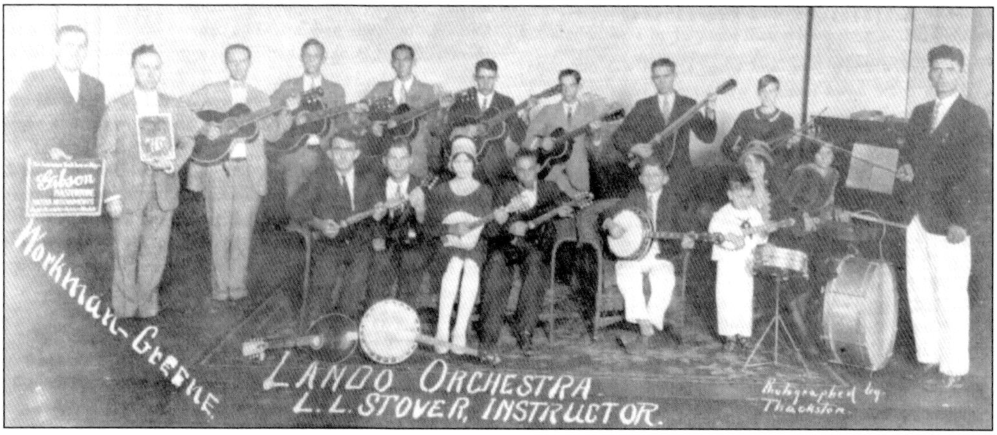

THE 1927 LANDO ORCHESTRA. Pictured are the following, from left to right: (seated) Jim Alley, Bud Sanders, ? Stover, Homer Miller, two unidentified, ? Stover, and Pauline Miller Bolton (piano); (standing) unidentified, Carl Thomas, Grady Bolton, Dewey Sanders, Alex Varnadore, Clyde Sanders, Walter Billy Haggerty, Lilia Saunders Mitchell, unidentified, and instructor L. A. Stover.

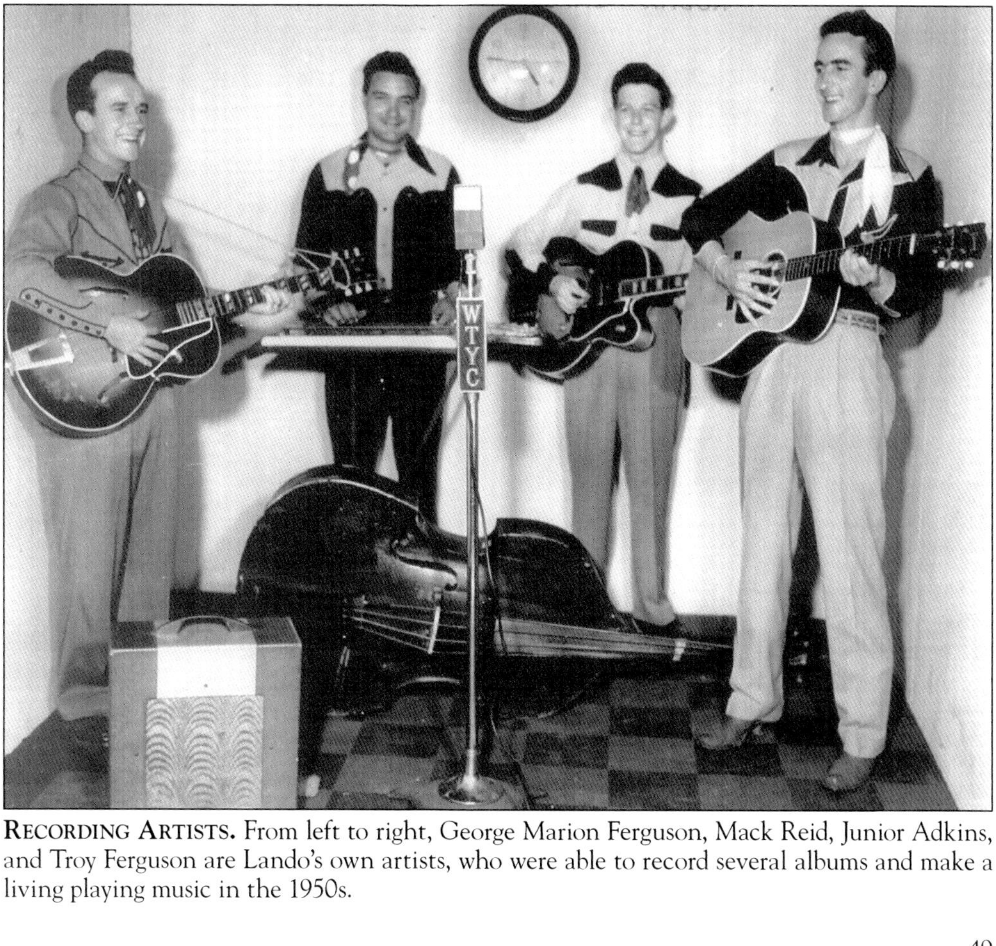

RECORDING ARTISTS. From left to right, George Marion Ferguson, Mack Reid, Junior Adkins, and Troy Ferguson are Lando's own artists, who were able to record several albums and make a living playing music in the 1950s.

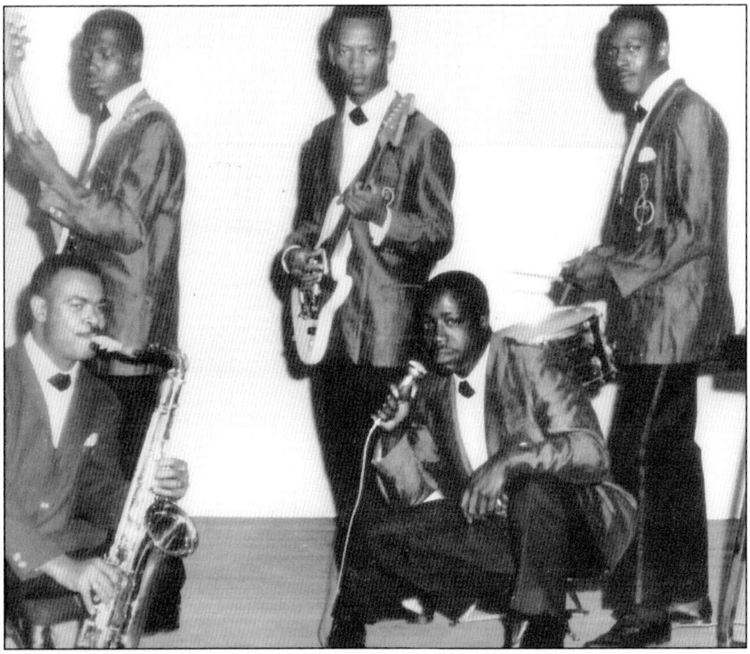

Bo Brown. Bobby Player (saxophone), Bo Brown (singer), Chick Hooper (bass), ? Brown (guitar), and Willie Dee (drums) constituted another group of Lando's talented musicians in the 1960s.

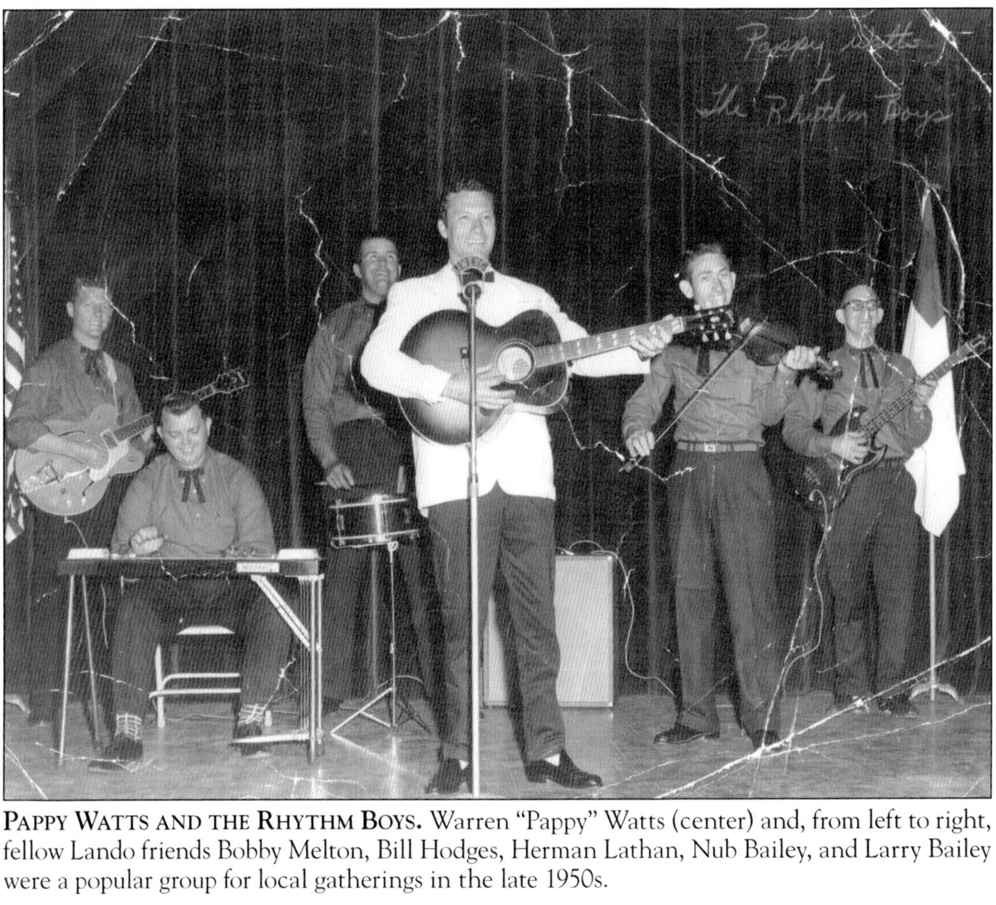

Pappy Watts and the Rhythm Boys. Warren "Pappy" Watts (center) and, from left to right, fellow Lando friends Bobby Melton, Bill Hodges, Herman Lathan, Nub Bailey, and Larry Bailey were a popular group for local gatherings in the late 1950s.

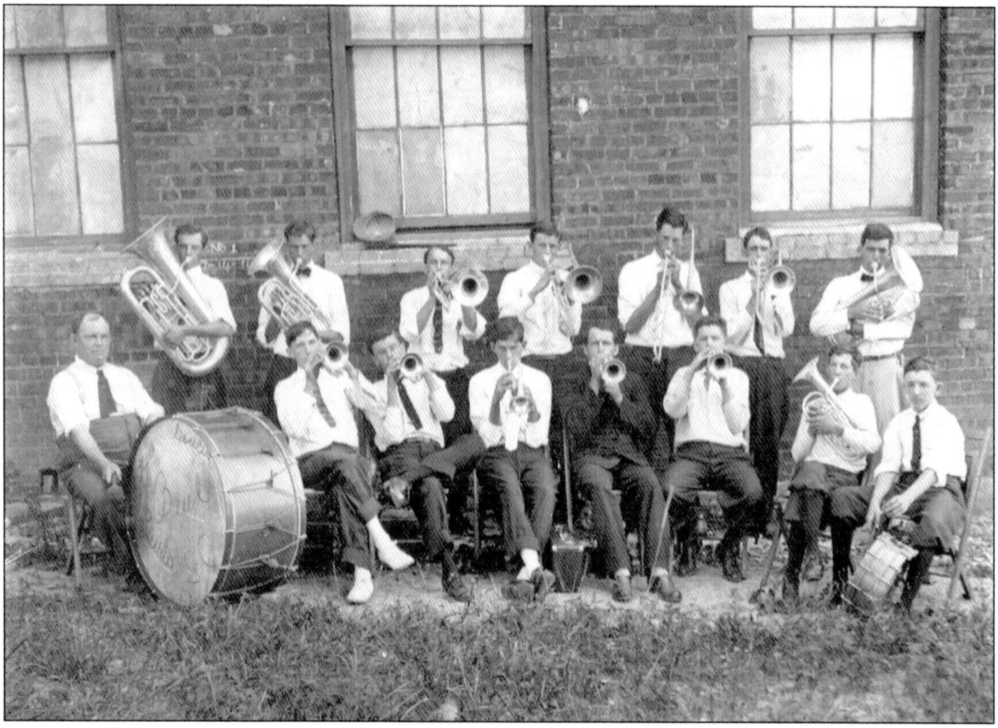

LANDO'S BRASS BAND. The Lando Brass Band would practice and play at the bandstand, and the music could be heard throughout Lando in the 1920s.

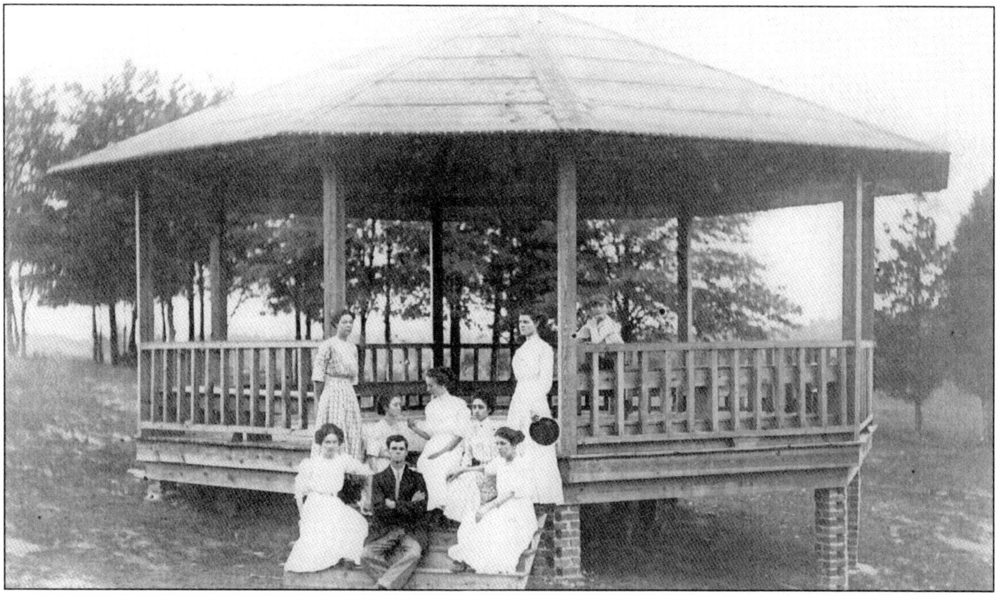

LANDO BANDSTAND. A group of Lando residents enjoy the bandstand in 1920. The bandstand was located in a field between the Lando schoolhouse and Main Street.

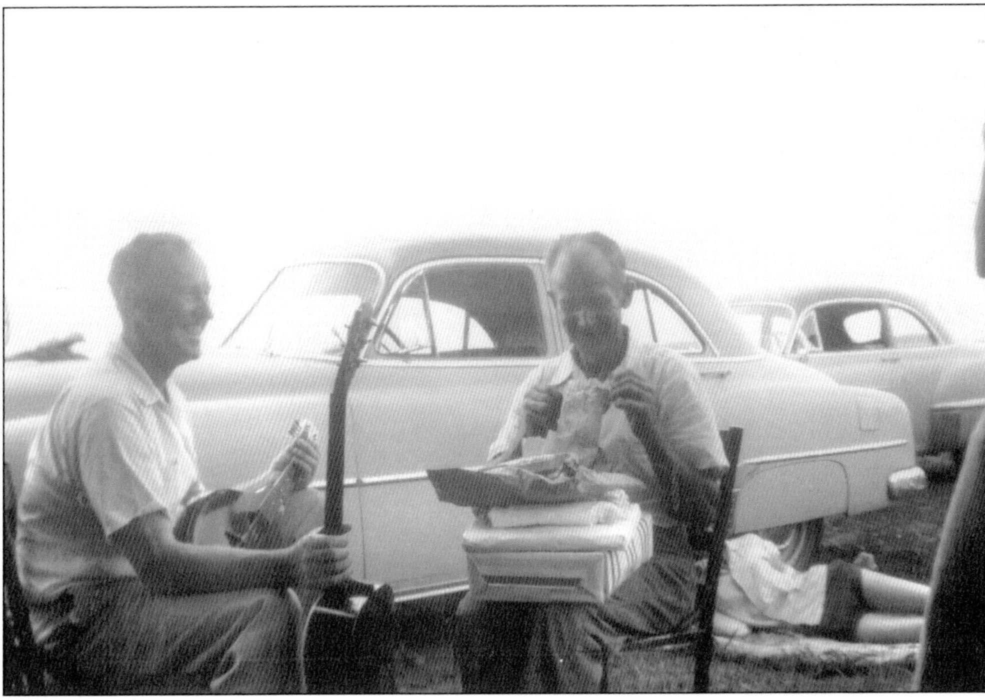

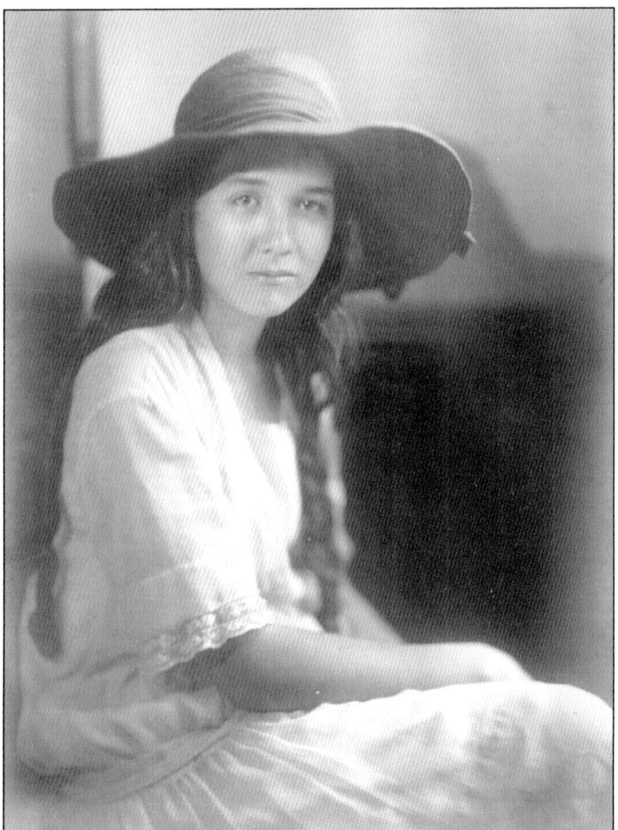

HAPPY BIRTHDAY. Billy Haggerty (on left) and Elvin Wallace (opening presents) enjoy playing music at a birthday party for Wallace in the 1950s. Haggerty was seldom seen without a musical instrument nearby.

TEACHERS. Miss Stoner was the music teacher at the Lando School in 1923. The Lando School was built by Manetta Mills, but the teachers were paid by the State of South Carolina. The school always employed five teachers. Former teachers at the Lando School include Flora Reid, Mattie Mae Whiteside Simpson, Kate Murphy, Eddie Burns, Louise McCrorey, Wil Lou Gray-Loftin, Mildred Nunnery Cox, Mattie Hicklin, Rosa Hoke, and Ethel Gaston.

Five

Economic Revolution

The growth of Lando as a community allowed many other entrepreneurs the opportunity to make a living in Lando. Manetta Mills was the foundation of Lando, but Manetta Mills did not provide Lando with everything it needed. Manetta Mills provided the Savings Bank of Lando and company store. The Heaths were able to help many families start a savings program, and for many folks who needed assistance, the mill provided company tokens known as "loonies," which employees could use to buy items from the company store. Loonies were advances on wages to help folks through tough times.

M. J. Tadlock also opened a general store near Lando. Many folks have nothing but kind words for Tadlock because of his understanding and generosity to the folks of Lando. Lando had barbers who set up shop inside the company office building and also a deputy sheriff of Chester County that resided in Lando.

One of the best-known people in Lando was Granny Thomas, who ran the boardinghouse. Most of the stories are from women, so Thomas must have really had an impact on the women of Lando. Thomas was not a big woman, but she was a strong woman with a big heart—and she has left a big positive impression on many people from Lando.

Another person with a big heart who left a positive impression was Dr. John Newton Gaston Sr. He had a basement office in the Manetta Mills office building, but it was his house calls, bedside manner, and kindness that made him memorable. Dr. Gaston would deliver babies in homes, prescribe and deliver medicines, and mend wounds. Dr. Gaston was a professional doctor who took care of the people of Lando, and the people of Lando loved and respected him.

Dr. Gaston's economic reward did not come from service to the people of Lando. Many times he would fix an illness and say, "Pay me when you can." The people of Lando were good, hard-working people and did repay him. Dr. Gaston will always be remembered as Lando's doctor.

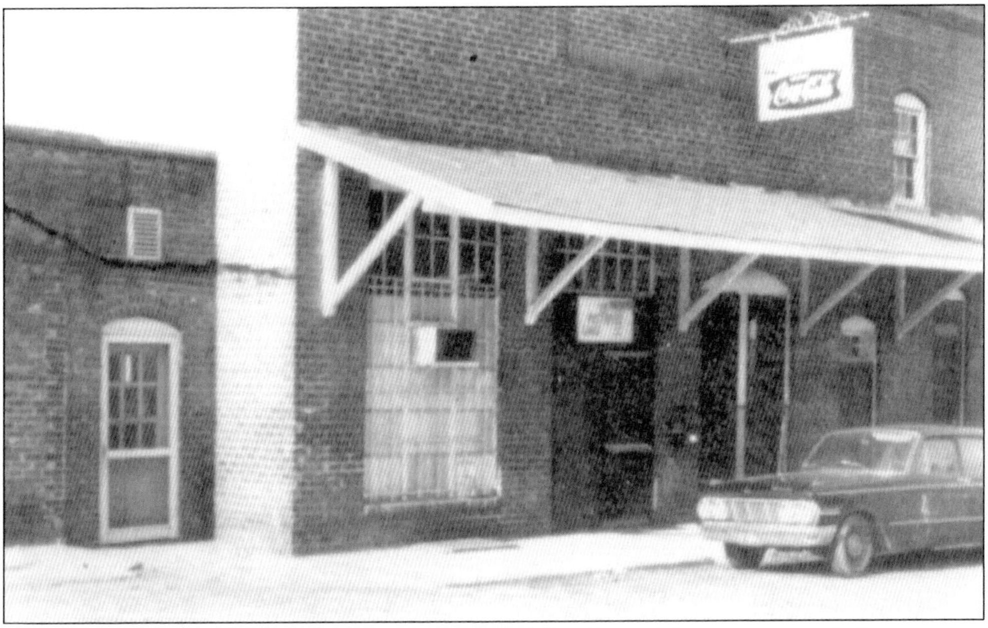

MANETTA MILLS OFFICE, 1940S. The Manetta Mills Office housed the executive and administrative offices on the right side of the building. The left side of the building is where the U.S. Postal Service has the Lando Post Office. During the operations of Manetta Mills, there was also a company store that sold everything from cookies to clothes to cough medicine to caskets. The far left door is where Manetta Mills had a filling station for gasoline and later a barbershop with a shower.

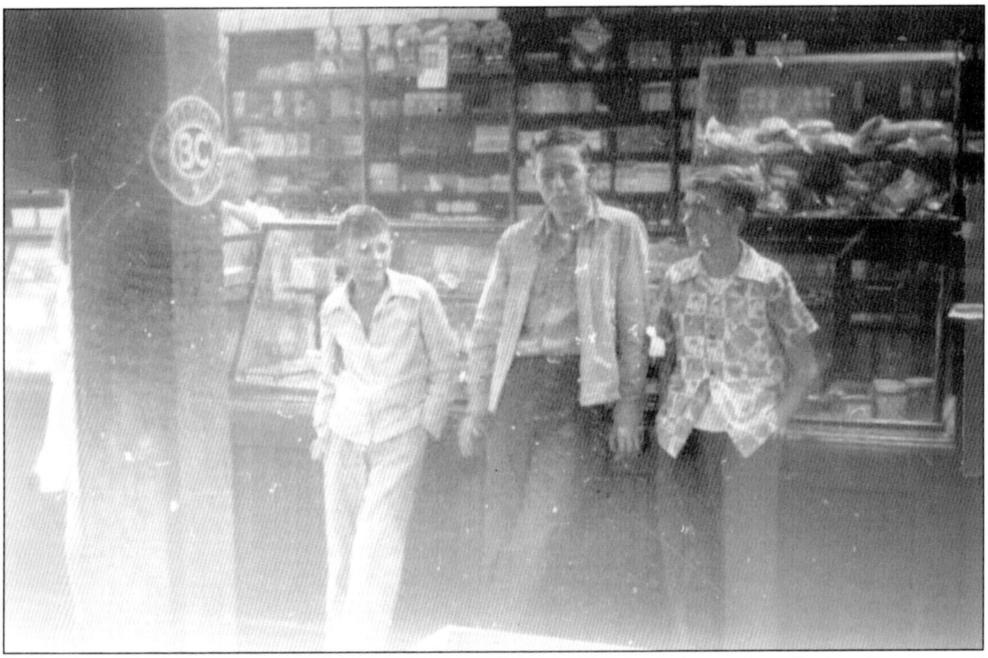

THE COMPANY STORE, LATE 1950S. Seen from left to right, Pete Hyatt, Sam Barber Guinn, and Tommy Ramsey stand in front of the candy counter in the Manetta Mills company store. Many folks from Lando depended on this store for household items.

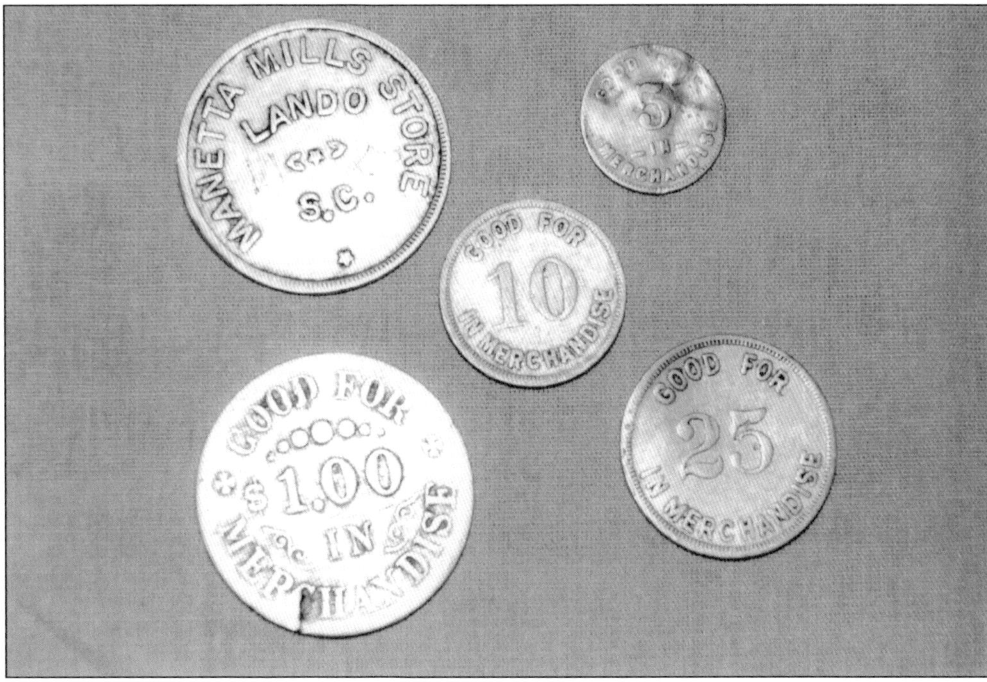

LOONIES. Manetta Mills offered aluminum coins known as "loonies" to employees who needed credit from the store until payday. The loonies could only be spent in the company store. Today textile mill tokens are rare collectable coins.

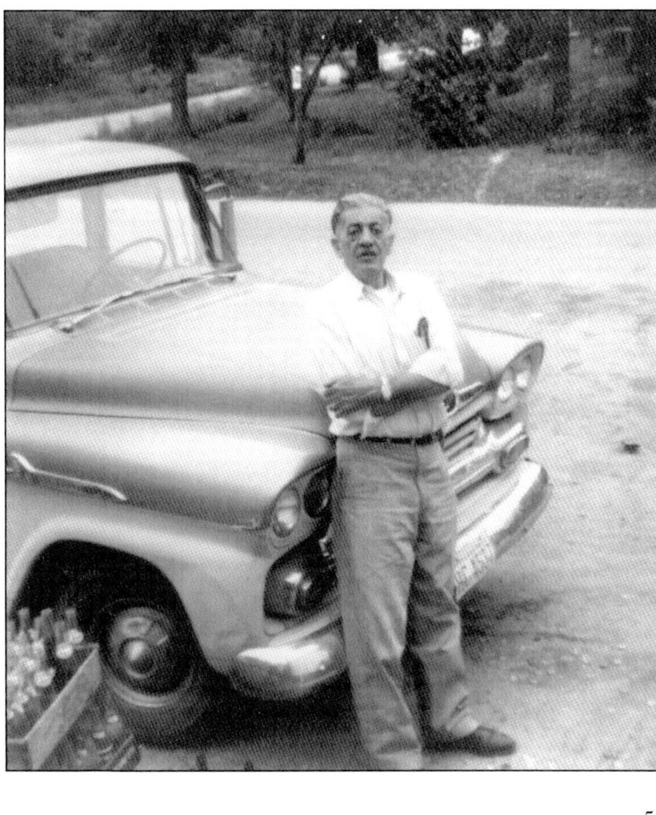

TADLOCK'S GENERAL STORE. In the 1960s, M. J. Tadlock owned and operated Tadlock's General Store just outside of Lando. Folks could always rely on Tadlock Store for items that were not available at the company store.

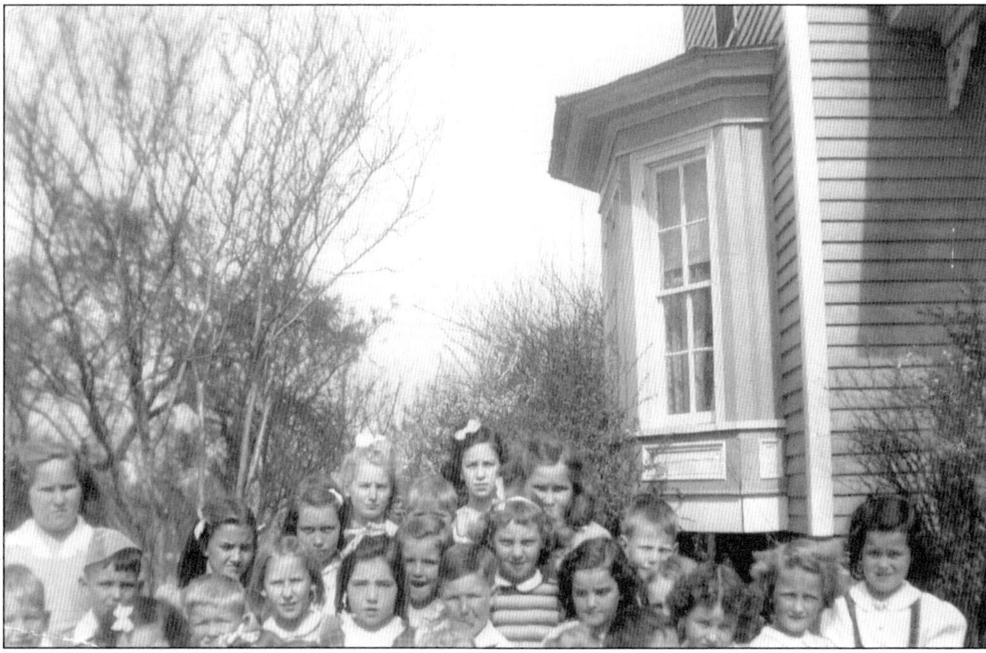

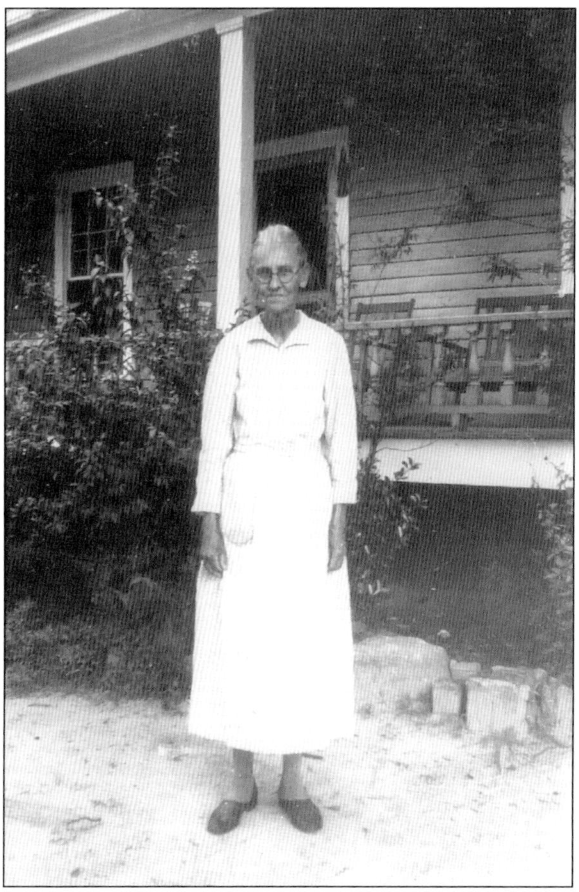

BOARDINGHOUSE. In the 1940s, a group of children celebrate at a birthday party for Sylvia Leckie in front of the boardinghouse. From left to right are the following: (first row) two unidentified, Alex Bolton, unidentified, Bobbie Polk, Eddie Orr, Sylvia Leckie, Shirley Thomas, Patricia Bailey, and Dotty Overby; (second row) Betty Coggins, Jennette Hefner, Betty Thomas, unidentified, Opal Coggins, Hope Allen, and Richard McKinney; (third row) Nell McKenny, Ruby Mosely, and unidentified.

GRANNY THOMAS. There were several businesses in Lando that were owned by the Heath family but operated by residents of Lando. The boardinghouse was run by Granny Thomas from 1922 to 1946. When the Heaths would come down from Charlotte, they would stay there. No one knows Thomas's real first name; she was "Granny" to everyone.

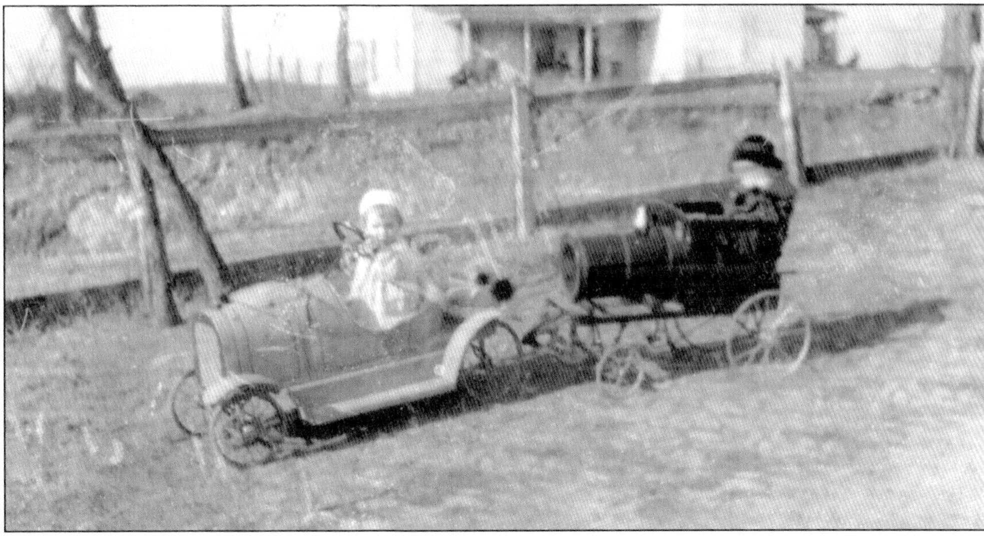

HEATH CHILDREN. Harry Heath and Genola Heath play at their childhood home in Lando in the 1920s.

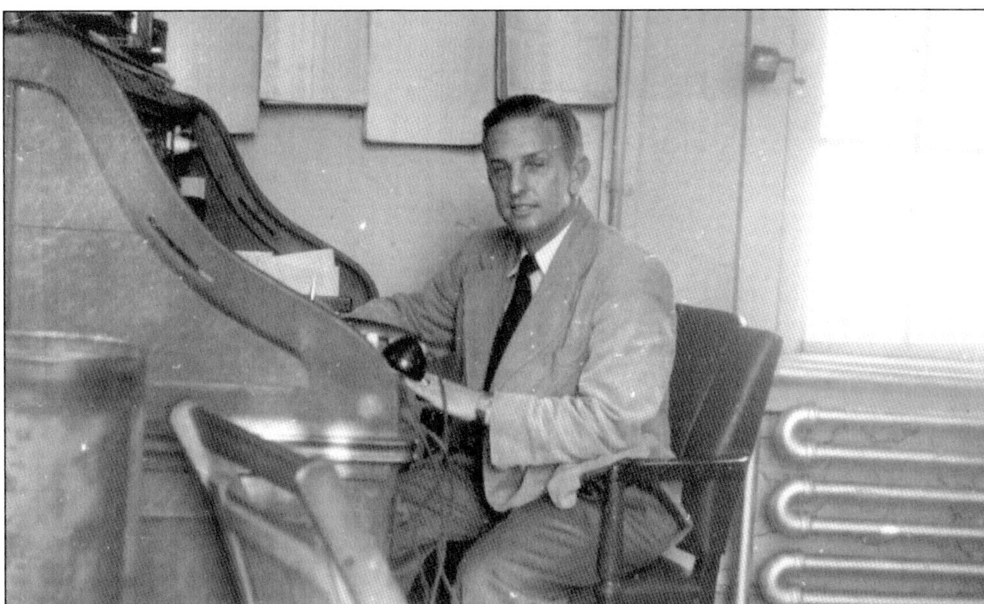

HARRY HEATH, 1950S. Harry Heath was the third generation of Heaths to run Manetta Mills. He was very familiar with all aspects of the mill and often visited the production facilities. Harry also made sure that his children Allen and Billy understood the operations of the mill, and he made both of his boys work in the mill in production.

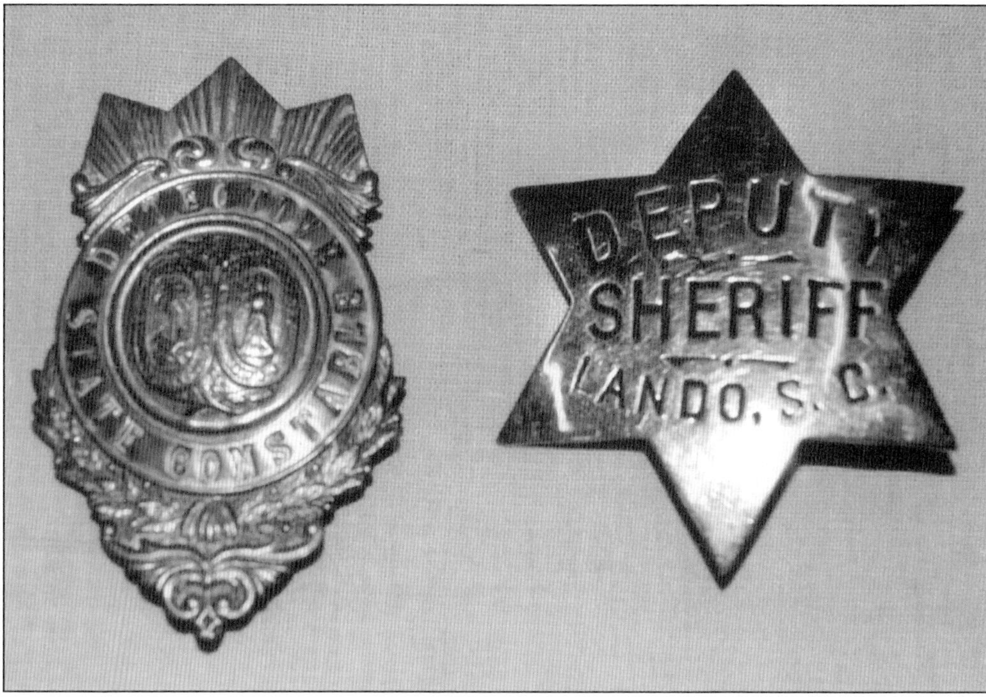

DEPUTY SHERIFF. W. H. Bailey was deputy sheriff in Lando in the 1930s. As peaceful as Lando was, occasionally there was a need for the law enforcement. Stewart McFadden was deputy sheriff from 1933 to 1943 and was also a loom fixer for Manetta Mills.

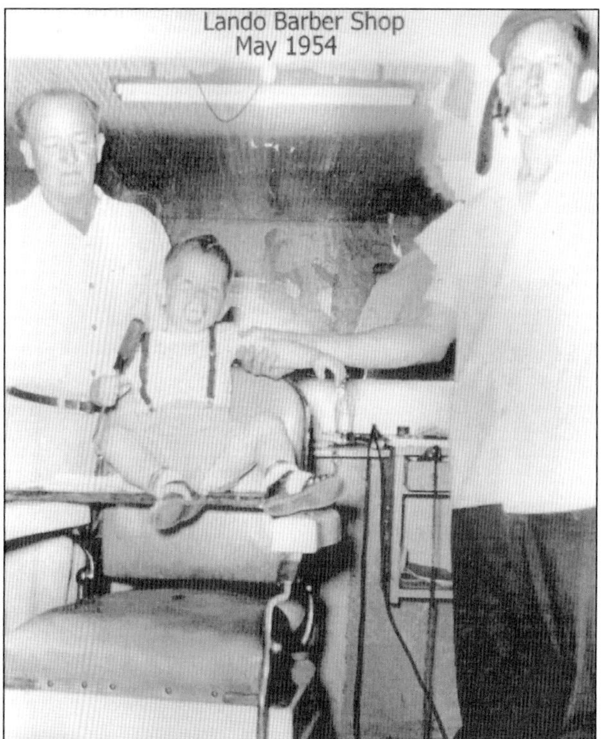

LANDO BARBERSHOP. Alan Laney Ernandez (in chair), son of Mouse (right) and Joyce Ernandez, receives his first haircut from Lando's barber, Fred Thomas Mosley (left), in 1954.

EXECUTIVES. Pictured is the executive and administrative team of Manetta Mills in 1943. From left to right are the following: (first row) Shaw Simpson, Harry Heath, and Bob Willis; (second row) James Whitesides, Harold Glass, Gilbert Heath, and Charlie Murphy.

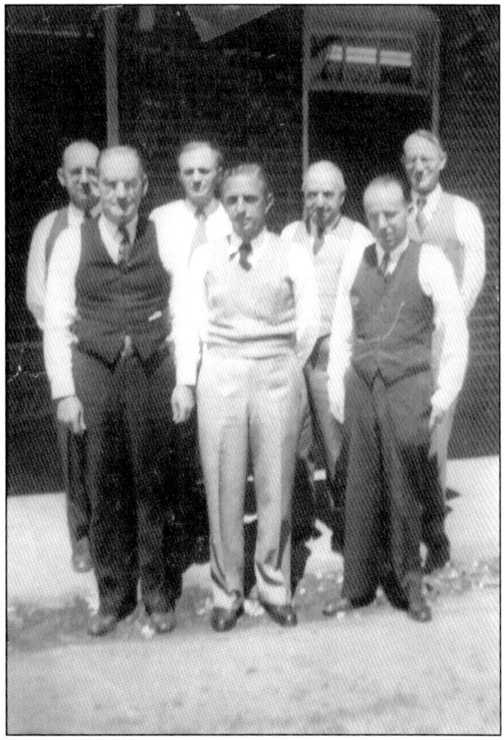

OFFICERS. The Heath family took great pride in their management staff. The Heaths' philosophy of and care for the community and its people was extended to the executive staff, who are pictured here. From left to right are unidentified, Harry Heath, ? Bucanon, John Tinker, Charlie Murphy, ? West, ? Stevenson, and ? Brown.

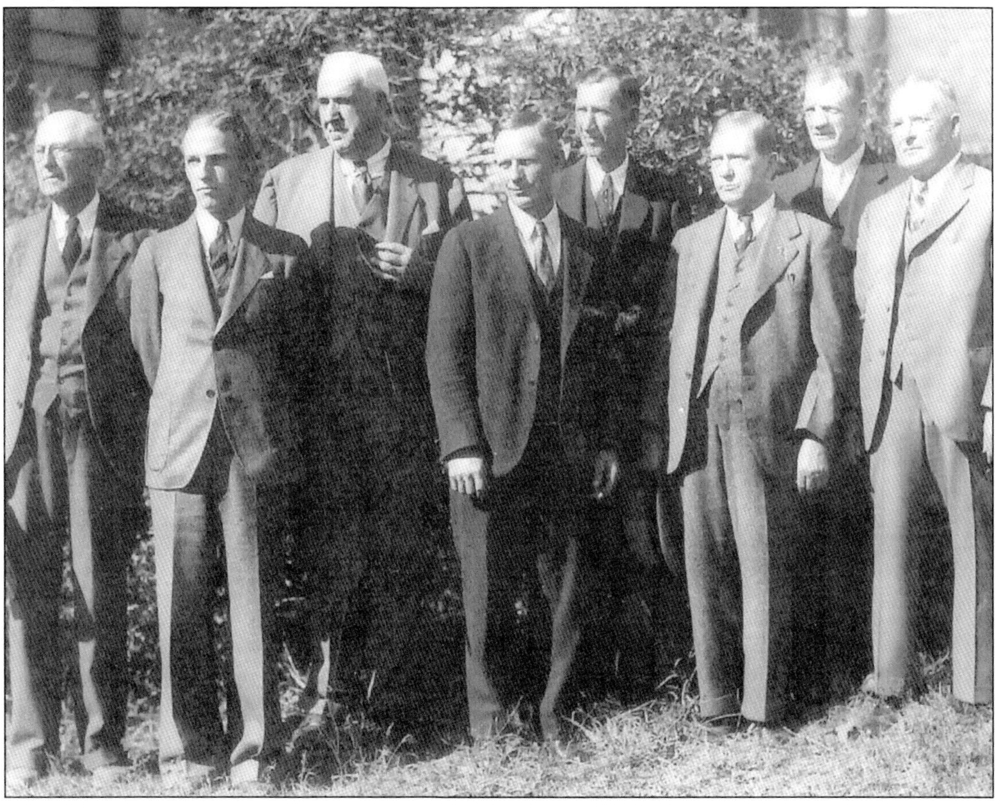

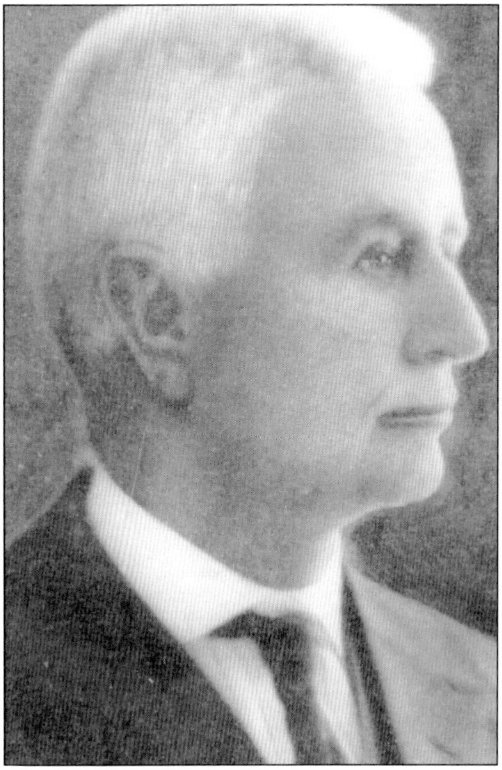

FIRST GENERATION. Benjamin Dawson Heath was the founder of Manetta Mills and a self-made businessman. Heath was born in upper Lancaster County, South Carolina, on July 26, 1849. He put himself through college; started his own mercantile business in Monroe, North Carolina; and built his business involvements to include the Charlotte National Bank (now Bank of America), Cliffside Mills, Jackson Mills, Stock Mutual Life Insurance Company, and Oakhurst Land Company, just to name a few. Heath always had a special interest in Manetta Mills.

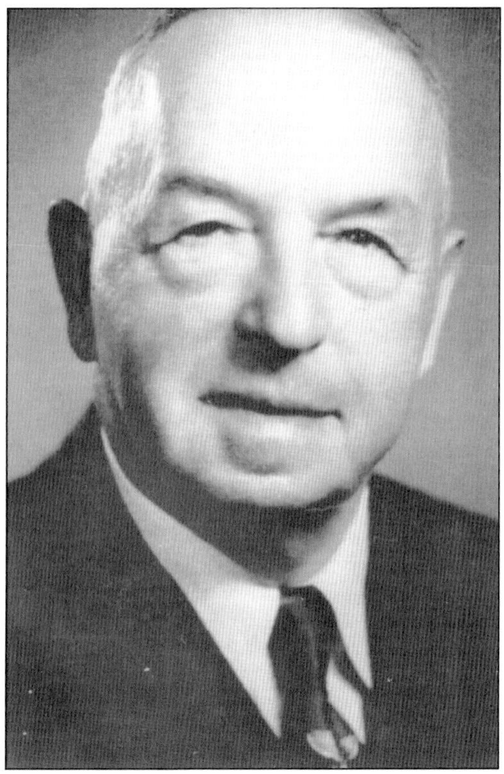

SECOND GENERATION. Gilbert Brown Heath became president of Manetta Mills in 1932 and remained there until he retired in 1955. Like his father, B. D. Heath, Gilbert was well educated and had a strong business sense. He took great interest in his church, Manetta Mills, and the people of Lando. Gilbert moved from Charlotte to Chester, South Carolina, where he became involved in the local banks.

THIRD GENERATION. Harry Heath became president of Manetta Mills in 1956. He sits on the desk in his office in front of a picture of his father, G. B. Heath.

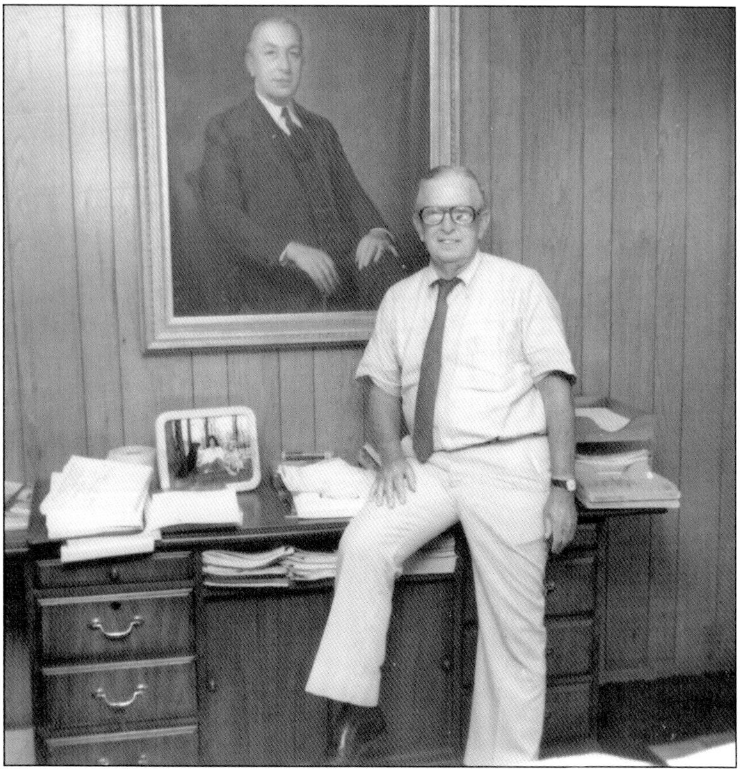

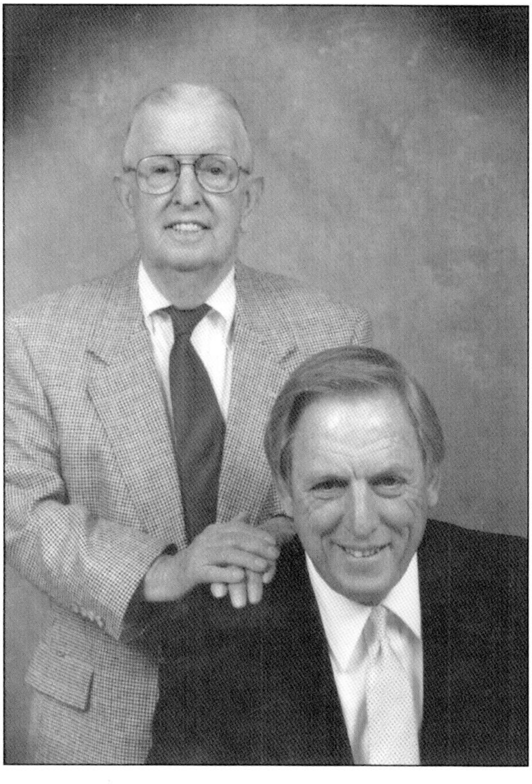

FORTH GENERATION. Pictured is Harry Heath (standing) with his son, Allen Heath. Allen became president of Manetta Mills in 1974. Both men started their working careers inside a mill, either pushing a broom or doffing spinning frames. Allen was the last president of Manetta Mills and the fourth generation of Heaths to operate Manetta Mills in Lando. The Heath family provided a good living for thousands of people in both Carolinas and took great pride in the communities they supported. Education, religion, recreation, and a good, safe place to work were the principles the Heath family held close while developing Lando and Manetta Mills.

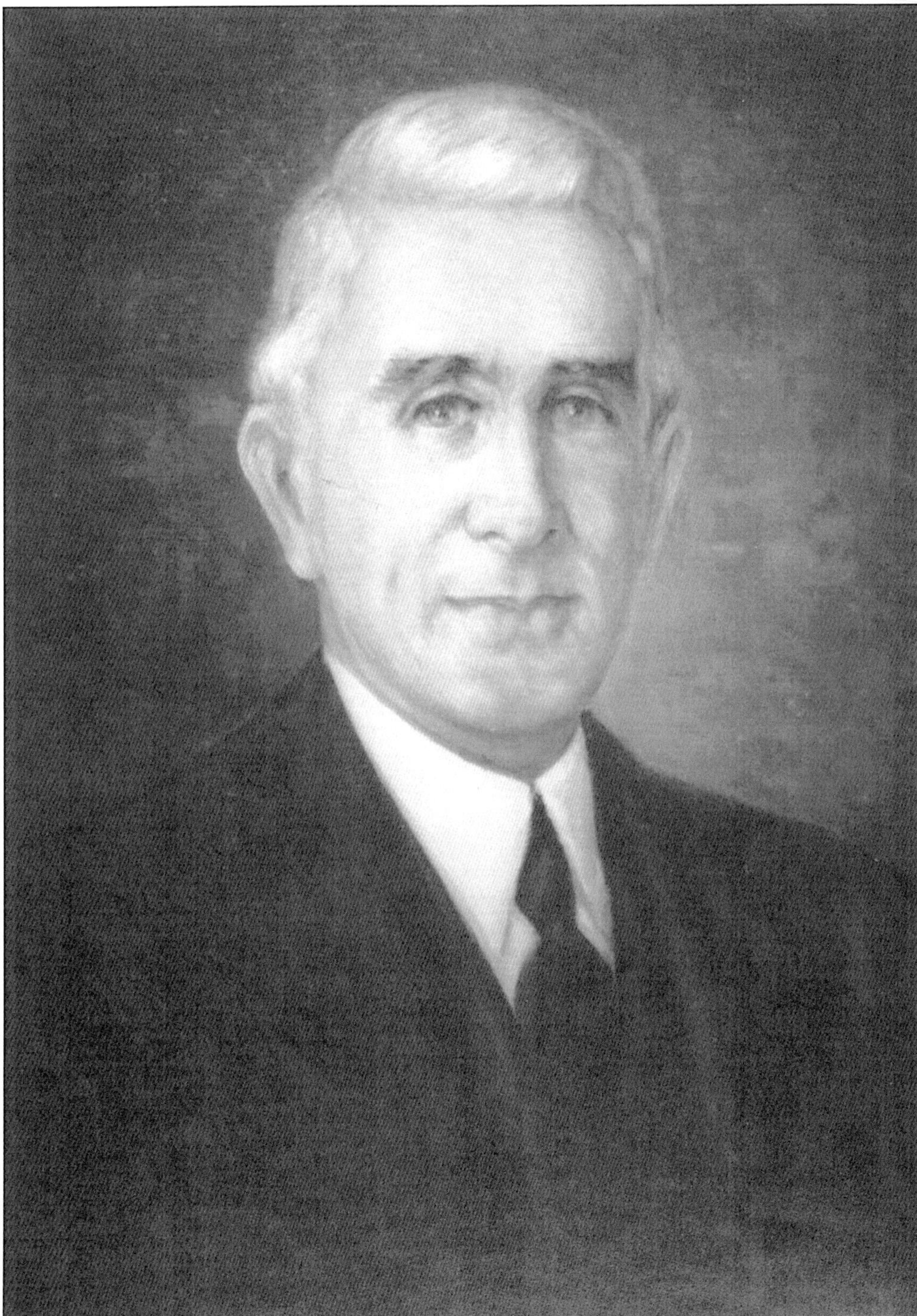

Dr. John Newton Gaston Sr. Dr. John Newton Gaston Sr. was respected and admired by all residents of Lando. He had an office in the basement of the Manetta Mills corporate office, where he held regular office hours several days a week. Gaston started practicing medicine in 1900 and worked as long as his health permitted.

Six

MILL WORKERS

During the early days of Fishing Creek Manufacturing, the first employees of the mill were mainly farmers from the rural countryside. These early families provided the labor needed to operate the mill. When the Heath family took ownership and created Manetta Mills, they provided an excellent work place. In 1904, Manetta Mills transformed into a state-of-the-art manufacturing facility that needed a dedicated, hardworking, and educated workforce.

Operating textile machinery such as a card machine, spinning frame, and a loom was a lot different than operating a mule and a plow. The Heath family knew the importance of education and made sure that all employees understood the proper ways to operate the equipment safely and properly. Once employees learned how to operate a piece of equipment, many of them became masters of the trade. Many folks took advantage of the diverse jobs inside a textile mill and learned more than one skill.

By the 1940s, many Manetta Mills employees were second- or third-generation mill workers. When World War II began, many young men left their jobs at Manetta Mills to serve in the military. The women of Lando filled many of the positions that were vacated. Some men, after returning from the war, decided to seek new jobs in the bigger cities like Rock Hill and Lancaster in South Carolina and Charlotte, Gastonia, and Monroe in North Carolina.

Textiles offered thousands of jobs throughout the South. Springs Industries, Cannon Mill, Burlington Industries, Cone Mill, and Carolina Mills are just a few of the large textile companies that offered jobs and competed for labor. Manetta Mills provided an excellent opportunity for a skilled mill worker to earn a living. Many employees worked for Manetta Mills for over 50 years and knew every aspect involved in the blanket-making process.

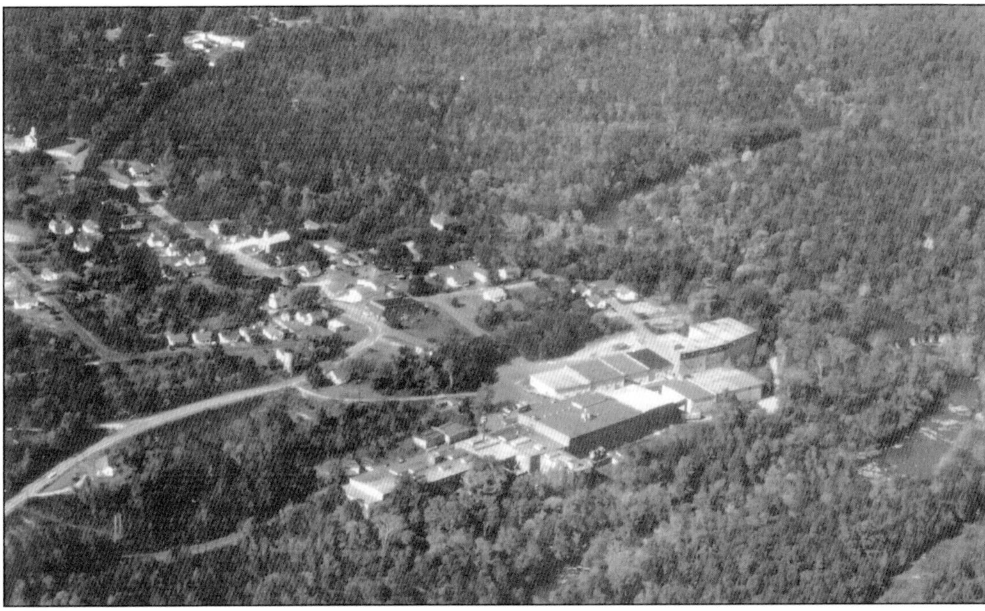

AERIAL VIEW OF LANDO. At the time of this 1989 view, the village is smaller, but Manetta Mills is still strong in blanket production. Many employees now can commute to and from work with their own cars and live in nearby communities.

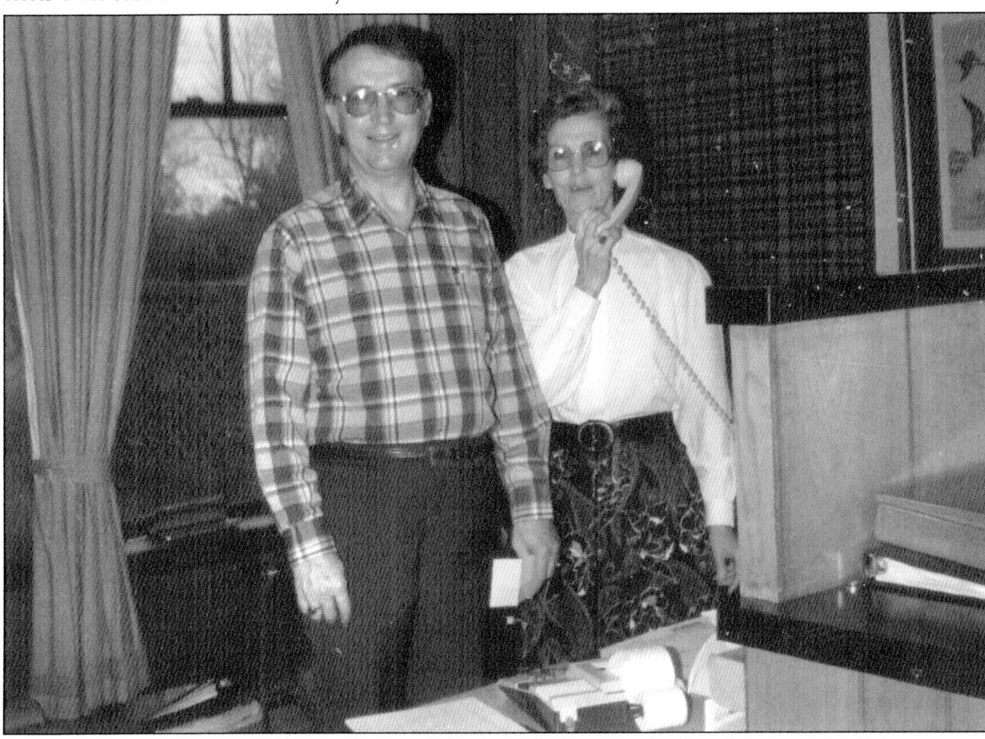

ONE MOMENT PLEASE. Ollie Hefner and Richard Bolton worked in Manetta Mills' corporate office in the early 1980s. Manetta Mills provided a silver dollar to each newborn in Lando, and a record of each birth and silver dollar was written down in a baby book that was maintained in the company office.

SUPERINTENDENTS. From left to right, (seated) Curtis, Leroy, and Bill Bolton and (standing) twins Richard and Ronnie Bolton relax on the porch of the superintendent's house in the 1940s.

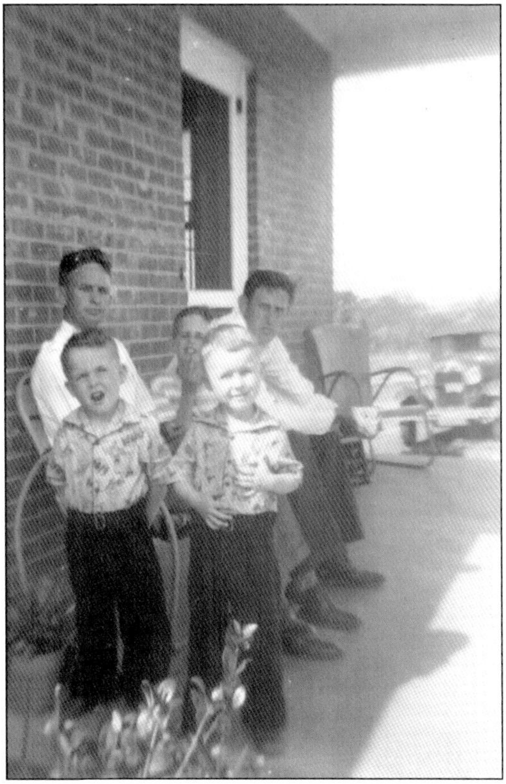

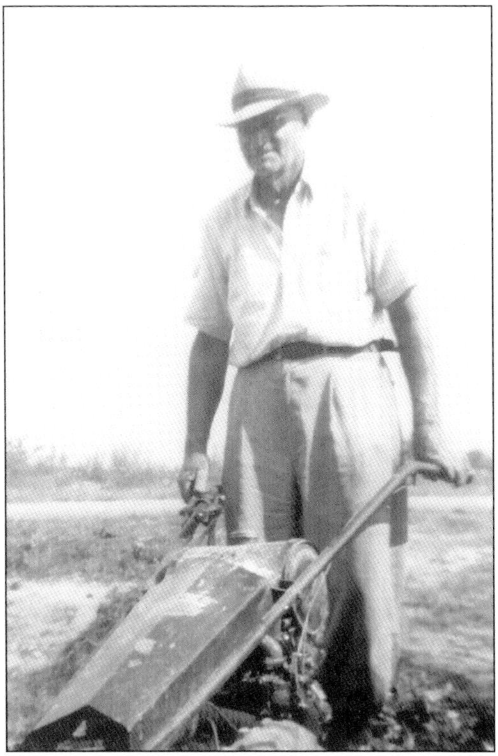

SUPERINTENDENT. Will Morgan tills his backyard garden in the 1950s. The superintendents' houses were the only brick houses in Lando, and there were four of them.

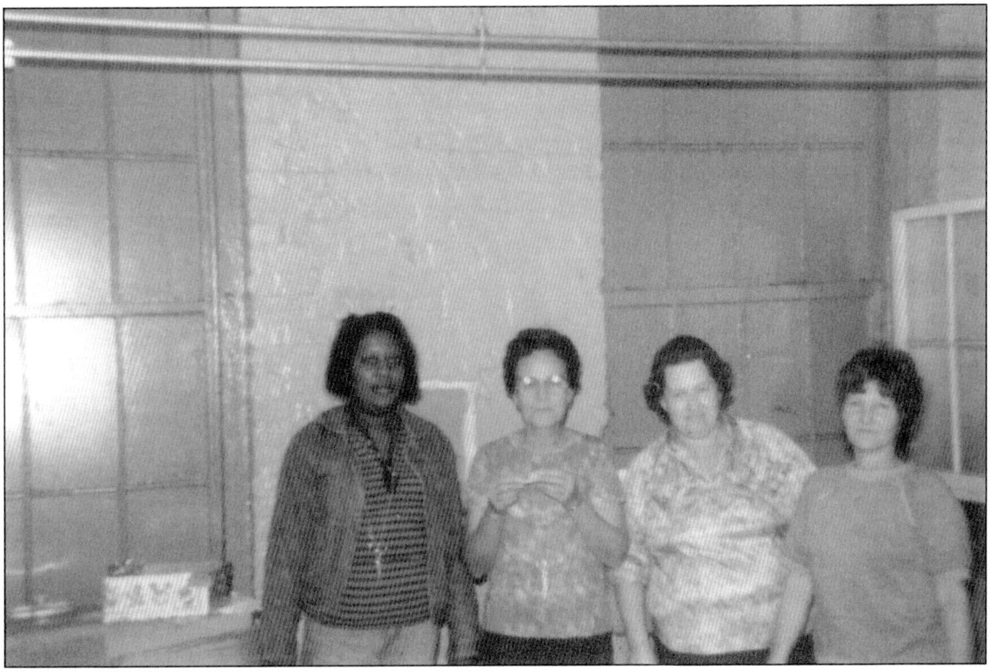

Christmas Party, 1970s. From left to right, Lillie Mae Dunham, Janie Ratterree, Betty Broome and Carol Lanier take time to exchange gifts during their break. At one time, Manetta Mills ran three shifts and employed over 800 people.

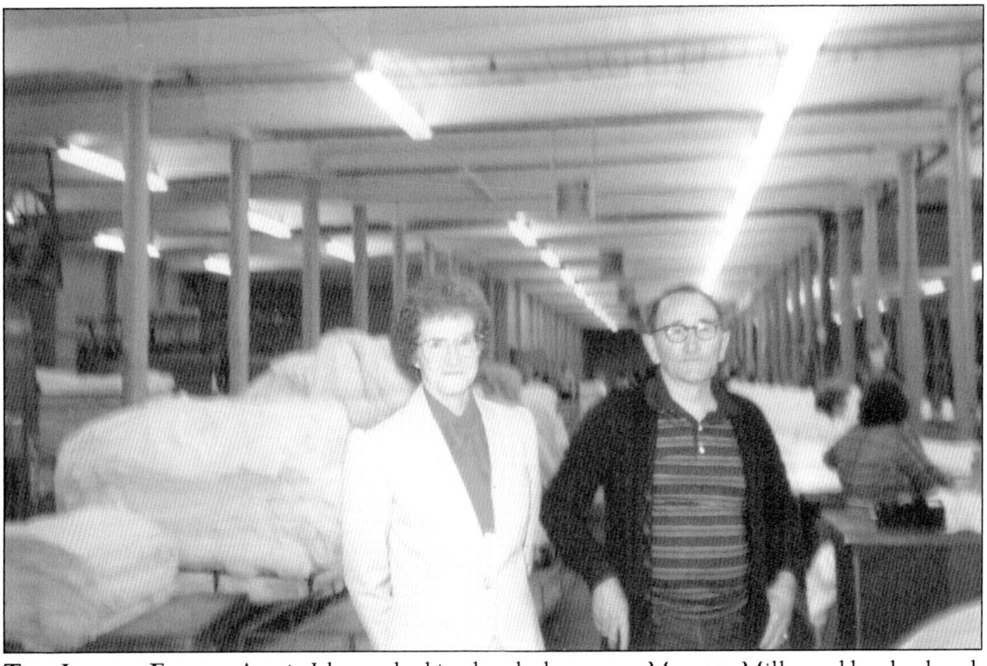

Two-Income Family. Annie Irby worked in the cloth room at Manetta Mills, and her husband, Ray, was a commercial painter in the 1970s.

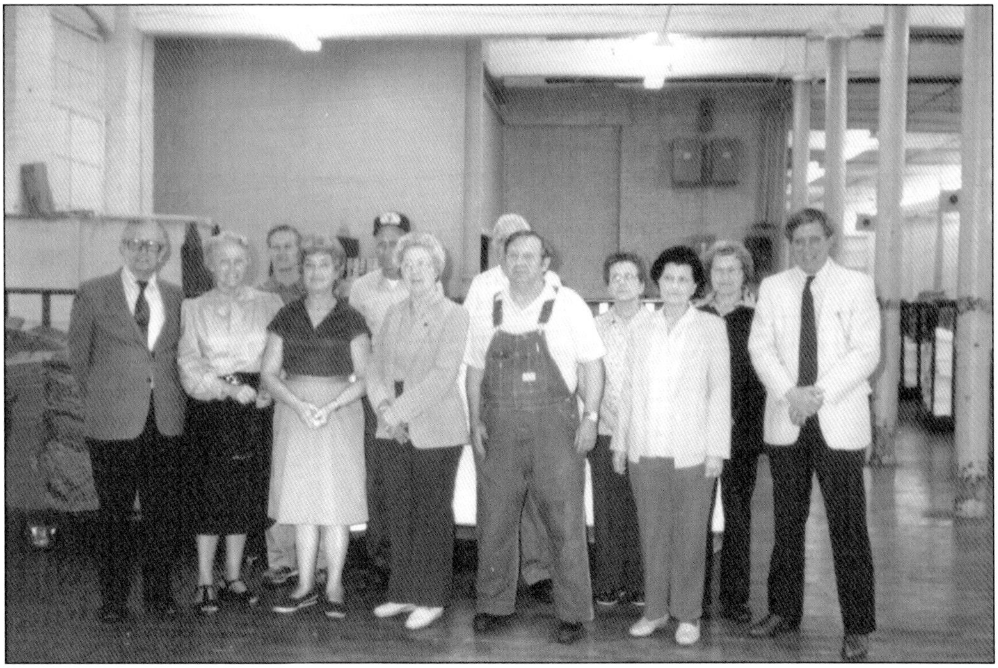

CLOTH ROOM. Pictured from left to right in the cloth room around 1984 are the following: (first row) Harry Heath, Temmer Ramsey, Gladys Hough, Effie Pate, Fred Miller, Janie Nunnery, and Allen Heath; (second row) Norman Ernandez, James Blanks, Jimmy Nunnery, Genola Collins, and Fannie Ernandez.

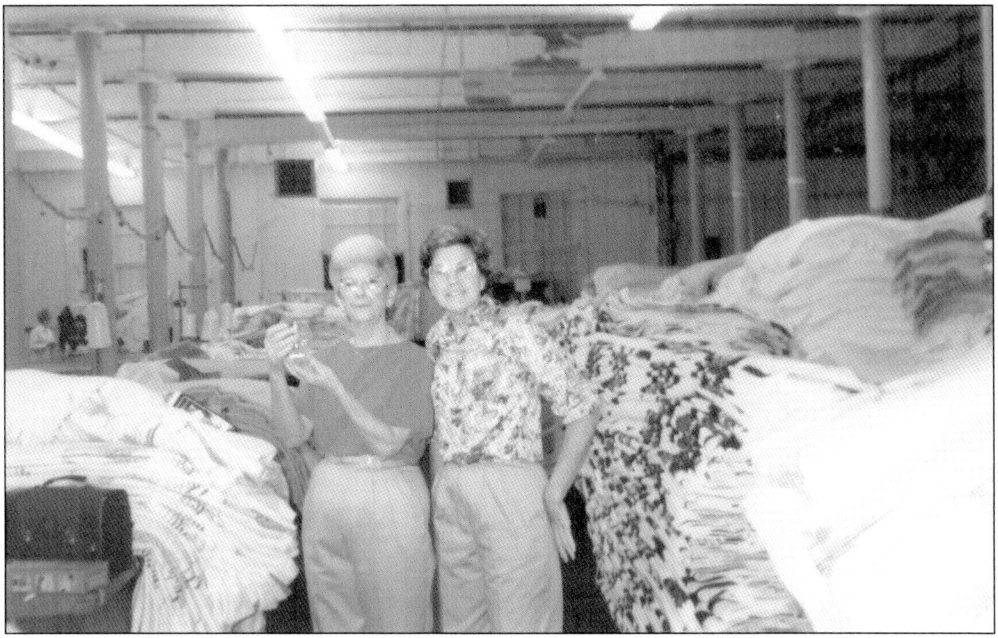

SMILE FOR THE CAMERA. Louise Hyatt (left) and Carrie Faust stand among piles of blankets in the 1980s. The Manetta Mills blankets were shipped to hospitals throughout the United States as well as to military bases all over the world. Thermal blankets, floral prints, and college logos were some of the many styles of blankets produced at Manetta Mills.

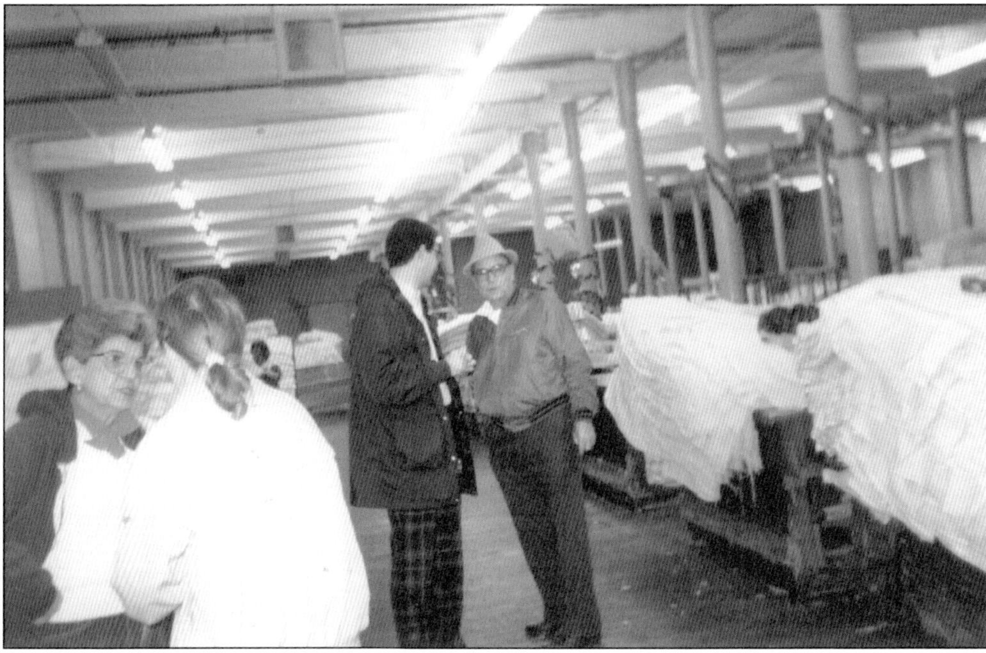

ON THE JOB. From left to right, Marian Tomberlin, Joe Simpson, and Wallace Benton talk in the cloth room in the 1980s. Manetta Mills also made a type of blanket that was sold to prisons. The "prison blankets" were made from extra cotton that was collected at the end of each shift. The cloth was then sent to the dye house to create a uniform color and then to the cloth room to make the blanket.

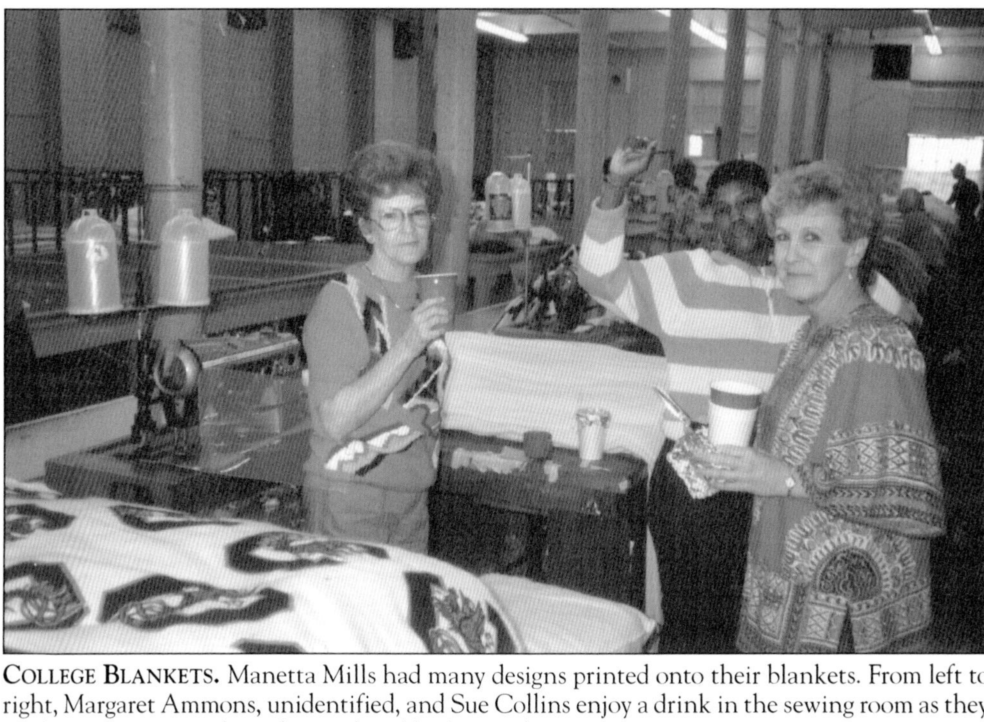

COLLEGE BLANKETS. Manetta Mills had many designs printed onto their blankets. From left to right, Margaret Ammons, unidentified, and Sue Collins enjoy a drink in the sewing room as they work on University of South Carolina blanket in the 1980s.

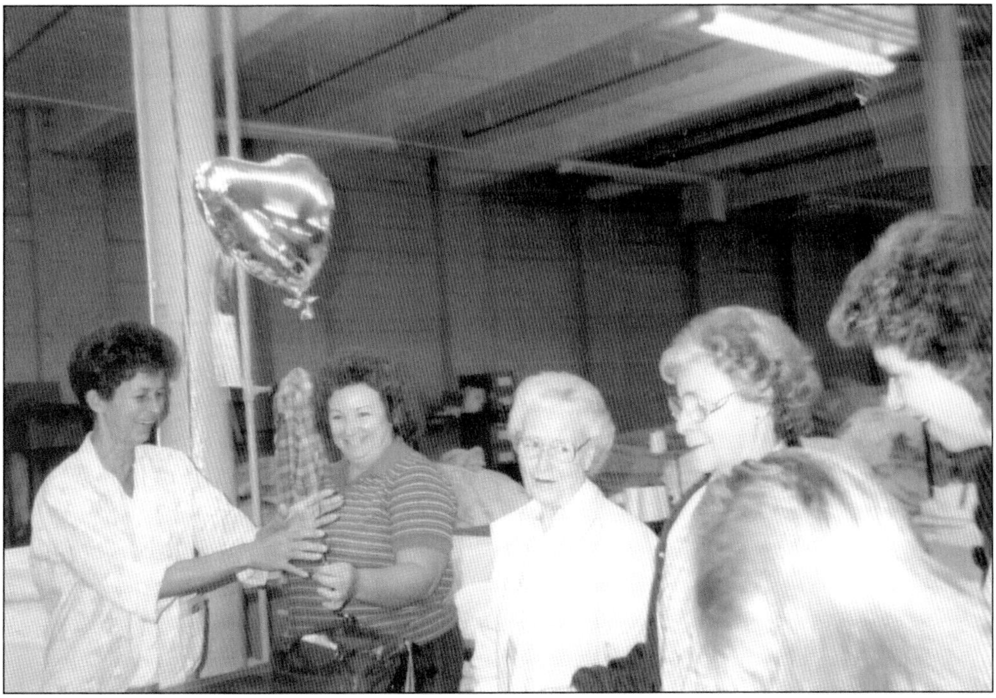

SHARING STORIES, 1980s. From left to right, Judy Gwinn Hefner, Patty Tadlock Harrelson, Ruth Hefner, Doris Scott, and Sherrie Coggins share a story during break time.

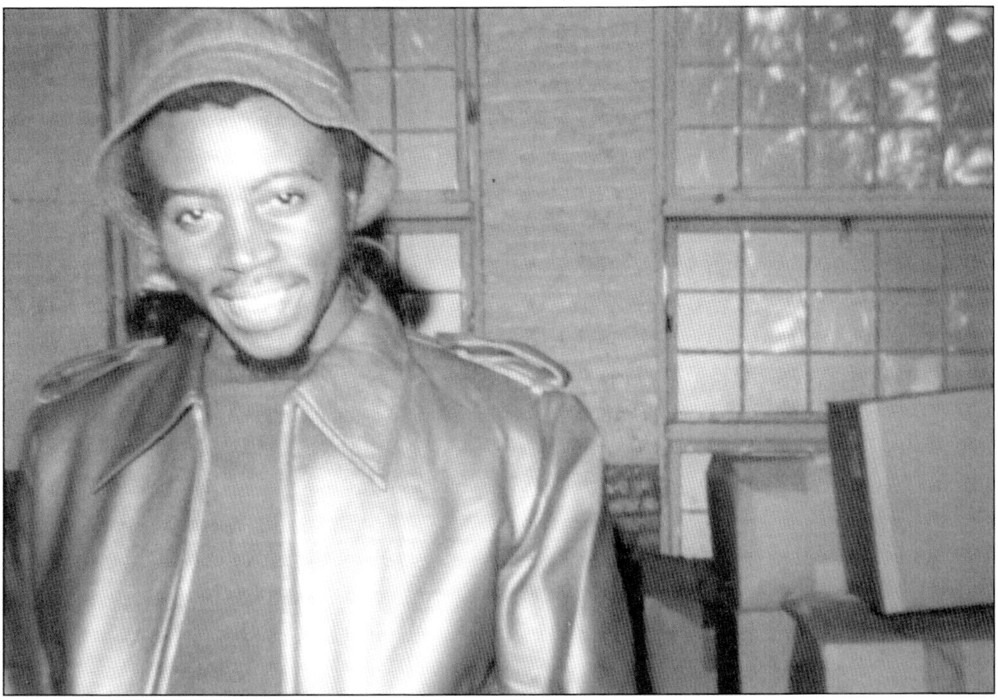

SHIPPING DEPARTMENT, 1980s. Tim Pressley worked in the shipping department at Manetta Mills. Each box had to be labeled with the destination of the shipment. A wall in the shipping department was covered with destinations all over the world where Manetta Mills shipped blankets.

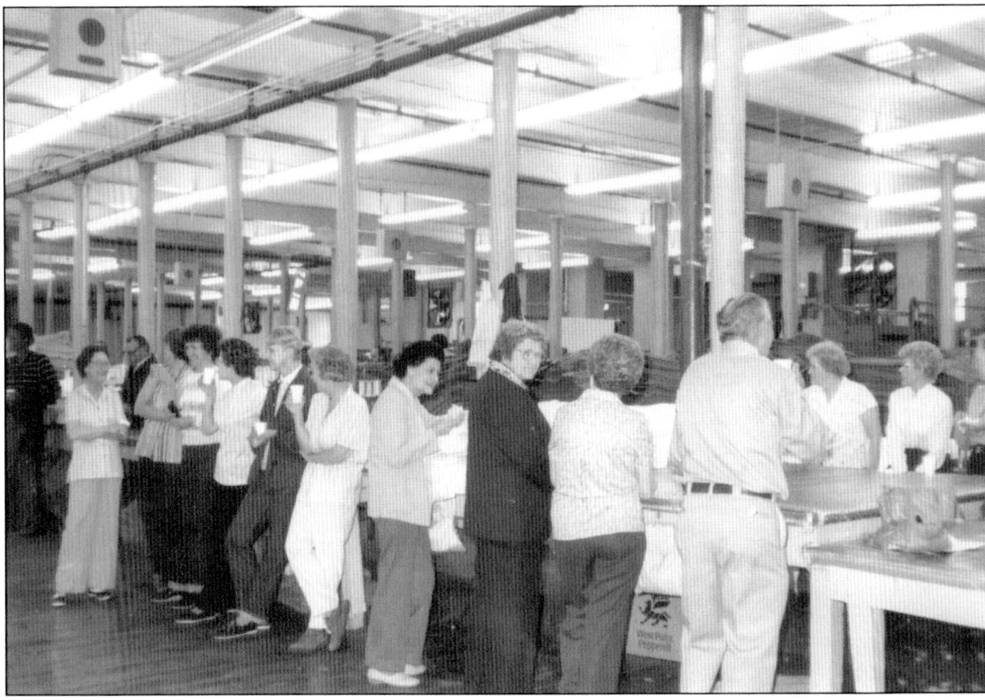

MEETINGS, 1980S. Manetta Mill employees enjoy a break during the first shift in Lando. Management would hold safety and training meetings on the mill floor.

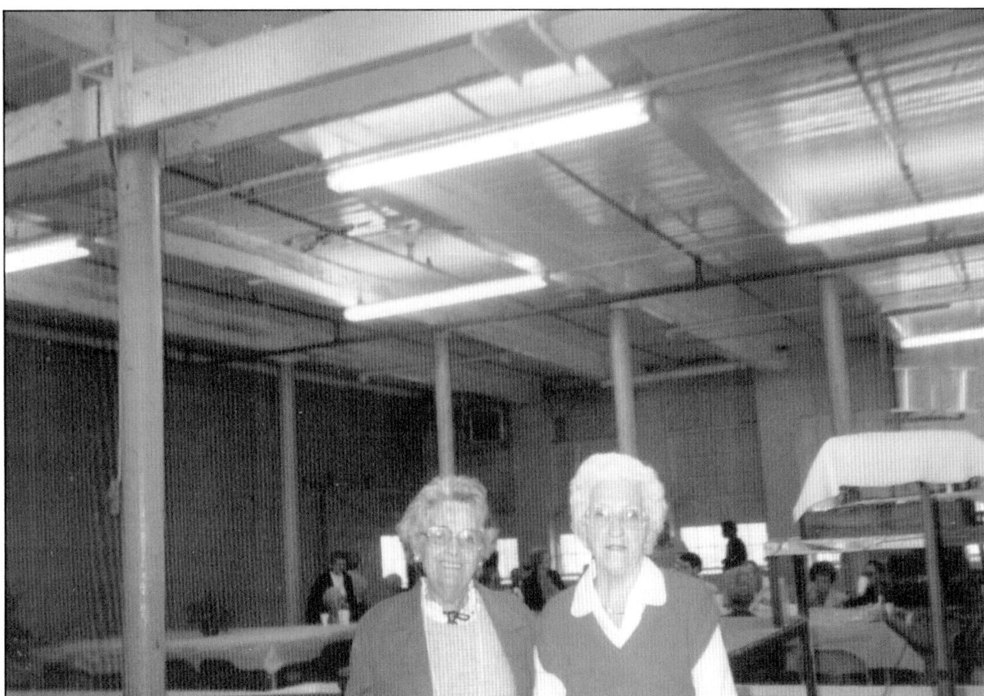

GOLDEN YEARS, 1980S. Idabelle "Ducky" Thomas Collins (left) and Effie Pate worked in Manetta Mills beyond retirement age.

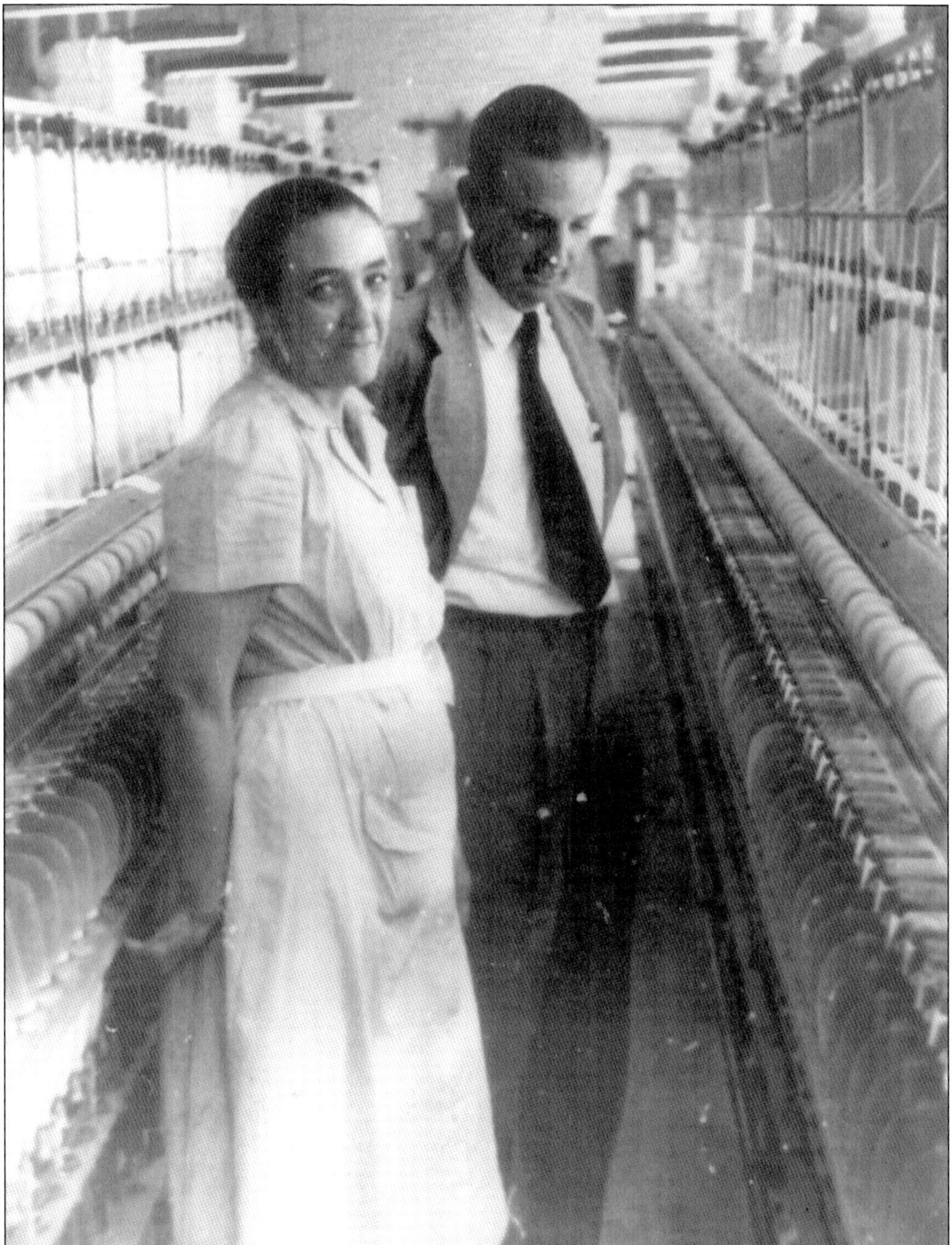

HAPPY EMPLOYEES. Dora Hefner and Harry Heath are standing among the spinning frames in the 1950s. Harry Heath was president of Manetta Mills, but to the employees of Manetta Mills in Lando, he was known as just plain "Harry."

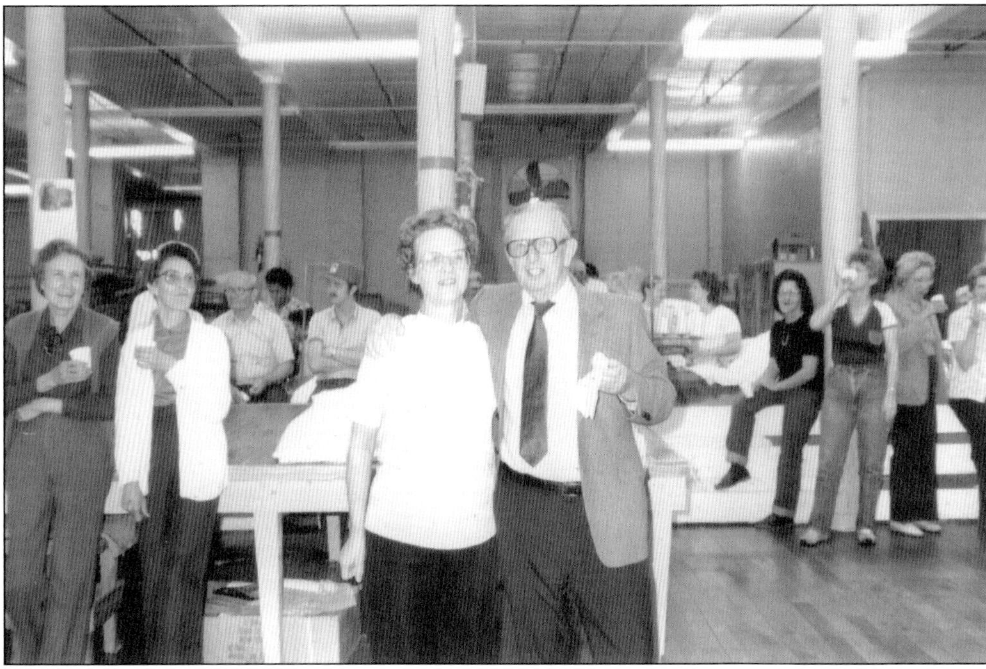

AWARDS DAY. In the 1980s, Harry Heath recognizes Abbie Kee Turner during a company meeting. Included in the background are Genola Clinton, Betty Jo Bishop, and Mary Etta Kee.

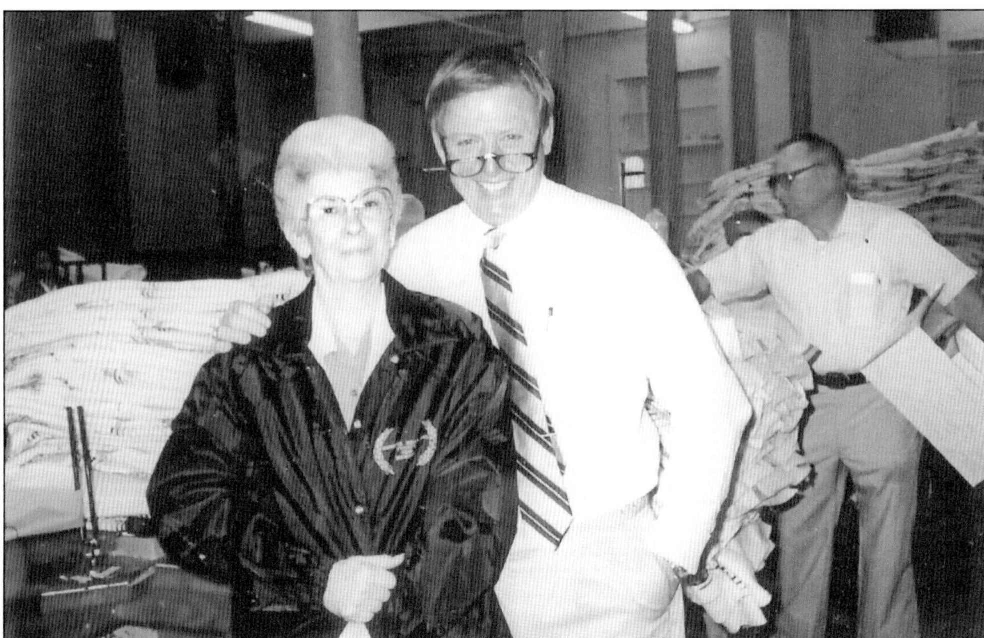

COMPANY JACKET. Allen Heath awards Louise Hyatt with a 25-year service jacket in the 1980s. Wallace Benton inspects blankets.

STANDING PROUD. Manetta Mills was the heart of the community and was in the hearts of many of the folks in Lando. Carl Curtis stands on the ramp to the weave room in the 1950s.

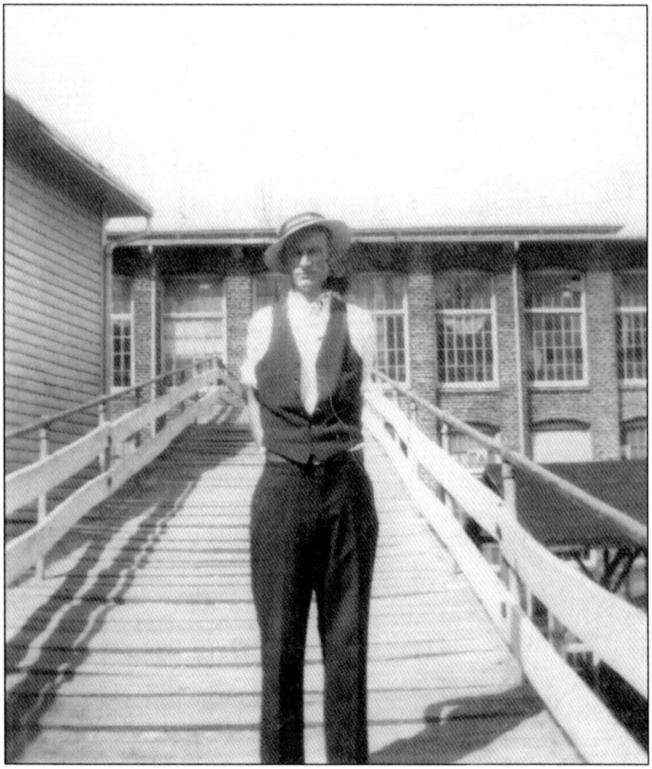

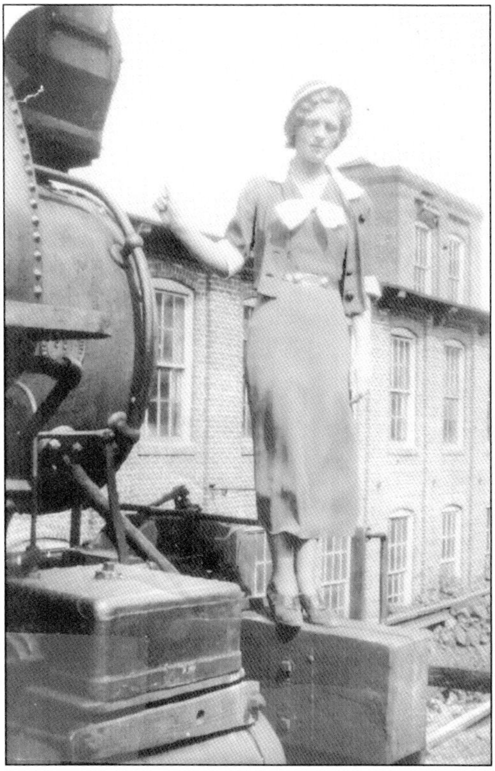

COMPANY CANTEEN. Margaret Starnes stands on the Dummy in front of the old section of Manetta Mills in the late 1930s. Starnes ran the canteen inside Manetta Mills for more than 20 years.

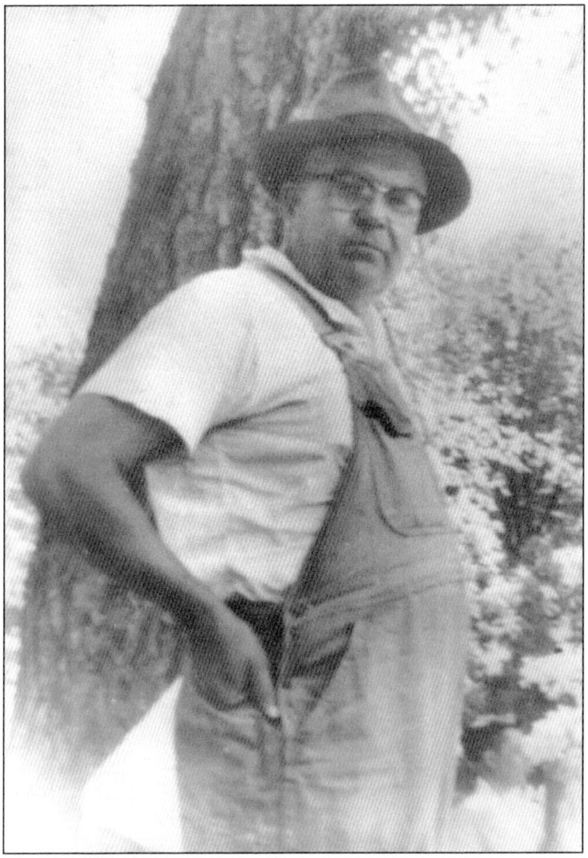

Doc Rainer, 1950s. Doc Rainer ran the tie-end machine for looms in the weave room. One month before he was to retire, he died of a heart attack on the mill floor.

Career Family, 1980s. Ben Ernandez worked in the mill for over 50 years. Jessie Ernandez lived in Lando and raised eight children on the mill hill.

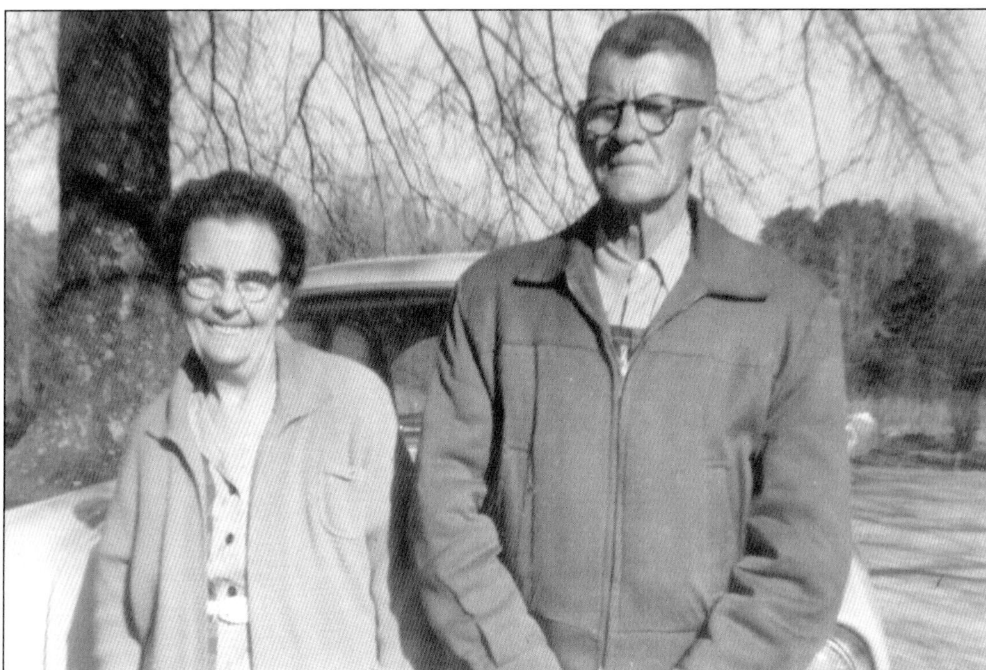

CAREER CHANGE, 1940s. Brothers James (Red) (left) and Fred (Bud) Hefner started working in Manetta Mills as young boys. After World War II, James decided to change careers, while Bud worked in the mill until it closed in 1991.

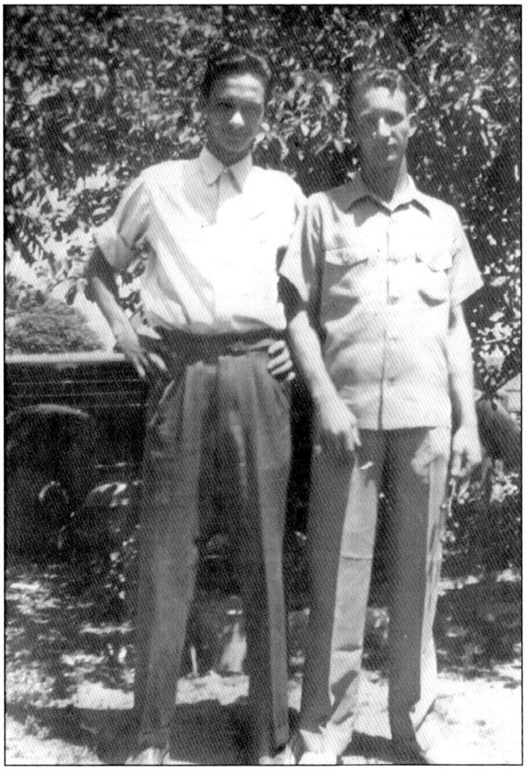

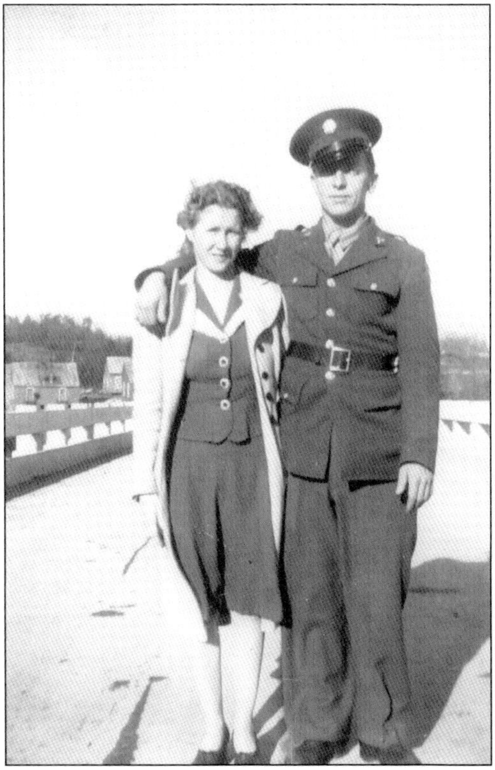

MILITARY SERVICE, 1940s. Tillman and Willie Mae Catoe have their picture taken on the Highway 901 bridge, with the Quarters visible in the background at left.

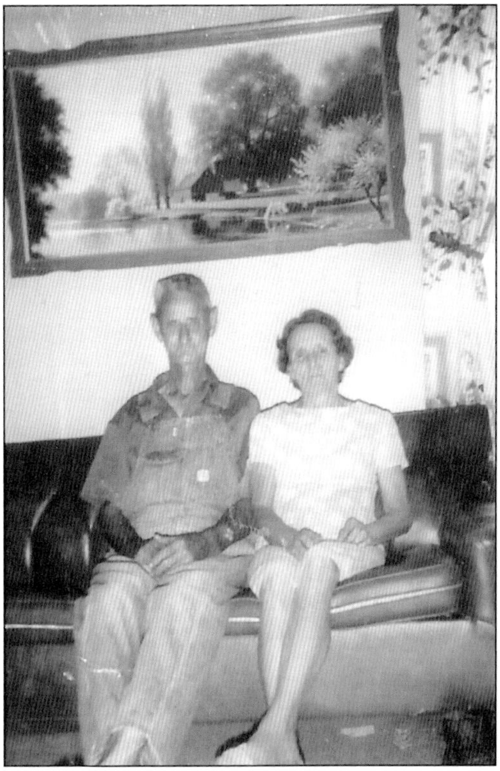

CARD-ROOM TENDER. Jim Lanier and his wife, Ollie, relax at their Lando home in the 1960s. Jim worked the card room in Manetta Mills for over 30 years. He trained hundreds of new employees and was a dedicated worker.

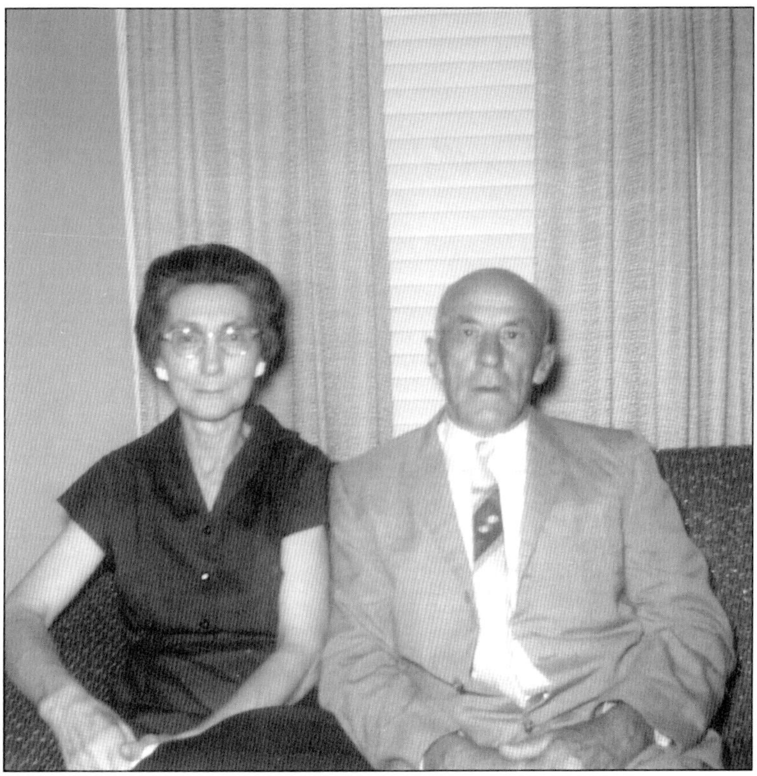

ON CALL, 1950S. Clarence and Willie Mae Irby worked in the cloth room and lived in Lando. Often employees were called to help raise motors and equipment above floodwaters inside the mill during the rainy season.

Seven

LANDO DAYS

Lando Days are remembered by many as a community festival. The first organized Lando Days was in 1982 and continued annually for the next seven years.

Lando Days refers to a way of life that residents of Lando experienced for many years. Lando was a community where people respected each other and had the true neighborly qualities that many communities strive to obtain. Lando was a place where neighbors would actually walk next door to borrow a cup of sugar or flour. Freshly baked pies would cool in windowsills as children played in the yard. Lando Days was a celebration of this sense of community.

Everyone who knows the area says Lando was the perfect place to raise a family. The area had a strong religious base, good schools, and good jobs. There were always plenty of children to play with, and good, safe areas in which the children could play. In the 1970s, a community pool and park was built in Lando by the Heath family. The pool was safer than swimming in Fishing Creek, because Manetta Mills provided lifeguards.

There are many folks who are waiting for a return of Lando. Now that the mill and abandoned houses are gone, the plans are in the works for rebuilding Lando. In 2006, several major residential developers have chosen Lancaster and Chester Counties as sites for residential communities. Joe and Gayle Lanford and Lando Properties, LLC, have plans to redevelop Lando as a residential community. The Lanfords are working with environmental, historical, and local groups to make sure that Lando is reestablished as a community where families can once again raise their children in a healthy and pleasant environment.

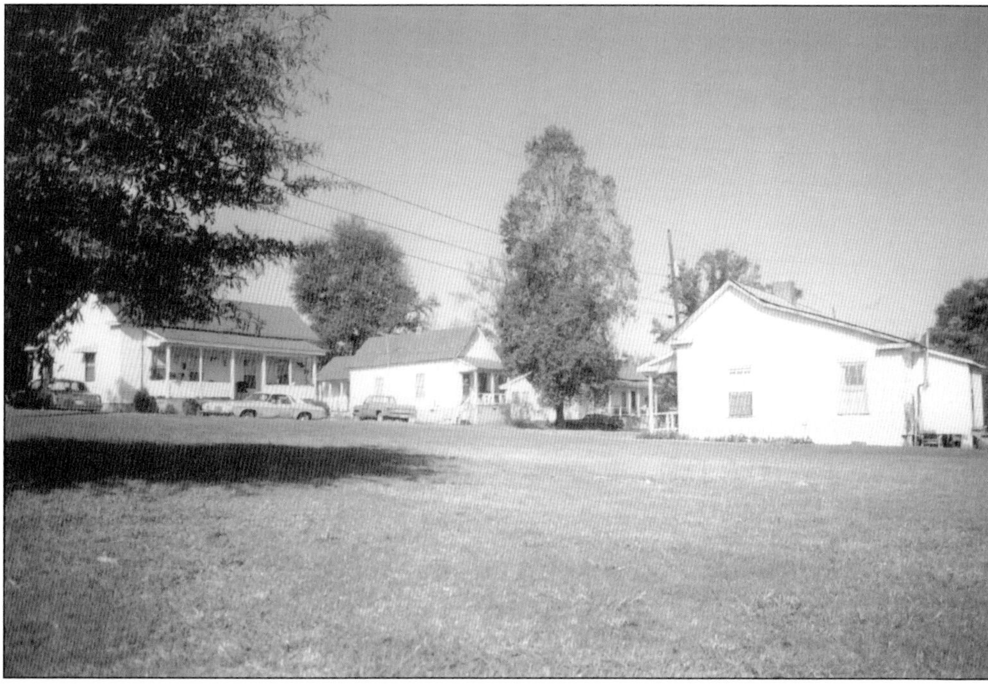

Frog Town, 1980s. When Manetta Mills was prosperous, Lando prospered as well. The hundreds of people that called Lando home took great pride in their community. This section of Lando was known as "Frog Town."

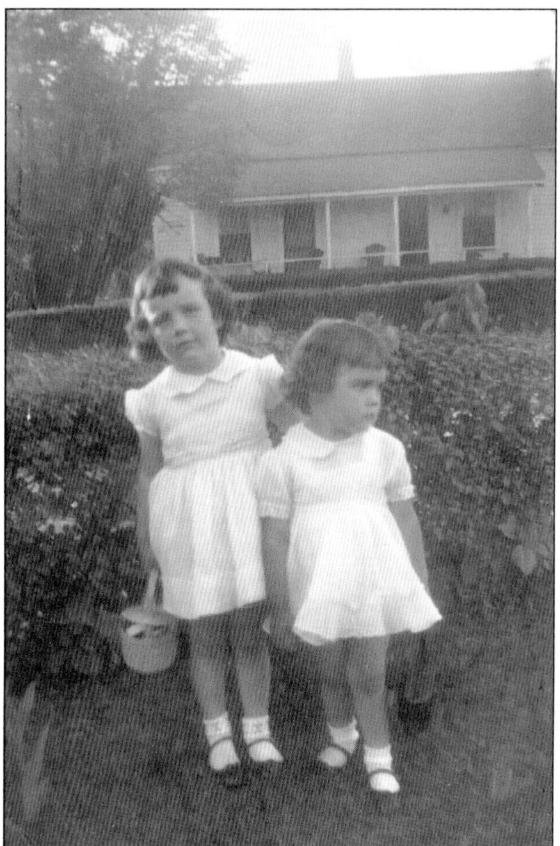

Sunday Best. Patty (left) and Roxann Yarborough stand in front of the Cooper house dressed in their Sunday best in the 1950s. Many folks in Lando could walk to church from their homes. Most families went to church in the morning, went home for lunch, and returned to church Sunday night.

FAMILY TIME. Pictured from left to right are Tessie McCorkle Bailey, Clarence "Hambone," Larry, and Margaret Lynn "Puddin" Bailey, and unidentified in Lando in the 1950s. The boardinghouse is visible in the background. The families of Lando tended to be very close. In the days before video games and cable television, siblings had to entertain one another. Families and neighbors relied on one another to help watch the children when they had to drive to Chester or Rock Hill or work overtime in the mill.

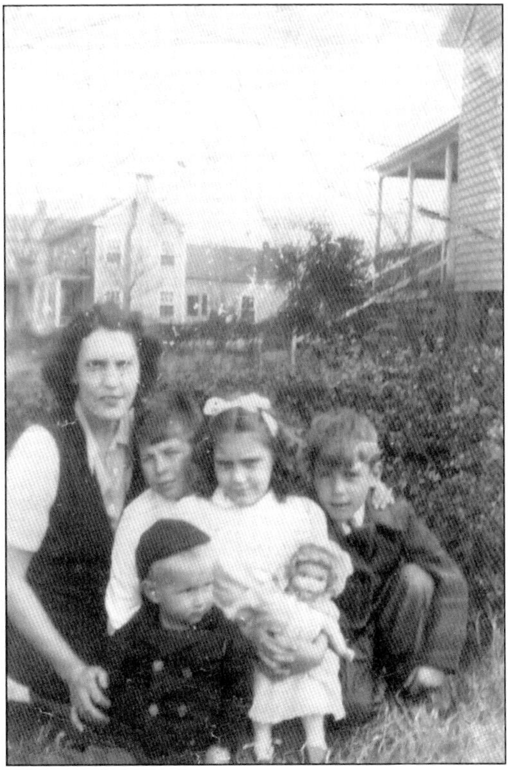

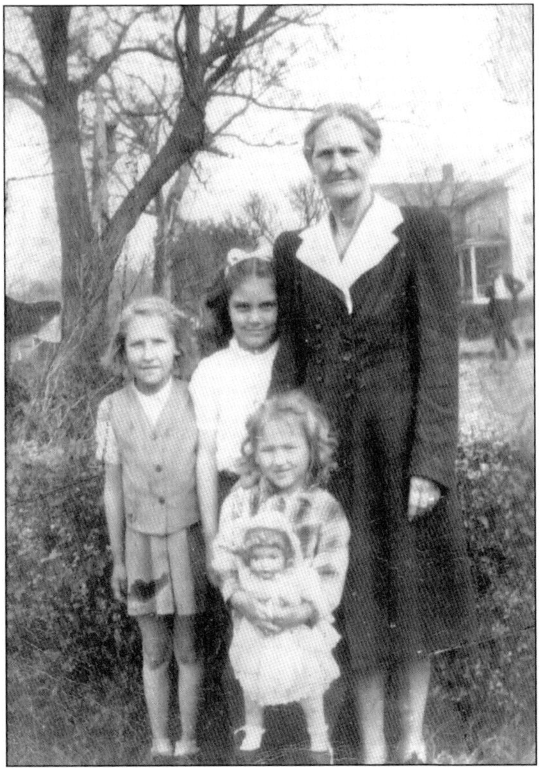

WOMAN'S WORK. From left to right, Mary Francis Black, Sally McCorkle, Margaret Lynn Bailey, and Joyce McCorkle stand in Lando before going to church in the 1950s. Women were the primary care givers in many homes. Cooking, cleaning, tending to the children's needs, and working in the mill were common for many wives and mothers in Lando.

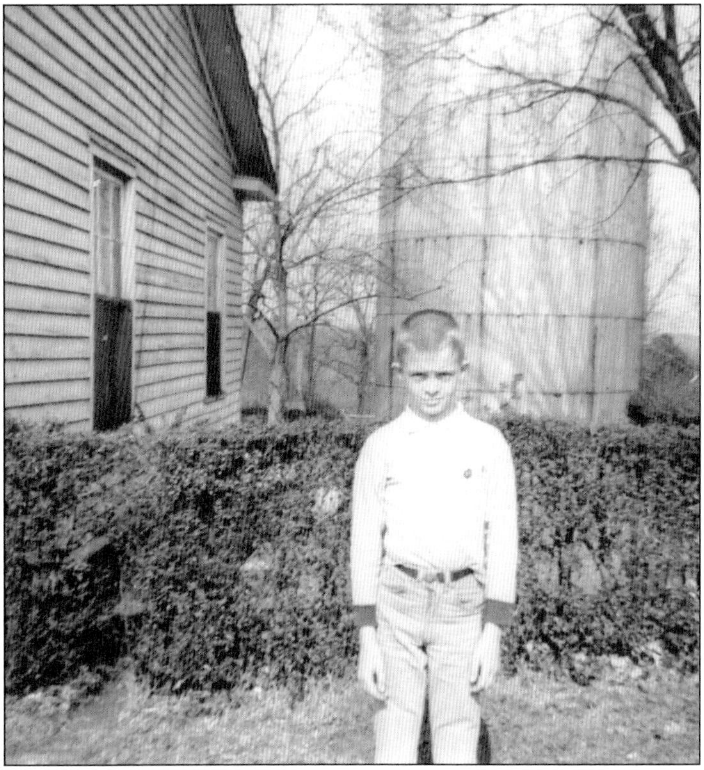

LANDO WATER. Robbie Rockholt stands near the water tower, which provided water for fire protection to Lando and Manetta Mills, in the late 1950s. Only a few longtime residents of Lando remember the freshwater spring that supplies the local creek with water. Bud Hefner said that "once you taste the fresh clean water of that spring you were in Lando to stay." Many families used to draw water from the spring and carry it up hill to their homes in Lando.

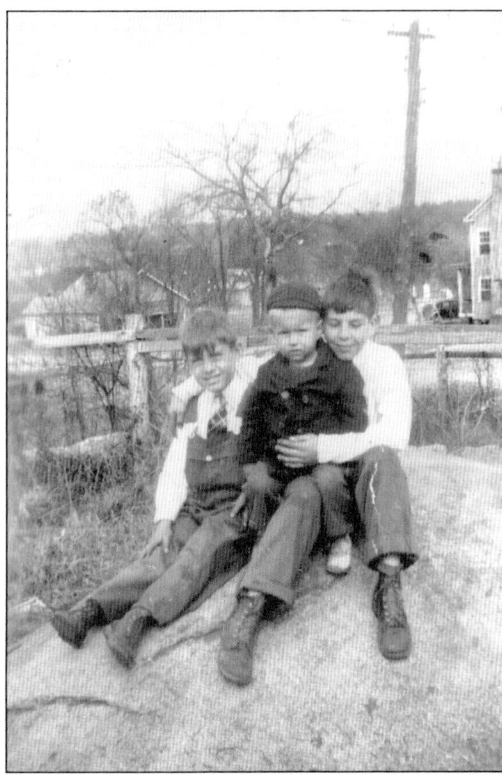

BROTHERLY LOVE. From left to right, Robert, Mack, and Sonny Black show true brotherly love in the 1940s. The closeness that existed between brothers also existed between neighbors. Longtime Lando resident Harold Tadlock tells of when the United States entered World War II; the young men of Lando all went together to enlist, and two men from Lando served in the navy with him.

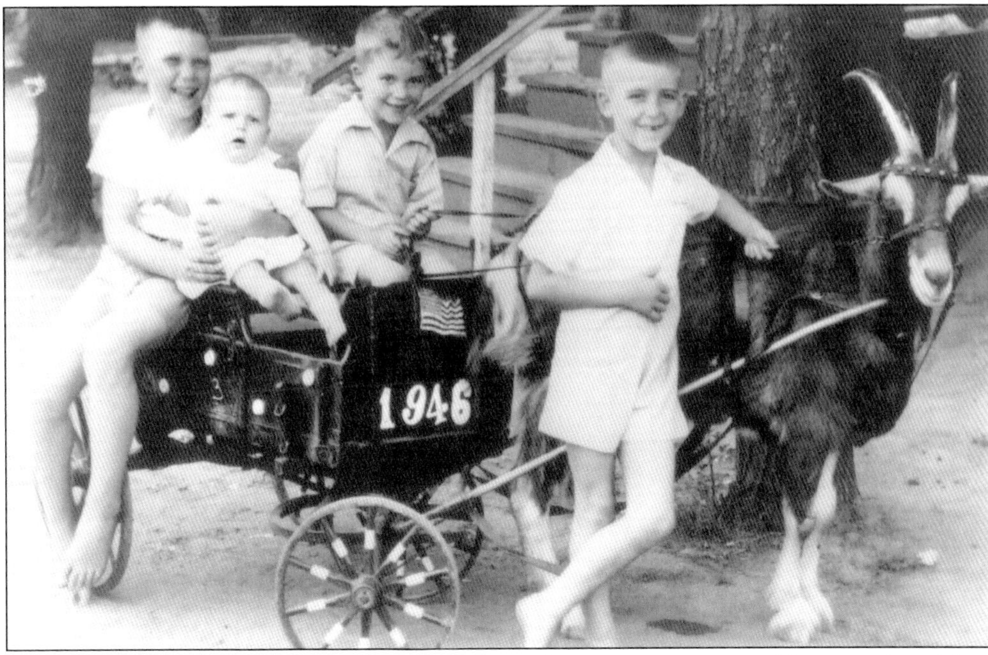

GOAT WAGON. Every mill town must have a goat-driven wagon picture. Here are, from left to right, Edward, Steve, and Jimmy Collins riding in the wagon with Harley Collins (guiding the goat) in 1946. Photographers would come to mill towns and let children have their picture taken in a goat-drawn wagon.

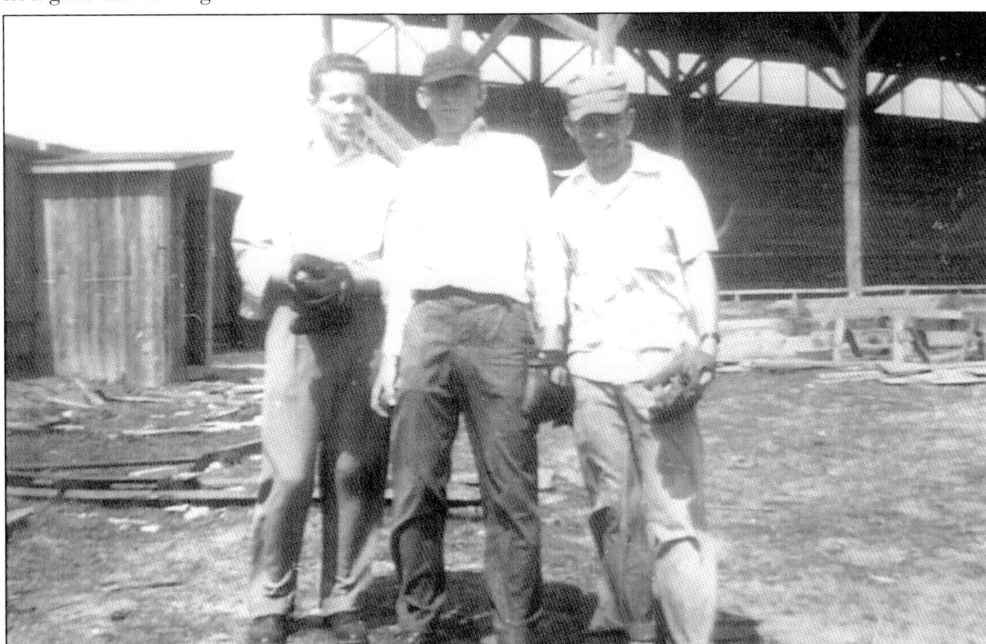

BASEBALL STADIUM. From left to right, O'Neal Bishop, Ruddey Blanks, and Roy Miller are ready to play baseball in the newly built Lando ball field in the 1950s. Manetta Mills, like many mills throughout the Carolinas, supported sports and recreation. This baseball field with stands for fans was funded by Manetta Mills and is where the Lando Blanketeers practiced and played.

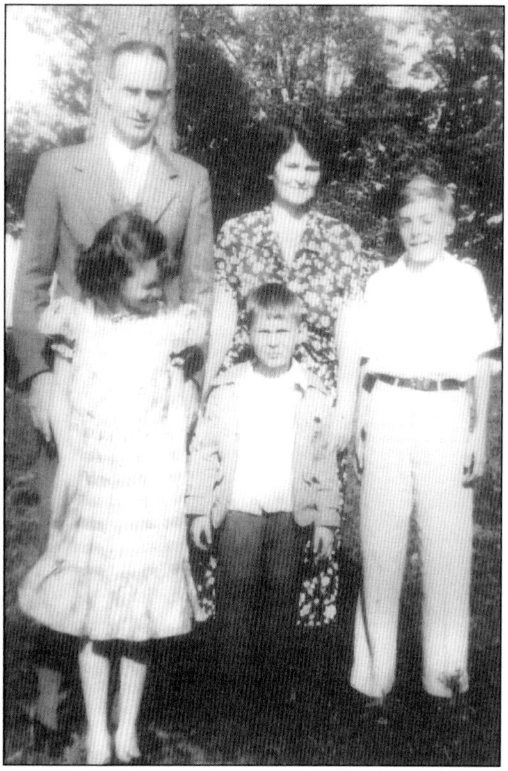

SIMPSON FAMILY. Pictured from left to right are (first row) Augusta and Jimmy; (second row) Harper, Amelia, and Harper Jr. Harper Simpson Sr. ran the company store starting in 1926.

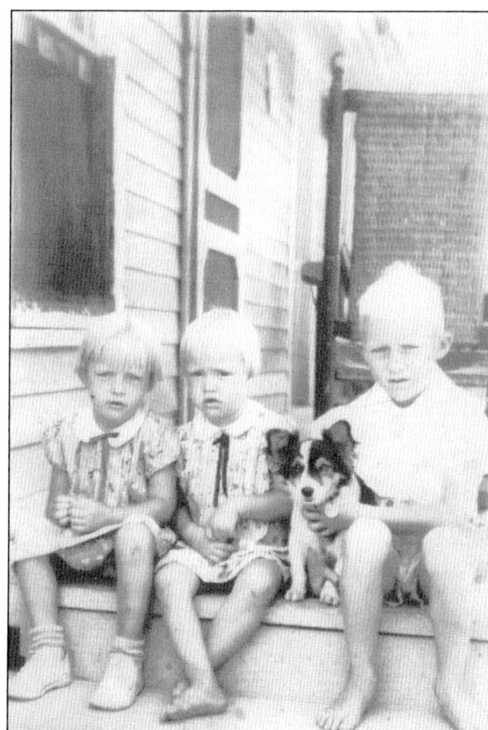

ON THE FRONT PORCH. From left to right, Lelia Hefner Black, Henrietta Hefner Lanier, and Fredrick Hefner pose with their dog on their front porch in the 1930s. The rocking chair in the background is an example of how many folks spent many leisure hours.

PLAYING IN THE STREETS. From left to right, Grover Cleveland, Madge Ramsey, and Ronnie and Rickey Bellue are having fun playing, as many children did in Lando. The last dirt road in Lando was paved in the 1950s. When Richard Miller and his friends saw the road paved, they decided to dig it up. They did not get far, but the patch in the road lasted for 30 years and was a reminder of their childish attempt.

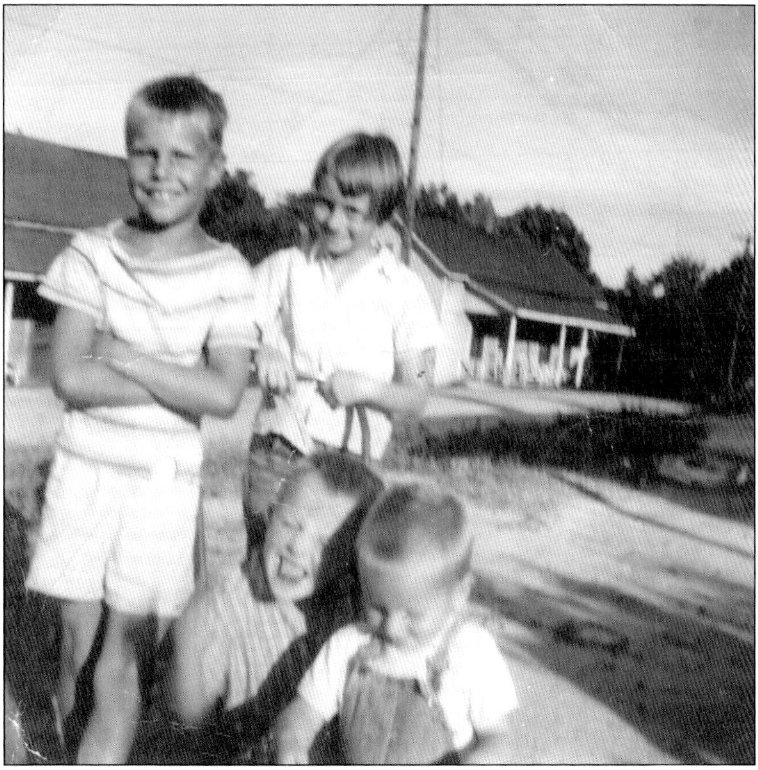

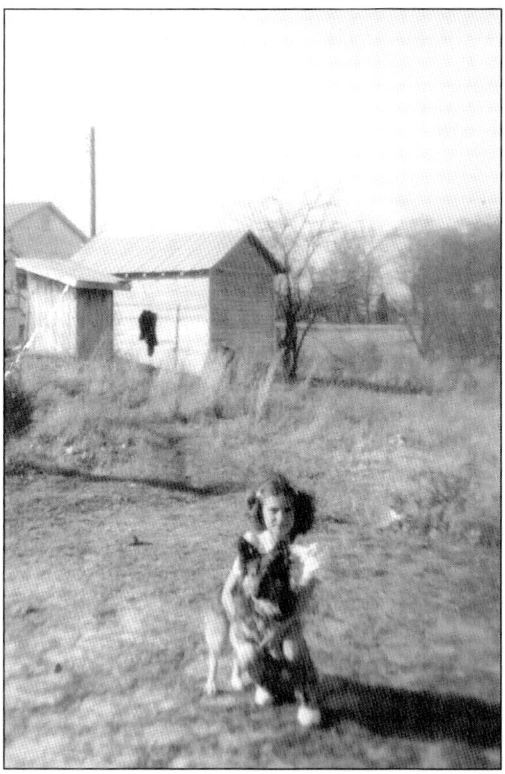

MODERN CONVENIENCES. Jenell Stroud poses with her dog in her backyard. Many homes did not have indoor plumbing until the 1950s. Electricity first came to the mill village by means of a waterwheel on the millrace where it exited Manetta Mills. It was a midshot wheel with a big cable that would turn a generator, which gave power to the village.

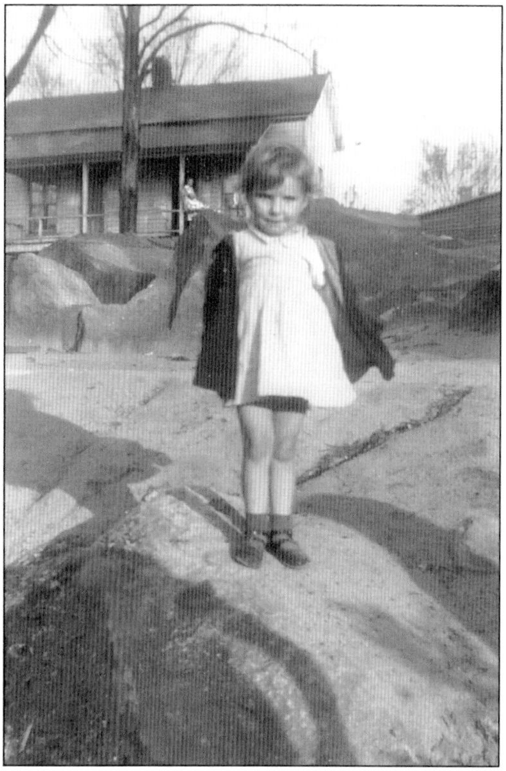

Rock Hopping. Peggy Scott plays on the rocks in front of her house. The area is 50 feet higher in elevation from the mill site and contains a granite bedrock which was used to make the millstones and foundations for many homes. Several outcrops of granite still have holes that were drilled into them by Manetta Mills' employees in the early 1900s to split the rocks into blocks for construction.

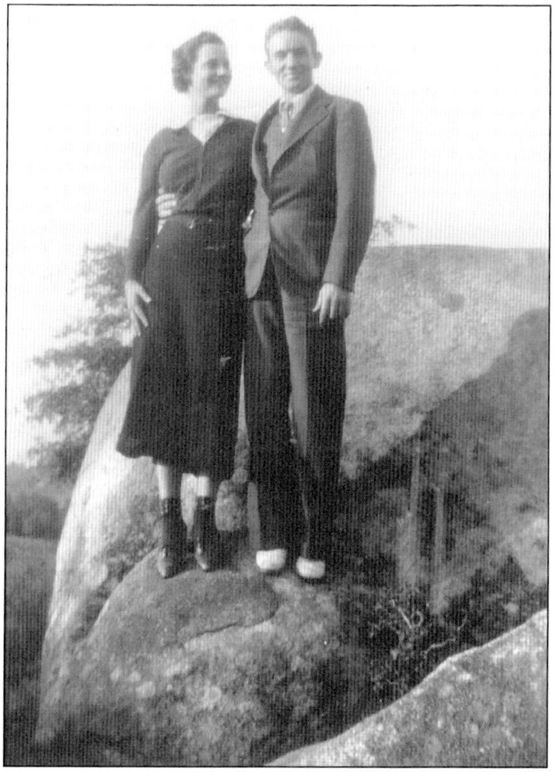

Devil's Footprint, 1920s. Some of the rock outcrops are over 10 feet tall and could be dangerous if a child fell off the rocks. In the area near the bandstand is a rock called the "Devil's Footprint." Parents like Manuel and Ella Hefner would tell their children that the devil had stomped on the rock, causing a dent, to help keep their children from playing there.

SUNNY DAYS. From left to right, Vergie Hefner Chappell, Jennette Hefner Ellis, and Corenna Hefner Bowers enjoy the beauty of the Lando countryside in the 1930s.

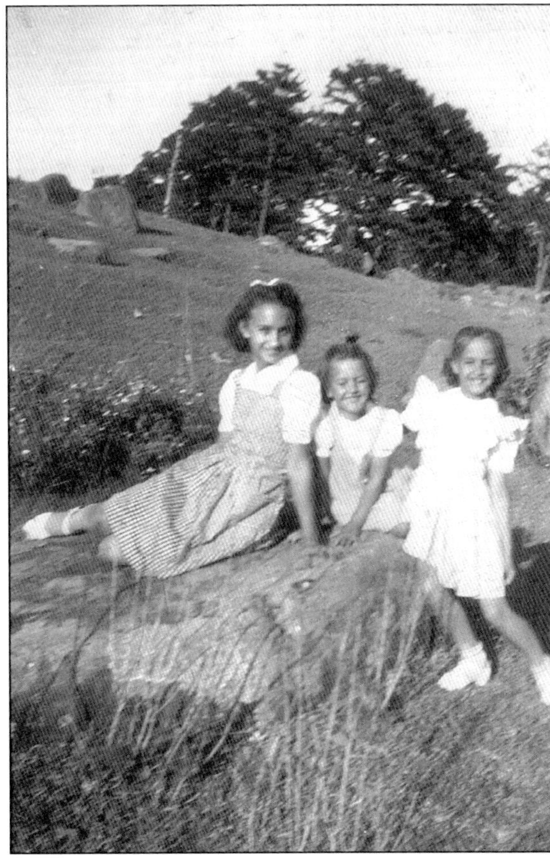

FRIENDS IN LANDO. From left to right, Betty McCrorey, Betsy Morgan, Flora Burns, Wilma Burns, Bessy Burns, Jane Reid, Eleanor Reid, and Sara Burns play on the banks of Fishing Creek in the late 1930s.

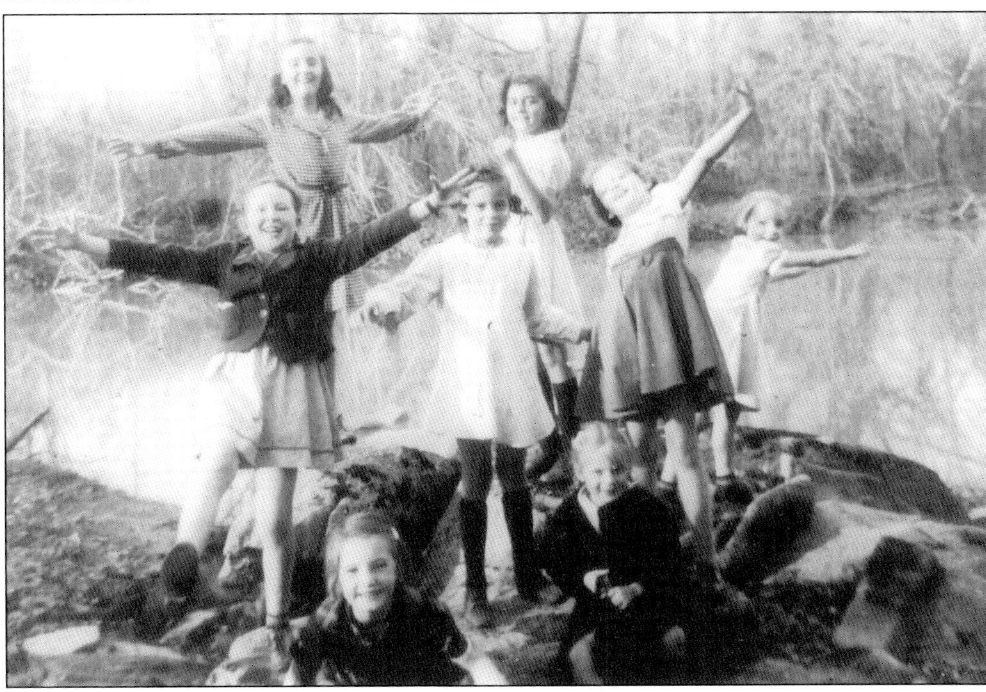

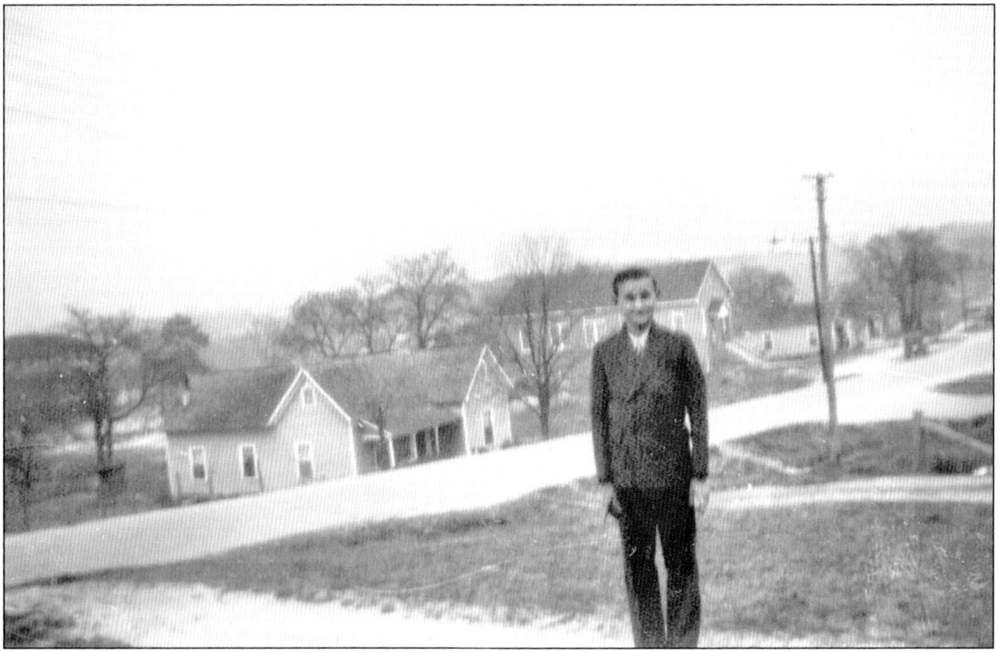

MAIN STREET. James Miller stands next to Main Street in Lando in the late 1950s.

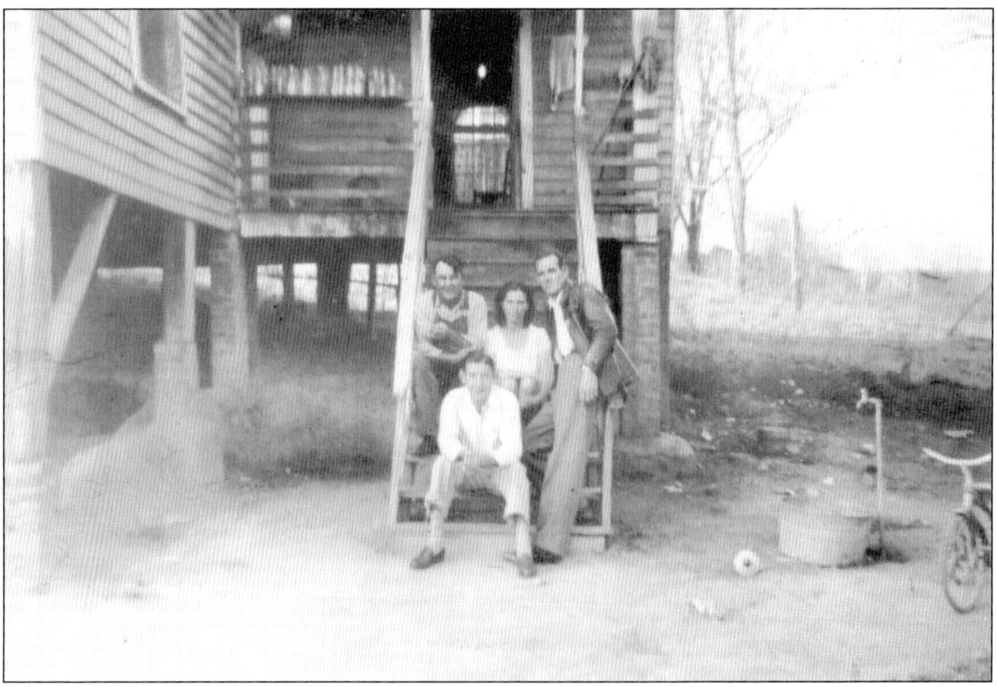

HAPPY HOLLER. From left to right, Walter and Hannah Rockholt, J. V. Coker, and Cecil Polk relax on the steps at a house in Happy Holler in the 1950s. The name Happy Holler originated when the Lando Church of God first started meeting at a home in the holler. People would hear the singing, praises, and happiness coming from the hollow, and someone said, "Listen to the happiness coming from the holler." From then on the area was known as "Happy Holler."

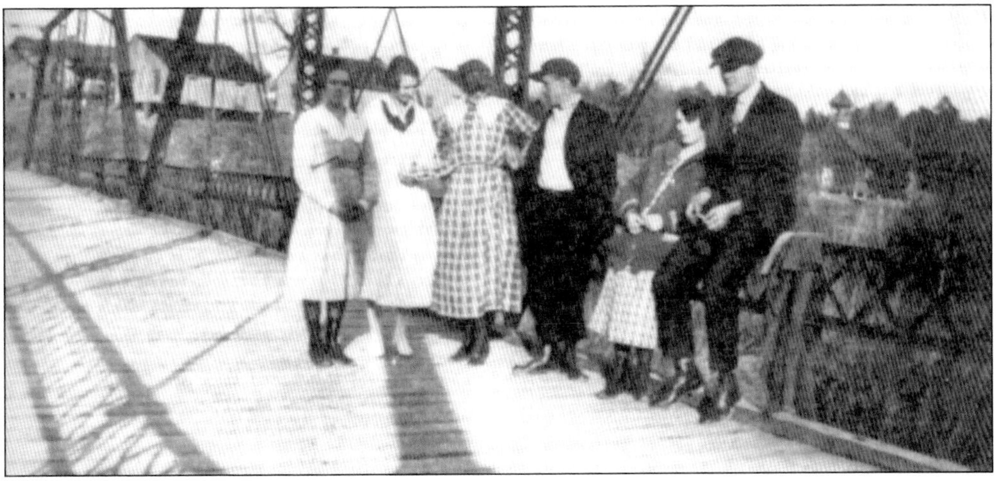

SUNDAY WALKS, C. 1919. A Sunday walk across the bridge to the Quarters was a common scene in Lando for much of the 20th century. Homes and Calvary Church, which existed on the Quarters side of Fishing Creek, are visible in the background of this image. Stories are told of how the people of the Quarters would chain down their houses and the church to keep them from floating away during hard rains.

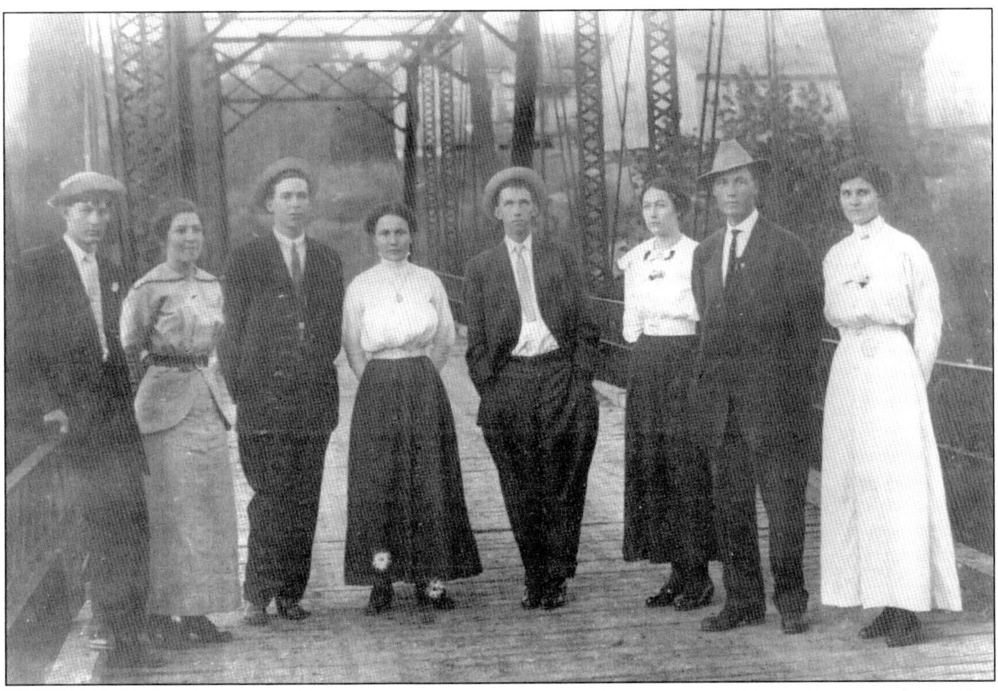

PLAYING ON THE BRIDGE. John Lewis, a resident of the Quarters, would climb up on the bridge and play his washboard. The music Lewis played could be heard throughout Lando. From left to right, Walt Hyatt, Myrt Long, Verna and Lillie Hough, Marshall Long, Rushie Ramsey, and Jim and Molly Ramsey stand on the bridge with Quarters houses in the background c. 1918.

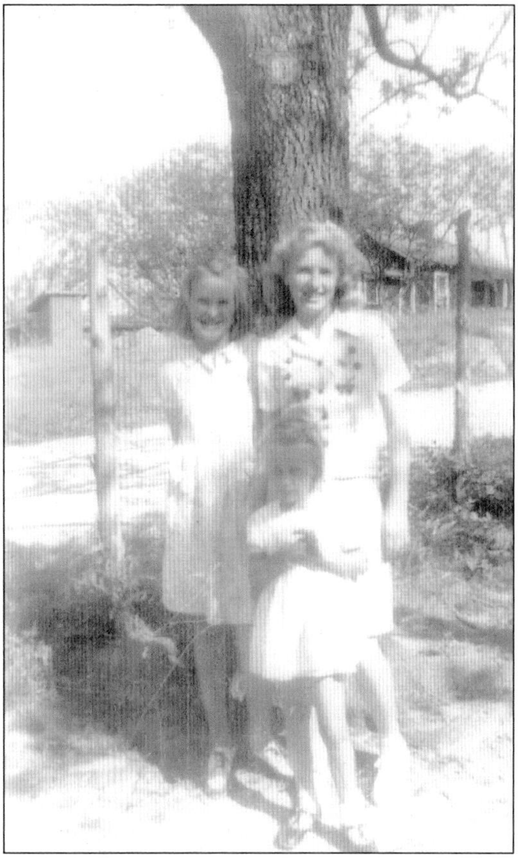

CONSTABLE. From left to right, Judy, Jeanette, and Jean Elliott lived and worked in Lando in the 1950s. Jack Elliott, father and husband, was the town's constable, and Jeanette worked in the weave room at Manetta Mills.

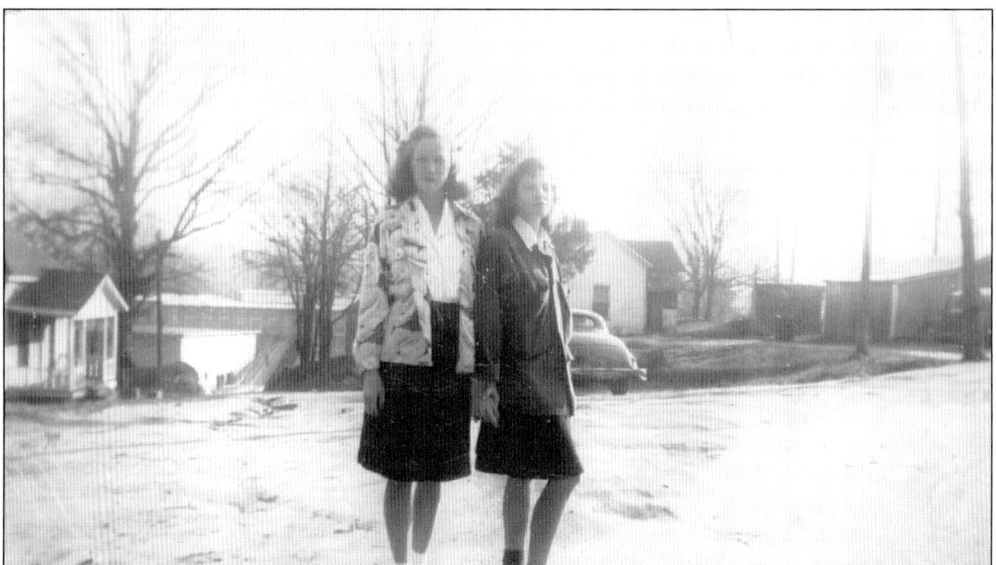

LANDO ROAD. Martha Ramsey Tadlock (left) and Carrie Lee Ernandez (right) stand in front of the company store with Helen Miller's home on right and Manetta Mills in the background in the 1940s.

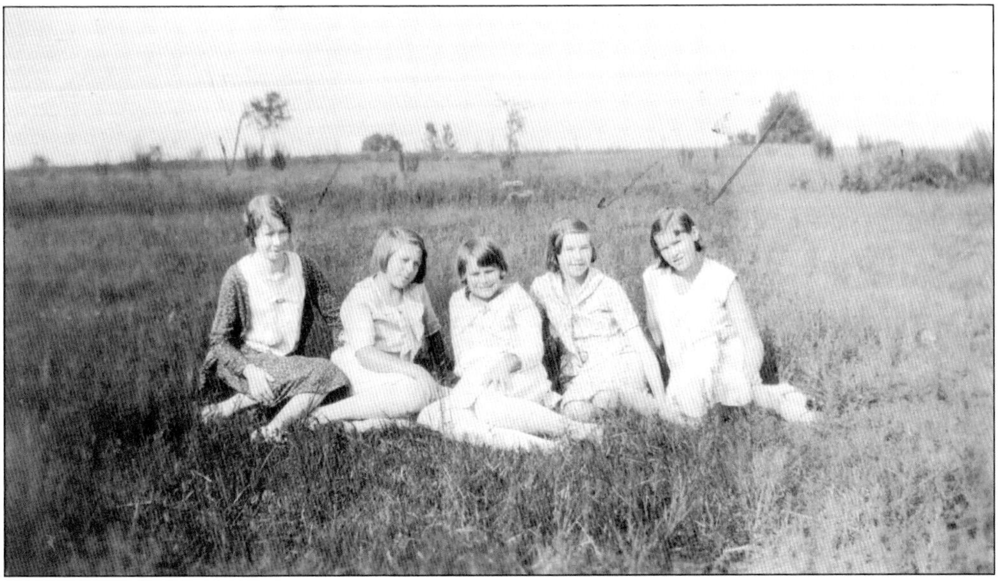

Lying in Green Pastures. From left to right, Willie Mae Catoe, Genola Ernandez Collins, Marie Hargrove, Iva Wallace Polk, and Fannie Ernandez relax in one of the many green pastures that surrounded Lando in the 1920s. Many young women would start working at Manetta Mills by age 15. Many couples met in the mill or in Lando.

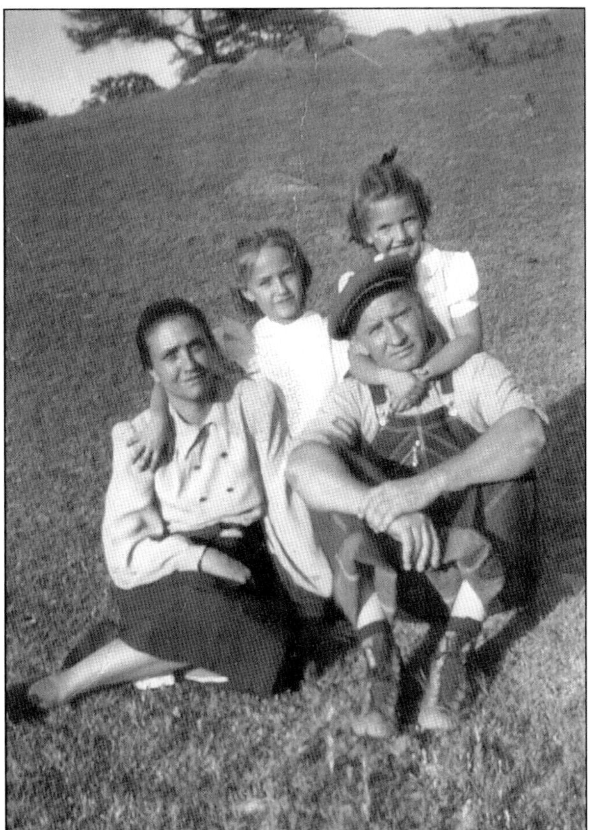

Hillside. Seen here from left to right, Dora, Corenna, Jim, and Jeanette Hefner have their picture taken on the hillside in Lando in the late 1930s. Jim Hefner was an excellent swimmer, and his son Fred often told the story of when Jim was awakened one night because the night supervisor had fallen in the millrace near the water wheel. Jim pulled the man from the water.

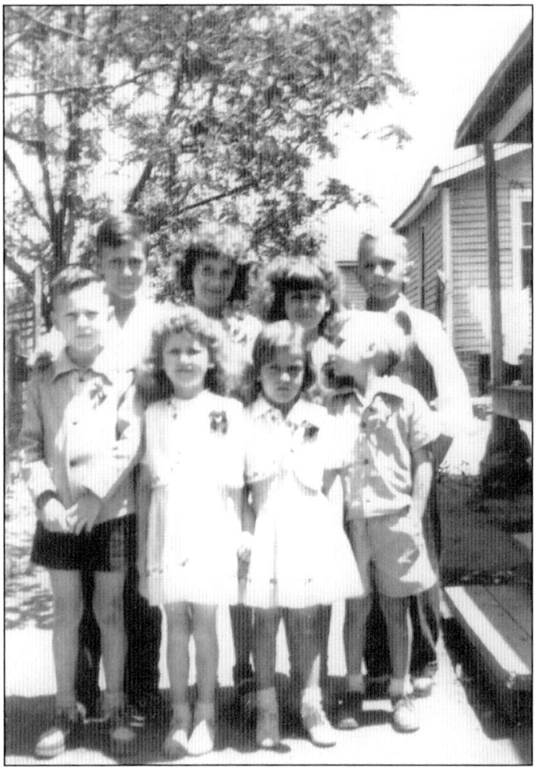

MILL HILL BRATS AND PROUD OF IT, 1940S. Pictured here, from left to right, are the following: (first row) Thomas Lee Byrd, Lauretta Ernandez, Jolane Byrd, and Ronnie Hargrove; (second row) Bobby Hargrove, Linda Ernandez, Donna Byrd, and Maxie Hargrove. The spirit of the community and lifestyle that many mill village children grew up in is still alive in the people who lived and worked in mill communities.

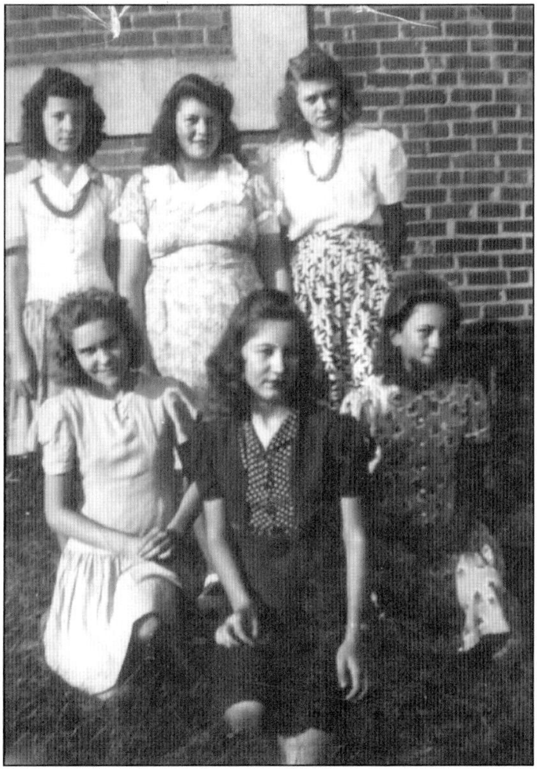

1942 GANG. Pictured from left to right are the following: (first row) Annie R. McFadden, Helen Moore, and Ruby Lee Starnes; (second row) Catherine Scott, Lillian Starnes, and Carrie Bigham. These ladies were part of a group known as the "1942 Gang." With many of the men serving during World War II, the women of Lando became a close-knit group.

A Fresh Start, 1920s. Many young couples started their families in Lando. Longtime Lando resident Louise Hyatt said that when a young couple from Lando got married and were ready to move into their new Manetta Mills house, their neighbors and friends would donate a piece of extra furniture to help the newly weds get started. Lillie Ramsey and Vernon Hough were one of many couples that fell in love in Lando.

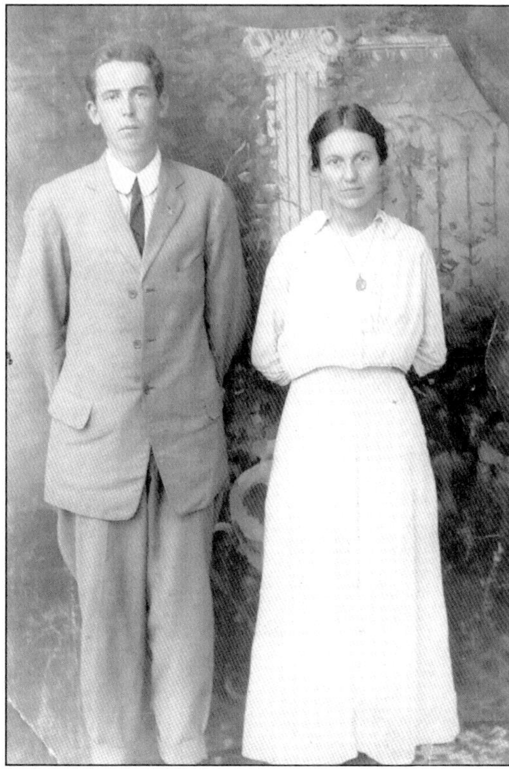

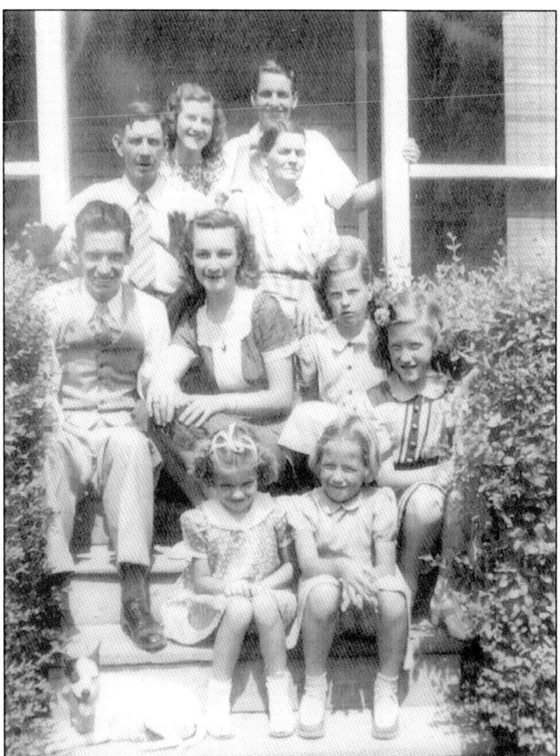

Big Happy Family, 1940s. From left to right, (first row) Bonnie and June Tinkler; (second row) Grady, Plummie, Carrie Lee, and Nancy; (third row) Willie, Faye, Tony, and Madge Ernandez were one big happy family. The Ernandez family adopted the Tinkler girls after the death of their father. Lando was a community where neighbors would look out for and help a neighbor in need.

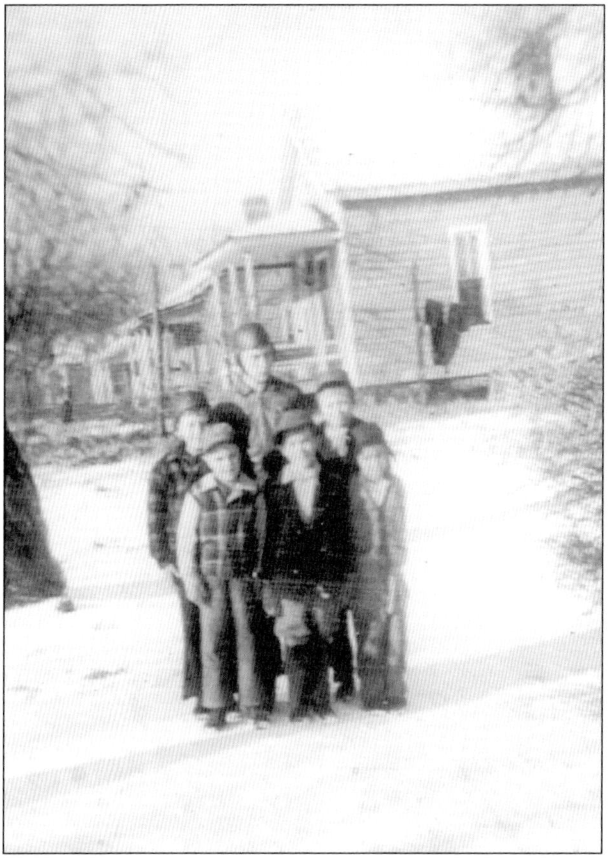

BENJAMIN STREET. Lando children often gathered on Benjamin Street to play. The steep hill was a perfect place for them to ride their homemade go-carts in the 1940s. The carts had pulleys for wheels, scrap metal for axles, and wood scraps for the body of the cart.

CHILDREN AT PLAY, 1930S. Pictured from left to right, Kirk Kirpatrick, Gracie Cooper, Wilma Morgan, Hambone Bailey (in wagon), Lucy Clawson, Tommy Ligon, and Allen Heath are ready to play everything from basketball to the drums. Longtime Lando resident James Coker says that when he was a child, he would keep bread in his pocket so that he would always have something to eat even when he was playing ball.

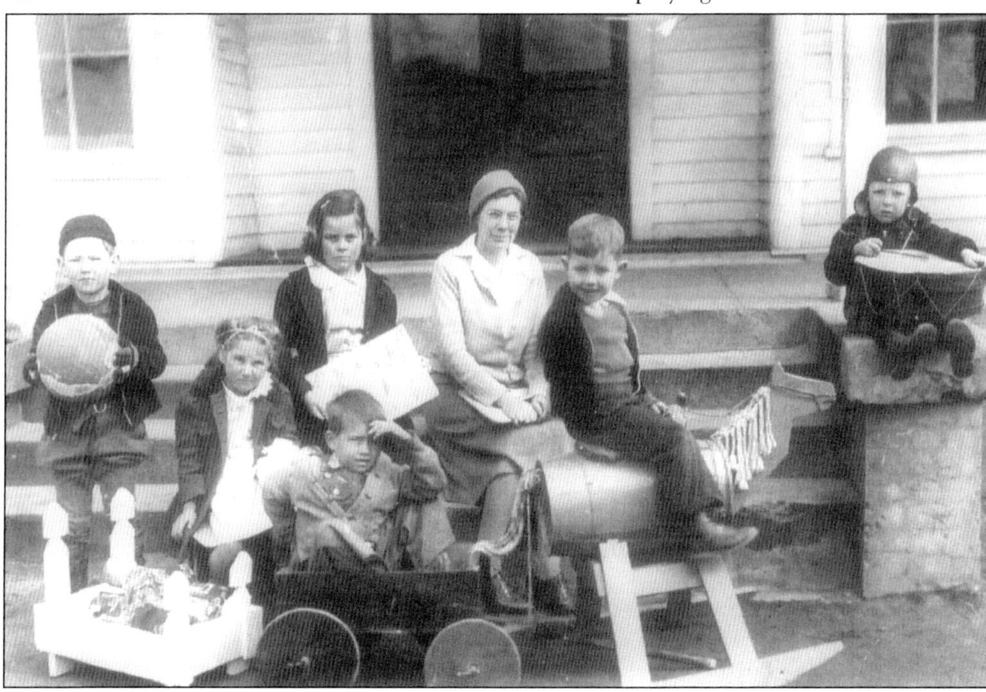

MAIN STREET. From left to right, Annie Ray Dawkins, Polly Culp, Dorothy Lee, and Annie Dell Dawkins sit on a bench near the baseball field in the 1930s. A story is told of a bench that sat outside the company store during World War II. Wives of the servicemen would gather on the bench and wait for the government checks to be delivered. The bench was known as the "widows bench."

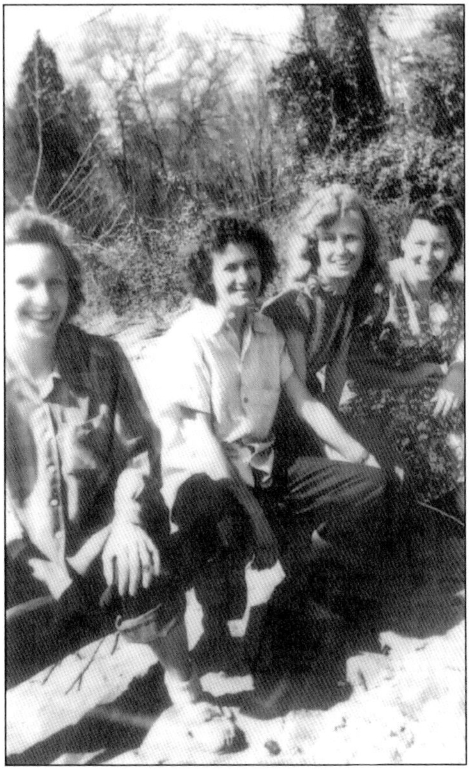

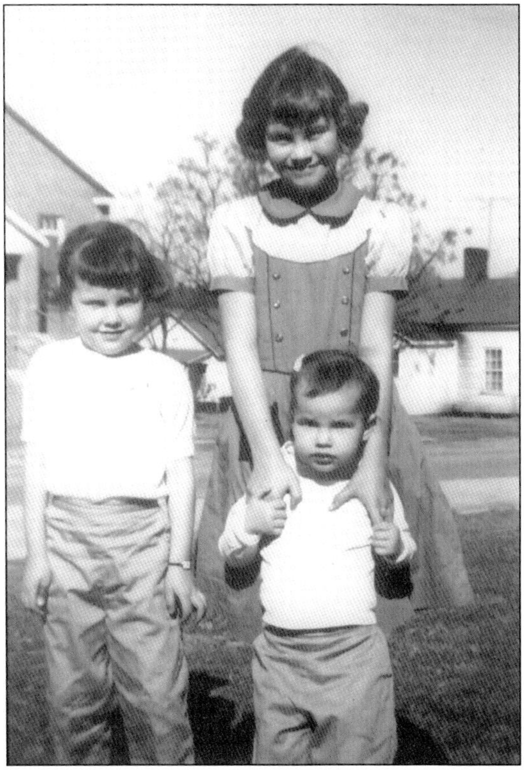

PLEASANT COMMUNITY. Sheila (left), Gloria (front right), and Shannon Ernandez stand if front of Heath Memorial Methodist Church in the 1960s. The white mill house, green grass, and blue sky make for a picture-perfect afternoon.

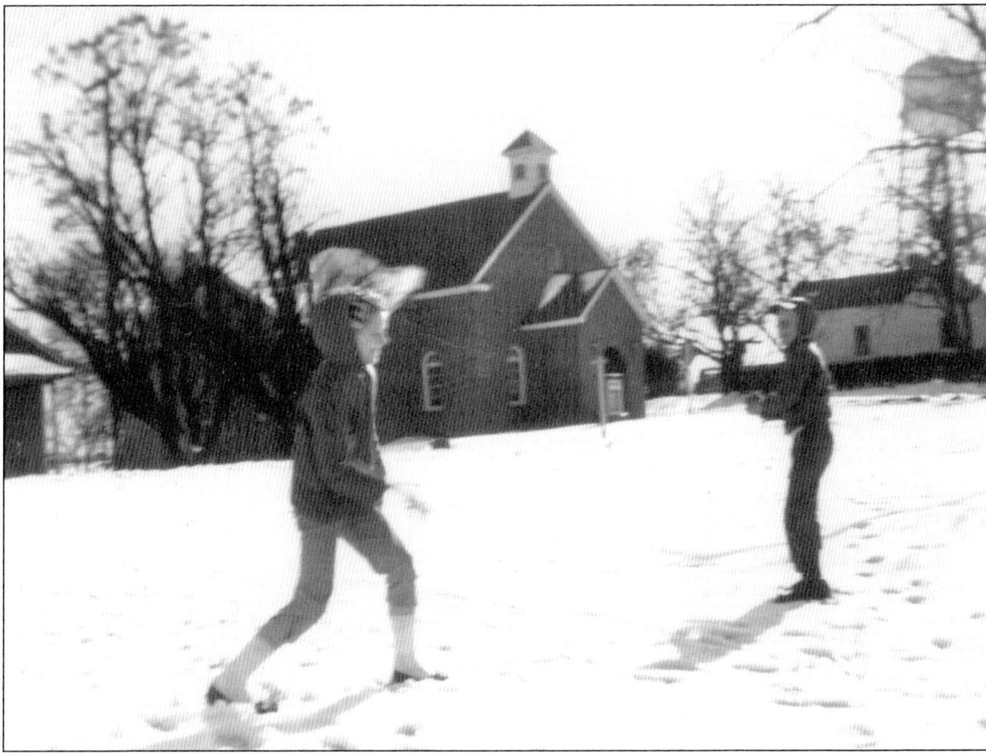

SNOW DAYS. Brenda and Bob Blanks play in the snow in Lando in the 1930s. John Coker tells a story of his mother's resourcefulness. One day during a hail storm, she asked her sons to gather hail stones for the ice cream churn because ice normally had to be purchased from the company store. The children did as their mother asked, and she churned them some fresh ice cream.

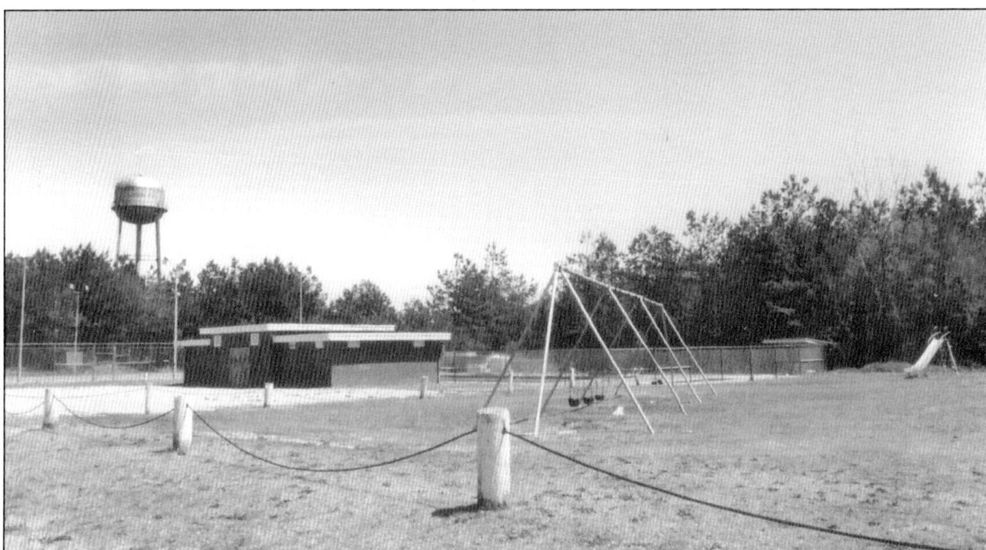

PLAYGROUND. Manetta Mills provided a playground equipped with swing sets, slides, seesaws, a baseball field, and a swimming pool in the 1950s. The water tower provided water to the mill village.

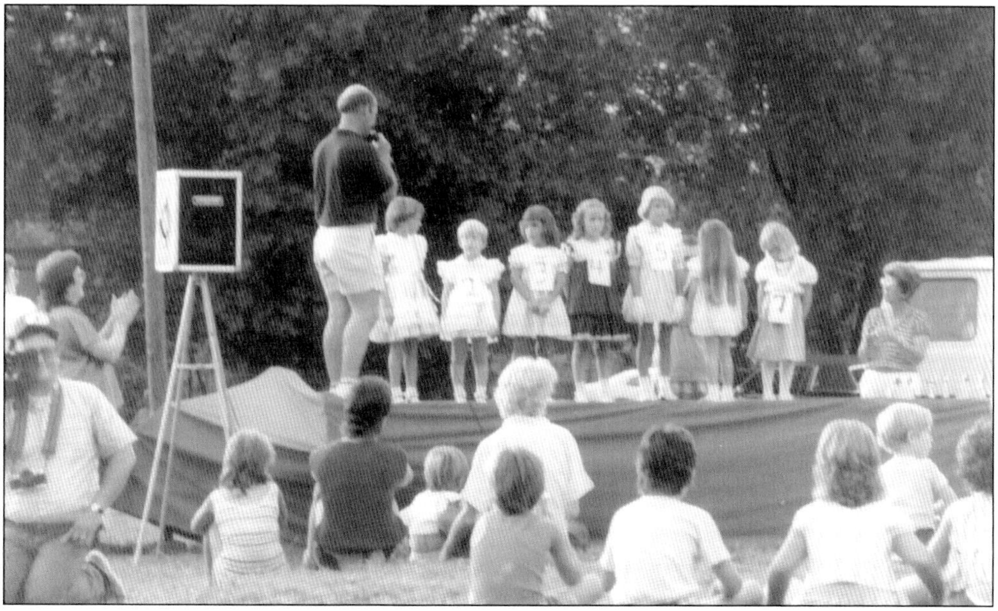

Wee Miss Lando. In 1988, Jennifer Murphy was crowned Wee Miss Lando. Today, Jennifer works at a local bank and is involved with the Lando Manetta Mills History Center. Jennifer is proud of her heritage in Lando and the memories of Lando Days, and her childhood in Lando will be passed down for generations.

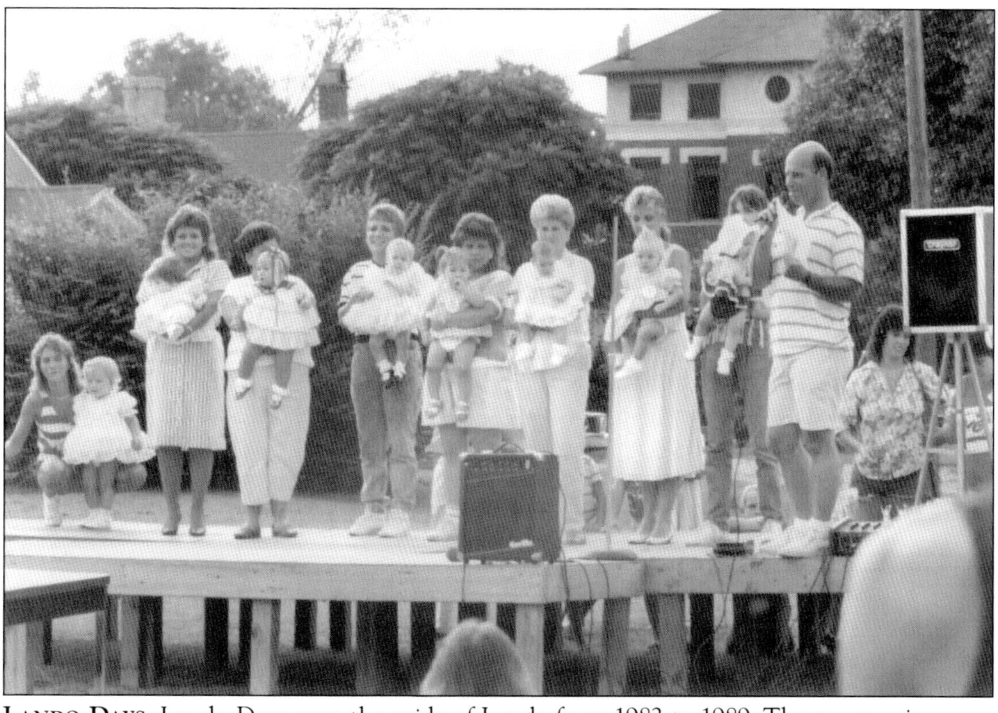

Lando Days. Lando Days were the pride of Lando from 1982 to 1989. The community came together for car shows, beauty pageants, mill tours, food, and games. Seen is the 1986 Lando Days baby contest, in which mom and baby try to impress the judges. Mike McBrayer emcees the pageant.

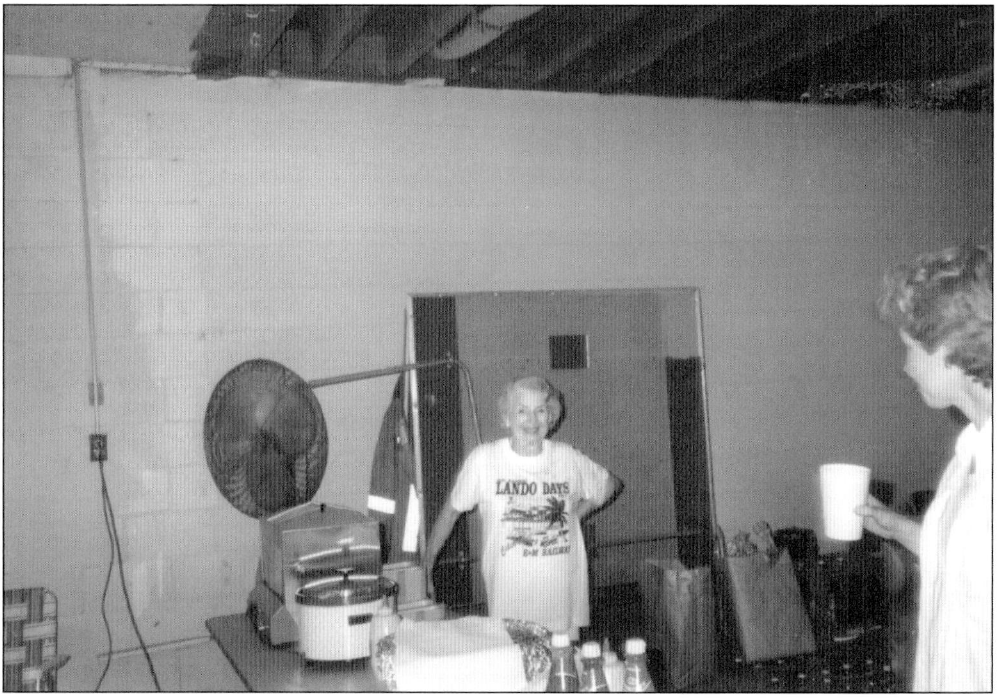

HOT DOG STAND. Helen Bolton sells hot dogs and hamburgers during Lando Days in 1987. The Lando Day celebration would go until midnight with music and dancing in the streets.

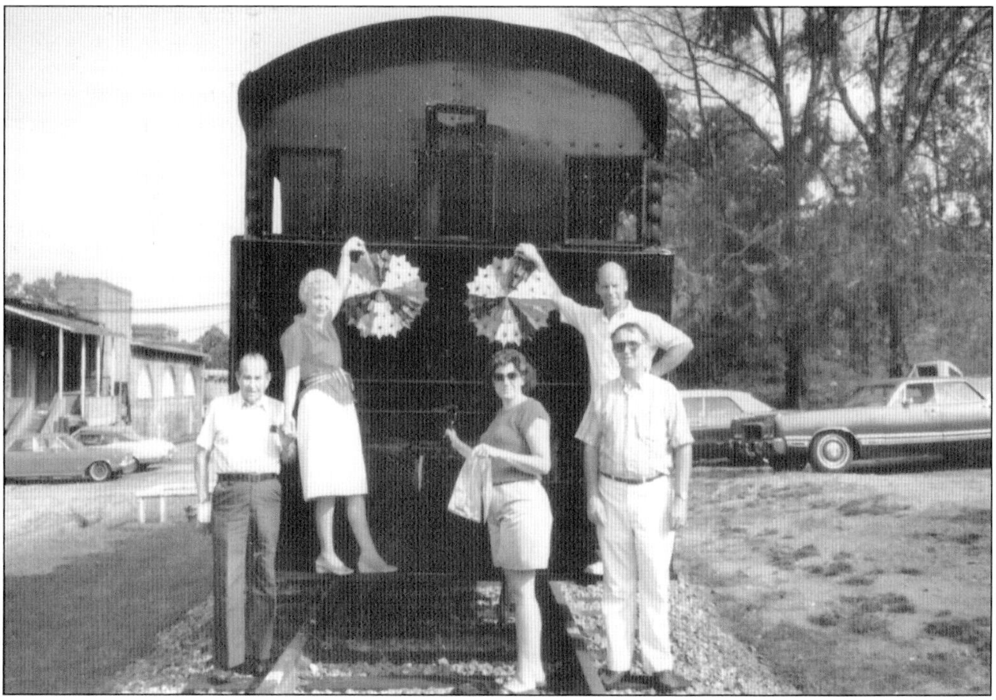

LANDO DAYS CELEBRATION. From left to right, Homer Miller, Ruby Ernandez, Brenda McBrayer, Mike McBrayer, and Richard Bolton (right front) decorate the Dummy for the Lando Days celebration in the 1980s.

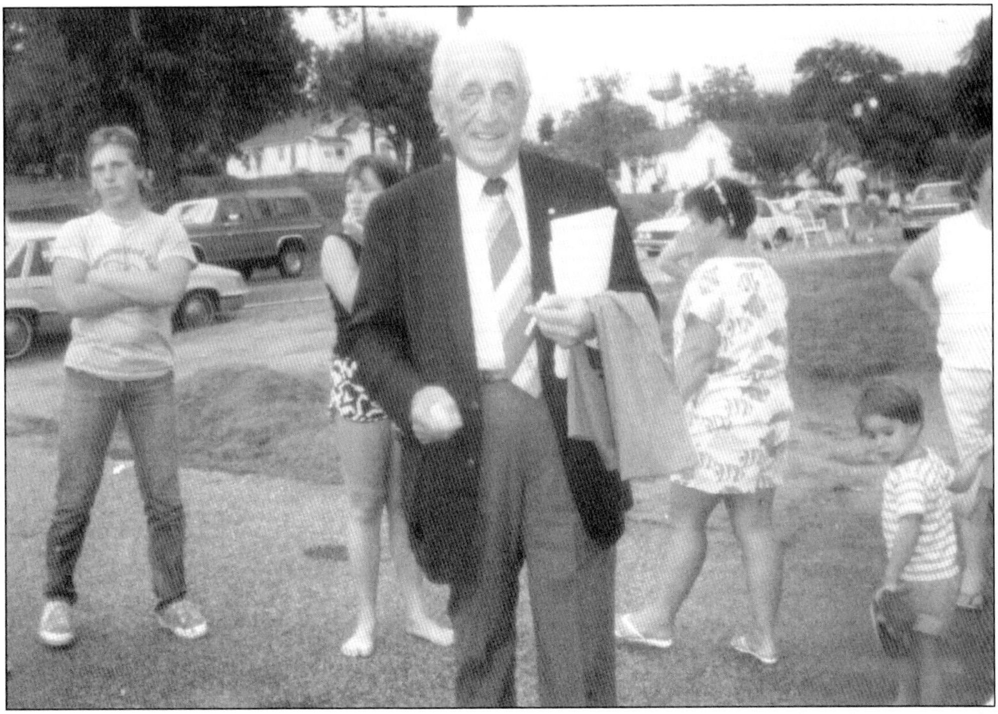

DR. GASTON JR. AT LANDO DAYS. Seen here is Dr. John N. Gaston Jr. (center) at the 1986 Lando Days with, from left to right, Todd Broome, Leslie Lanier, and Sybil Catoe in the background. His father was honored by the residents of Lando with a granite marker placed on Main Street.

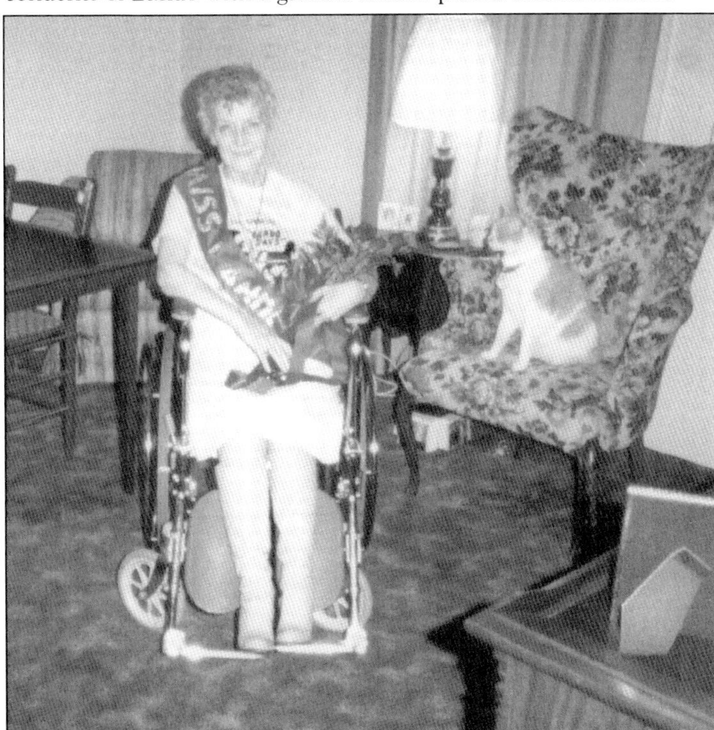

HELEN MILLER. Helen Miller was everyone's grandma. Recognized during Lando Days as Mrs. Lando Days 1986, Miller could always be counted on for kind words and comfort. She made homemade greeting cards that she gave to everyone.

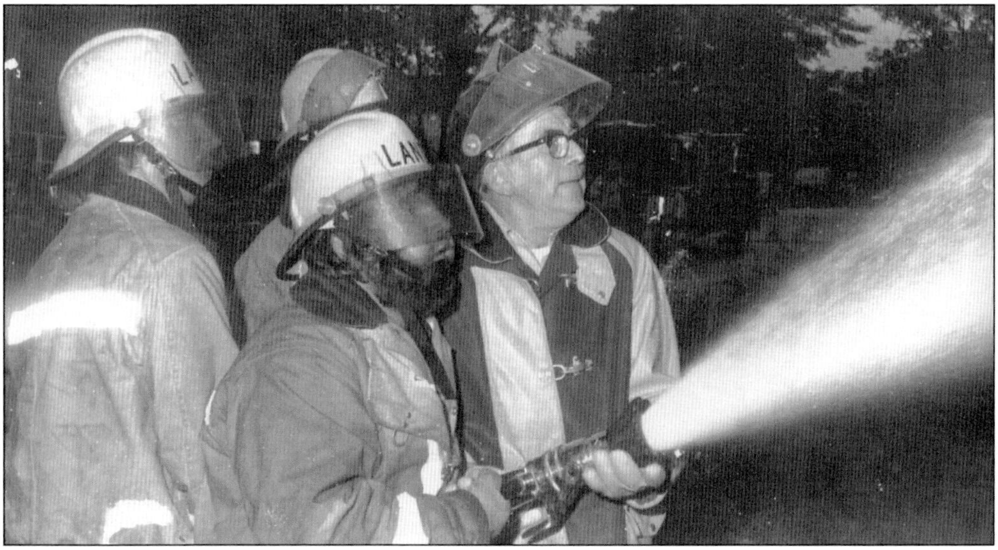

LANDO VOLUNTEER FIRE DEPARTMENT. Established in 1957 by Chester County, the Lando Volunteer Fire Department was one of three initial volunteer fire departments in the county. Manetta Mills respected the duties of the firefighters from the Lando Volunteer Fire Department and allowed any volunteers to leave their job when an emergency situation occurred.

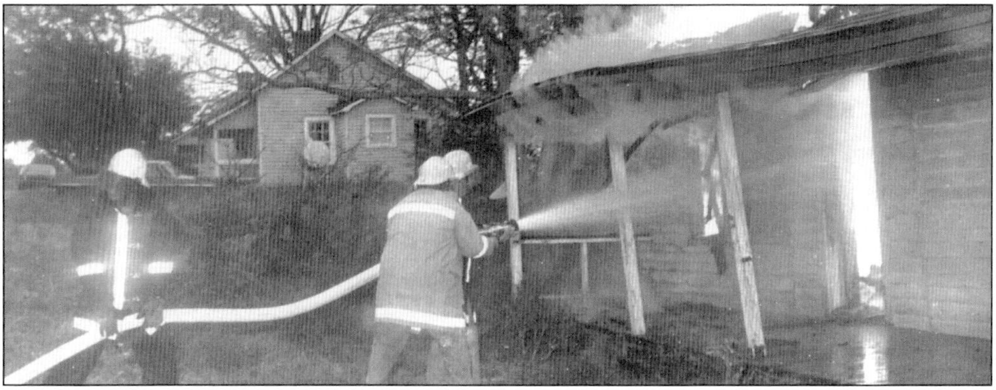

WELL-TRAINED AND READY, 1990S. The Lando Volunteer Fire Department spends hundreds of hours each year training for any type of situation. They also take great responsibility in educating residents of the county in fire safety and how to handle emergencies. The firefighters are always the first responders to emergency situations. The volunteer firefighters of the Lando Volunteer Fire Department have been serving the residents of Lando and eastern Chester County for more than 20 years.

Eight

Time Goes On

Just like water under a bridge, time moves on. Since the closing of Manetta Mills in 1992, Lando has undergone many changes. The mill is completely gone, 90 percent of the mill houses have been destroyed, and now only vacant lots remain. Even in 1998, during an extreme drought, Fishing Creek ran dry.

The water did return to Fishing Creek and continues to flow today. The majority of the lots in Lando are empty, and a large hole exists where Manetta Mills once produced millions of blankets. The railroad tracks of the E&M stop on the north side of Fishing Creek. For more than 10 years, Lando was a ghost town.

People left Lando in search of new jobs. Textiles production faded from many towns in the South, and North and South Carolina was greatly impacted. Young folks no longer had the security of Manetta Mills for a job, so they moved elsewhere.

With most of the houses deserted and dilapidated and Manetta Mills standing in ruins, a Rock Hill businessman saw the beauty and potential of Lando. Joe Lanford and a group of investors purchased the community of Lando and the buildings of Manetta Mills, encouraging the hopes and dreams of the folks from Lando for a revolution in their community.

Lando Properties, LLC, was formed with a vision of developing Lando as a family community. The Lanfords and Lando Properties, LLC, did not realize the deep history of Lando, but they both have come to respect and love the deep history that is Lando.

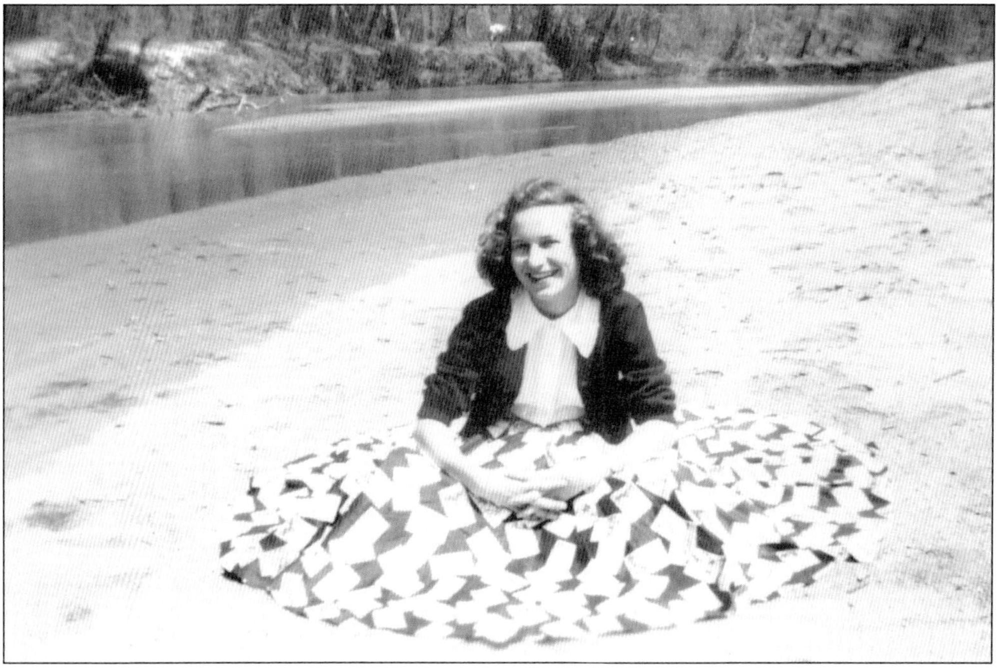

Picnic Spot. Willette Dawkins Ernandez has her picture taken at her family's favorite picnic spot on Fishing Creek in the 1940s.

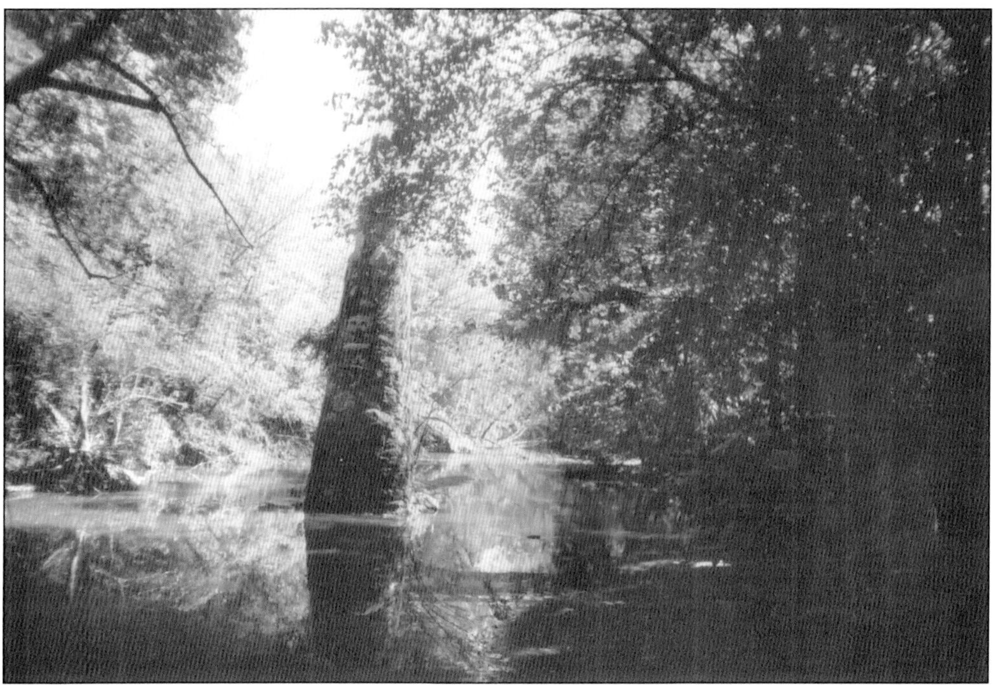

Trestle. A trestle from the Quarters bridge still stands on Fishing Creek. Several floods nearly destroyed the bridge in the early 20th century, and the final collapse came in the 1960s.

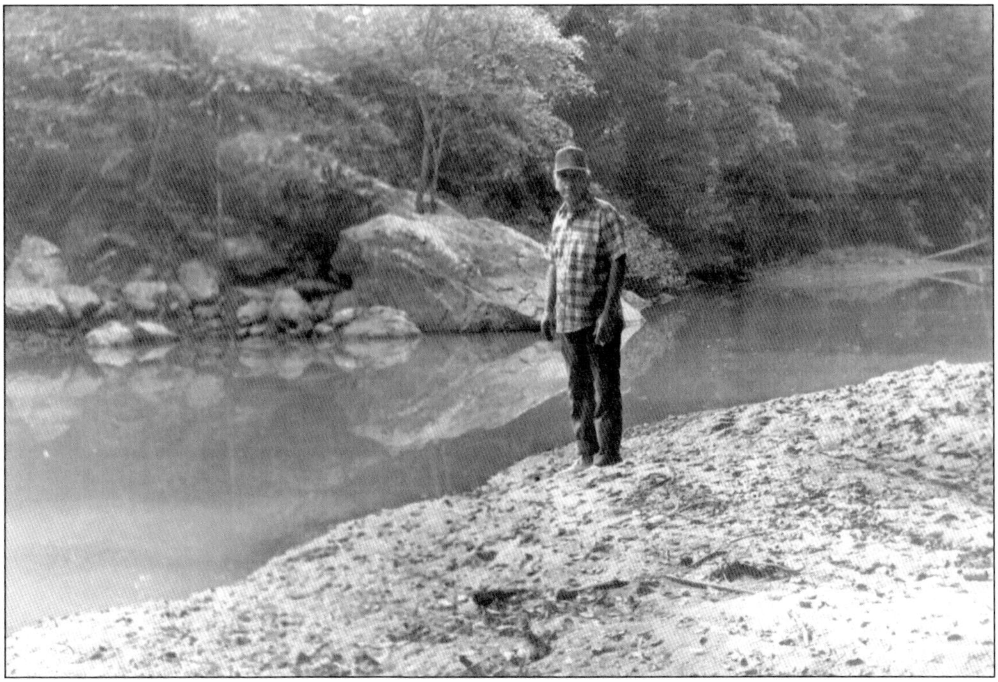

LANDO BEACH. Nub Bailey stands next to a peaceful flowing section of Fishing Creek known as "Lando Beach" in the 1980s. Wilbur Blanks and Arthur Stewart tells stories of a fish named "Big Mary" that was so big that Bud Hefner jumped on its back, and the fish pulled him underwater.

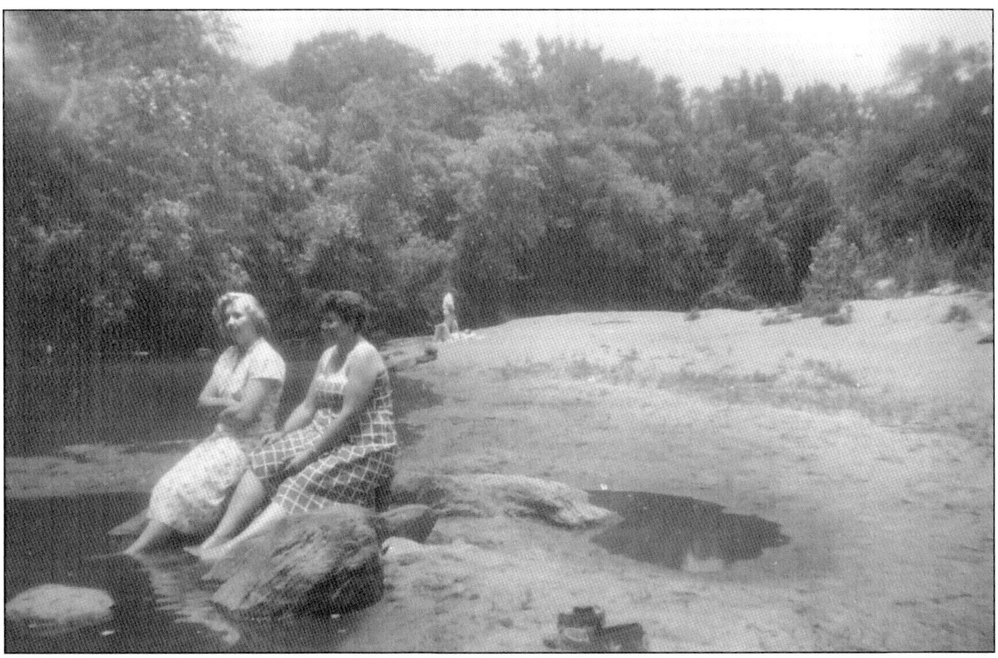

LANDO BEACH. From left to right, Iva Polk and Aggie and J. L. Wallace enjoy the peaceful and beautiful scenery of Lando Beach in the 1940s. This popular spot was enjoyed by generations of people from Lando.

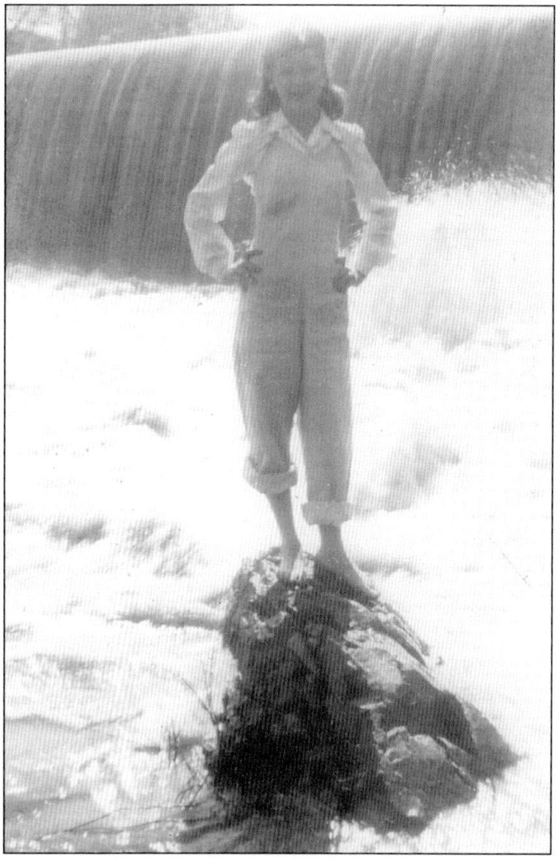

WATER POWER. Doris Scott stands on a rock below the dam and the roaring water of Fishing Creek in the 1930s. Unlike Manetta Mills in Monroe, North Carolina, which relied on steam engines for power, Lando had the luxury of Fishing Creek for power generation and recreation.

SWIMMING HOLE. From left to right, Lula, Martha, and Audrey Ramsey swim in Fishing Creek under the watchful eye of Benny Thorpe and photographer Harold Tadlock in the 1930s. All parents knew that the water could be dangerous and tried to teach their children to respect the waters of Fishing Creek.

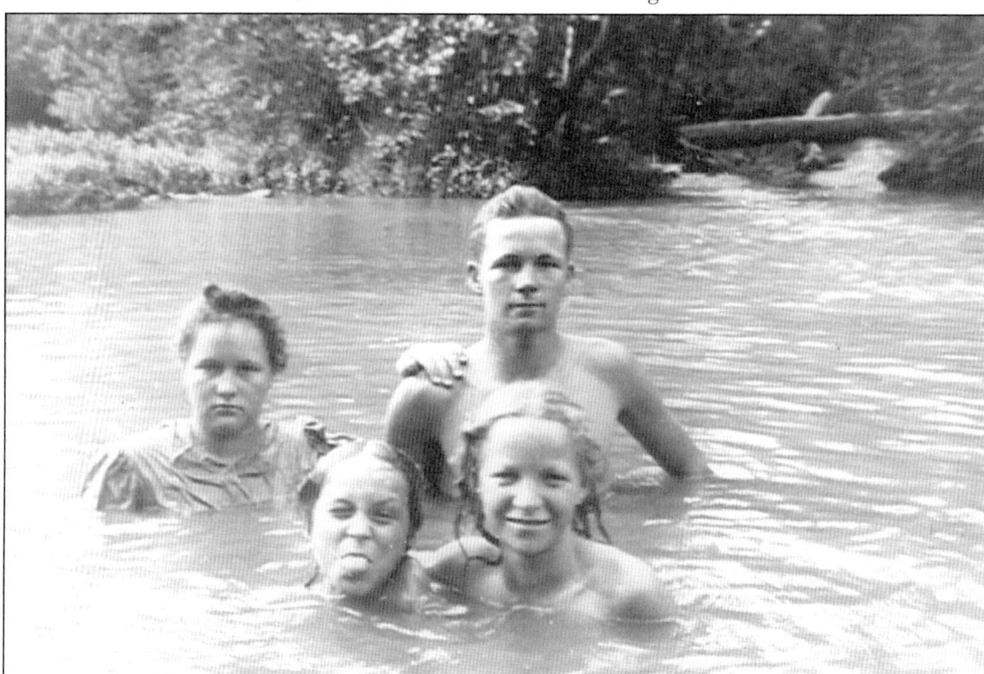

TRAIN BRIDGE. Jimmy Nunnery poses on the E&M tracks on the bridge over Fishing Creek in the 1940s. The millpond formed above the dam has provided fishing and swimming holes for over 100 years.

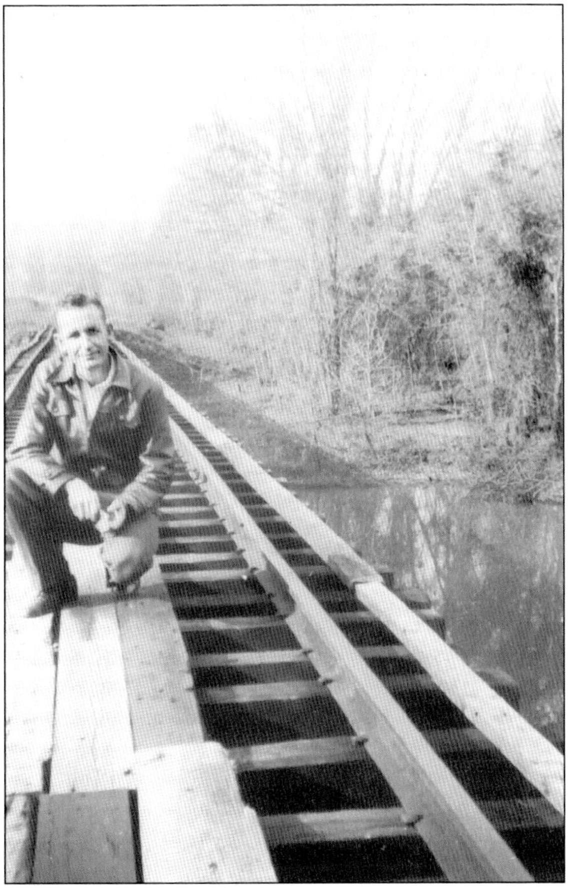

EASTER SUNDAY. From left to right, Dot Dawkins Mobley, Harold Tadlock, Willette Dawkins Ernandez, Ruddie Blanks, and Clyde Allen celebrate Easter Sunday on Fishing Creek in the 1940s.

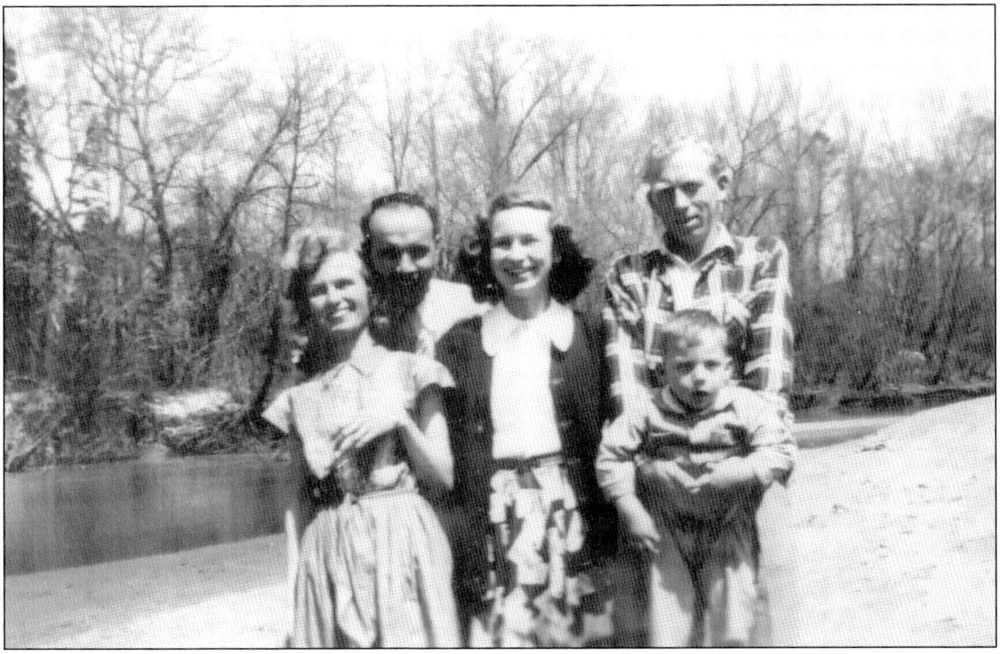

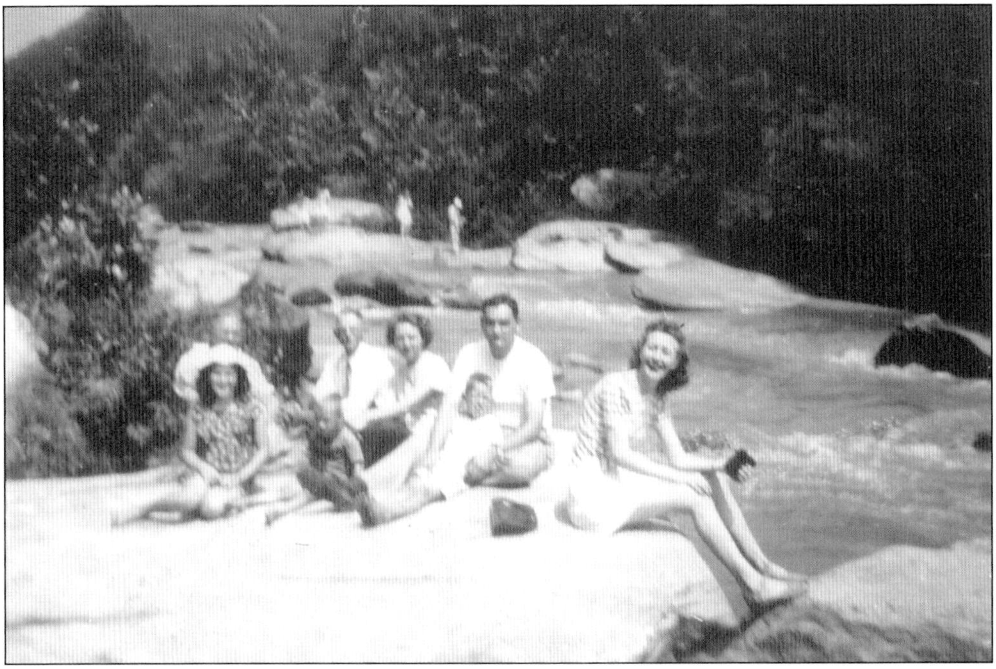

Big Shoals. Addie Kee (right) and friends enjoy a day in the sun on the big shoals in 1954. Lando residents did not have to travel to the mountains or beaches to get a relaxing vacation. Fishing Creek provided the color of changing leaves in the fall and the refreshing, cool water in the summer.

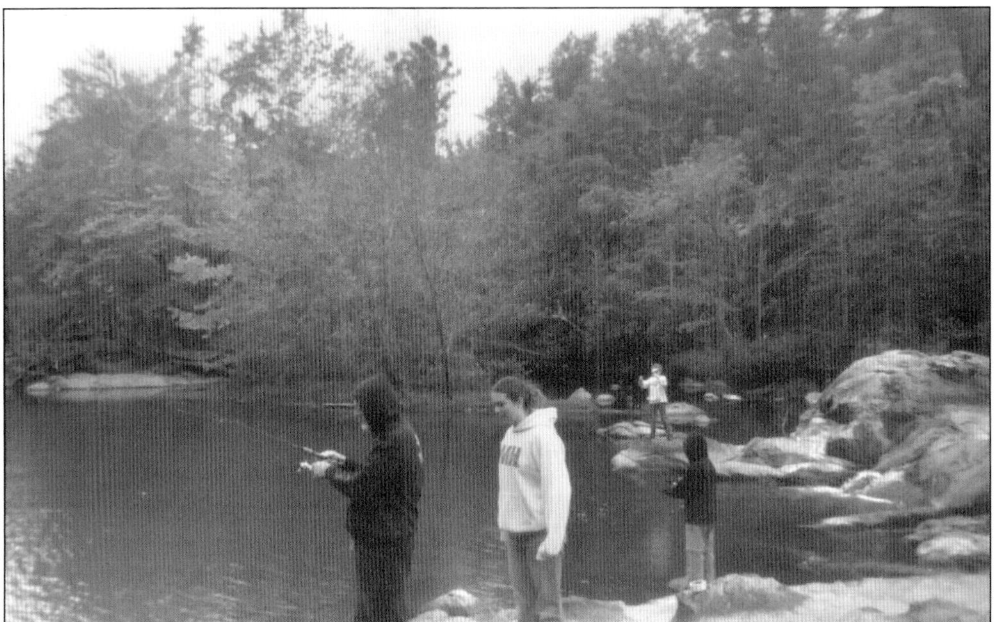

Fishing Hole. From left to right, Joe, Emma, and Ben Nelson fish, while Dillon Williams tells of the one that got away on the lower shoals in 2006. Fishing Creek feeds into the Catawba River, which allows for many species of fish to migrate up Fishing Creek to Lando, providing some excellent fishing holes.

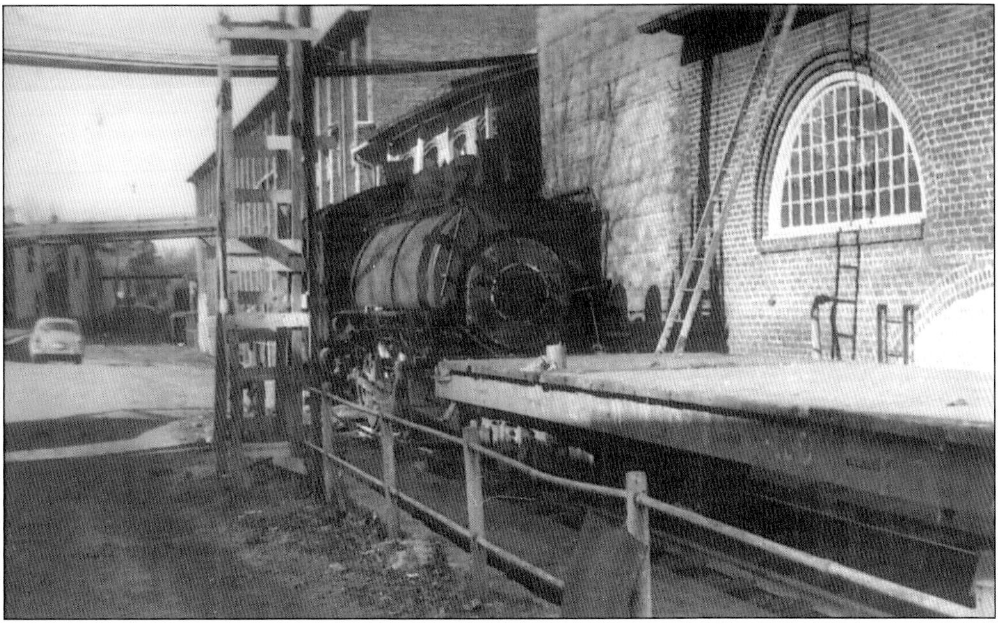

FULL CAPACITY. The Dummy and Manetta Mills are seen here in the early 1970s operating at full capacity.

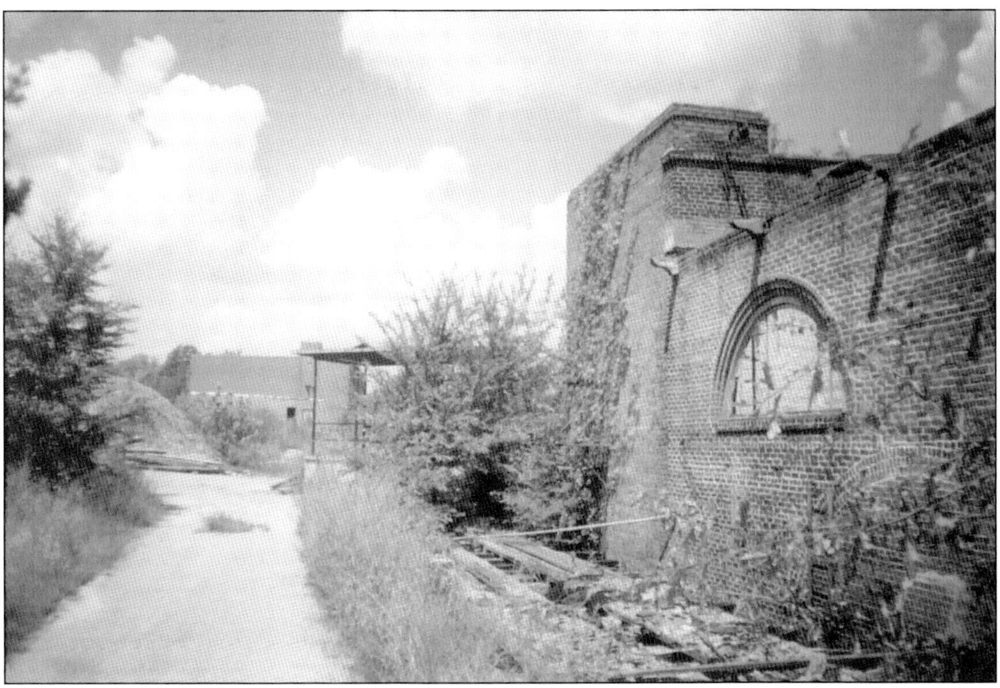

TIME GOES ON. Pictured here is the same spot at Manetta Mills, 30 years later.

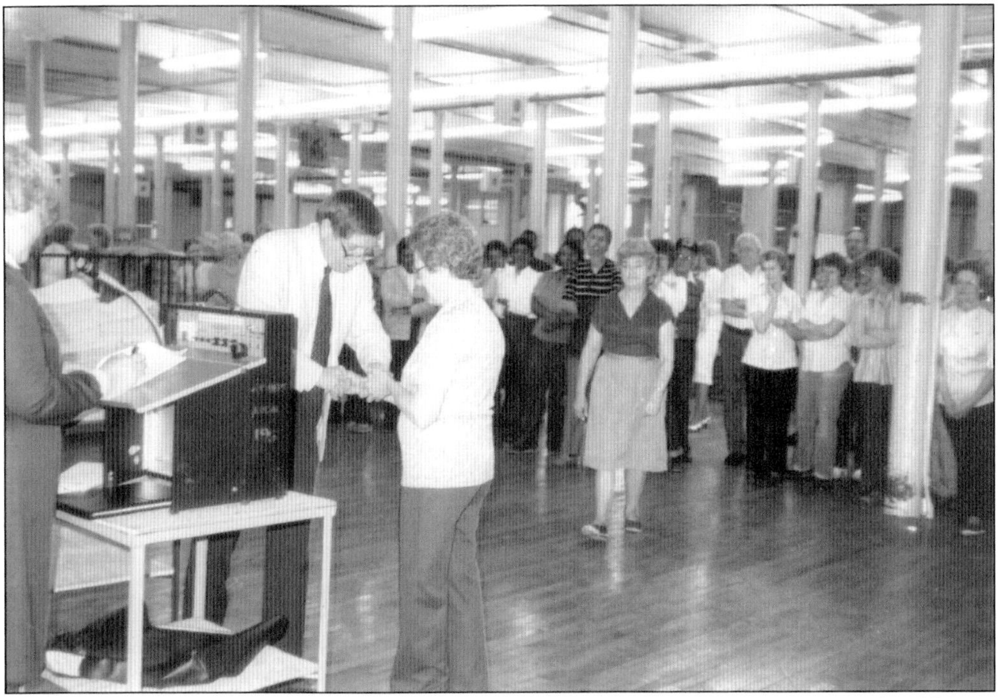

AWARDS DAY. Allen Heath recognizes Genola Collins as Gladys Hough walks up behind her in Manetta Mills during a recognition ceremony in the 1980s.

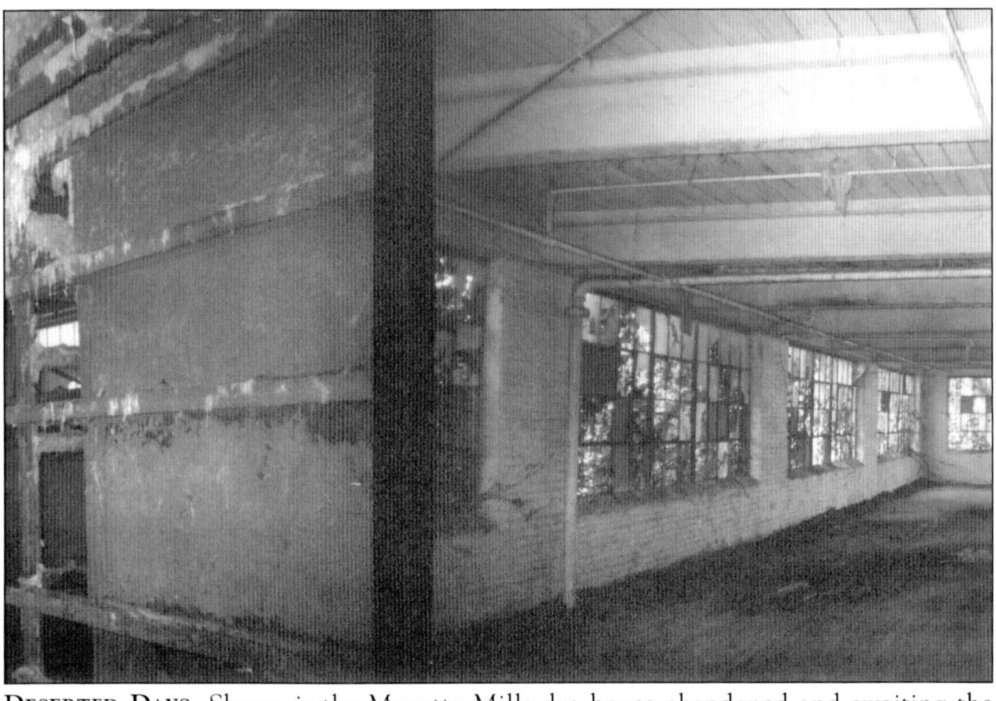

DESERTED DAYS. Shown is the Manetta Mills dye house abandoned and awaiting the wrecking ball in the 1990s.

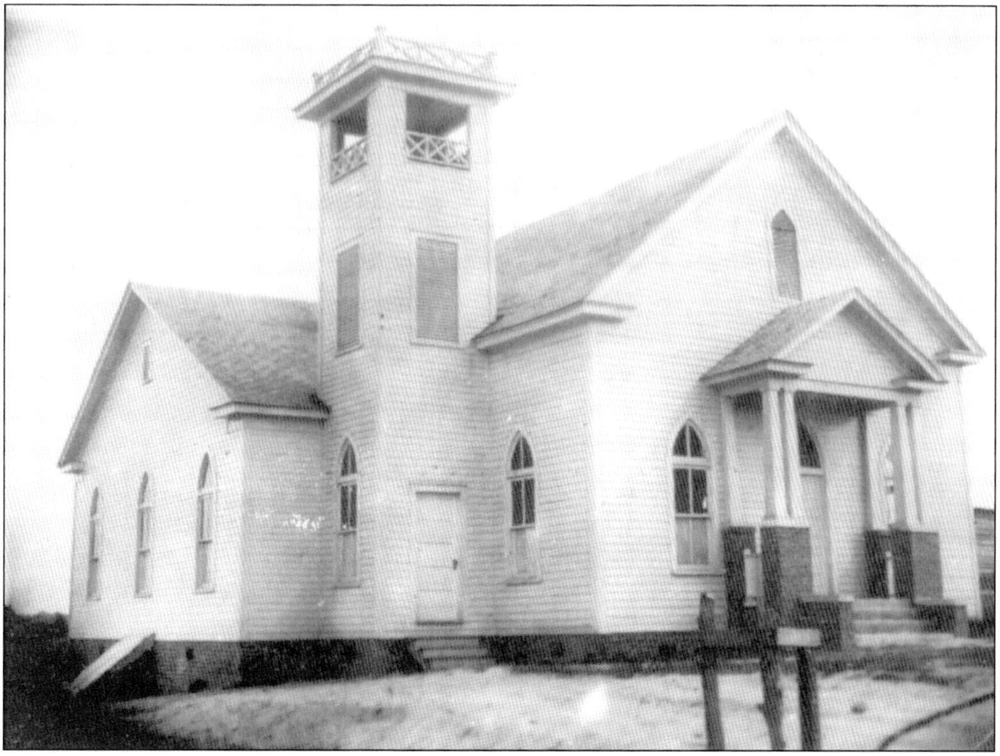

LANDO BAPTIST CHURCH. The Lando Baptist Church moved from the original building to a brick church on Main Street. The Lando Church of God purchased the wooden structure in the 1930s.

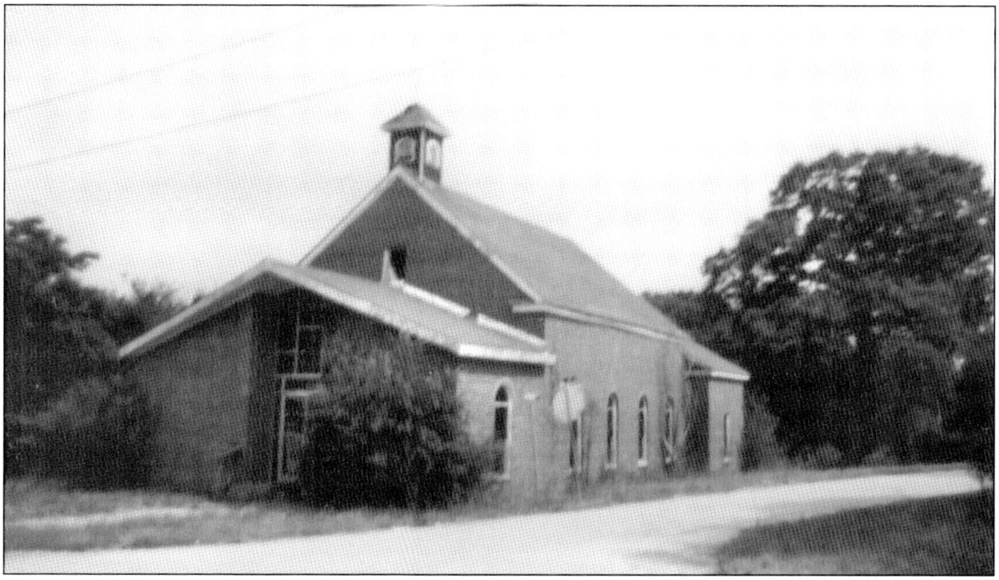

LANDO CHURCH OF GOD. The Lando Church of God built their church on the site of the original Lando Baptist Church. This brick structure was built around the original Baptist church building. The Lando Church of God moved to a new facility, and the old building remained deserted until it was torn down in 2006.

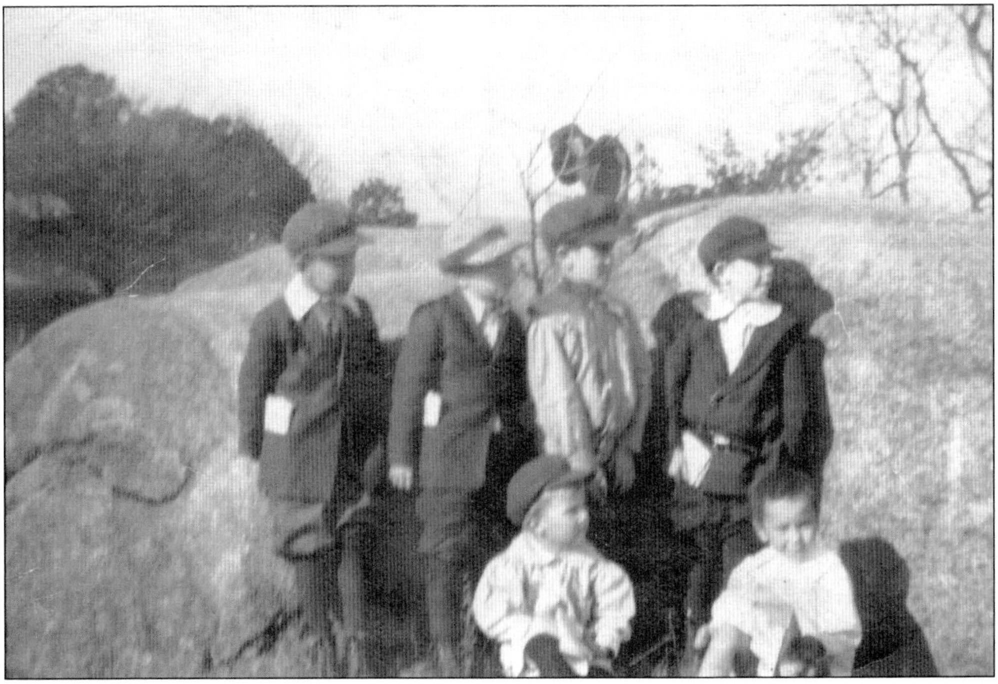

HANGING AROUND. A group of Lando schoolboys play hide-and-seek in Lando in the 1920s.

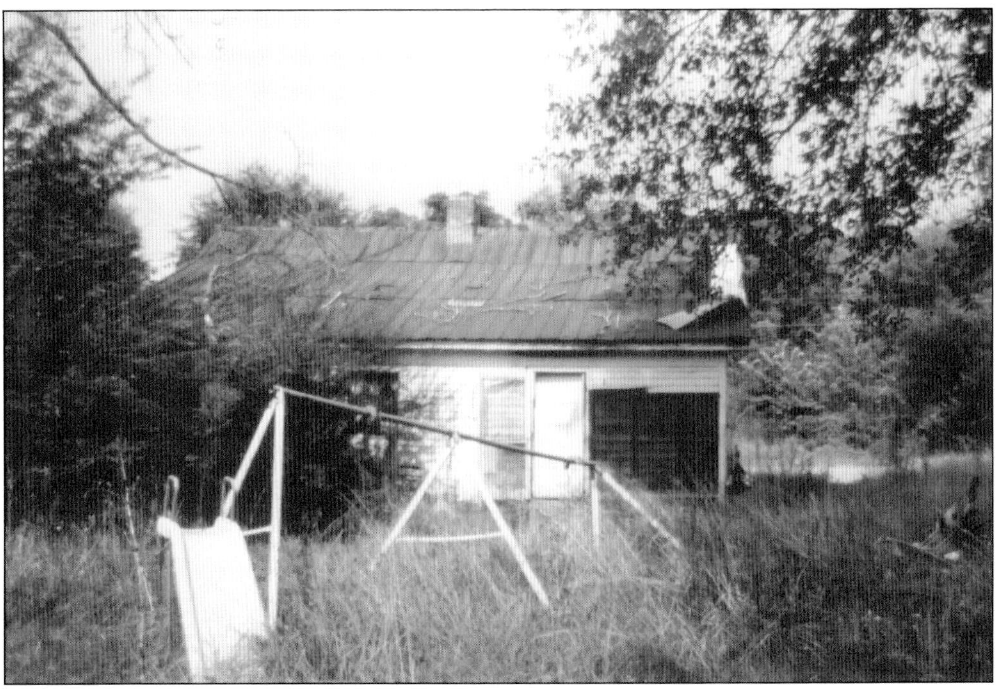

FALLING DOWN. This abandoned backyard in the 1990s evokes the ghost-town feel that exists in many mill towns throughout the Carolinas and much of the South.

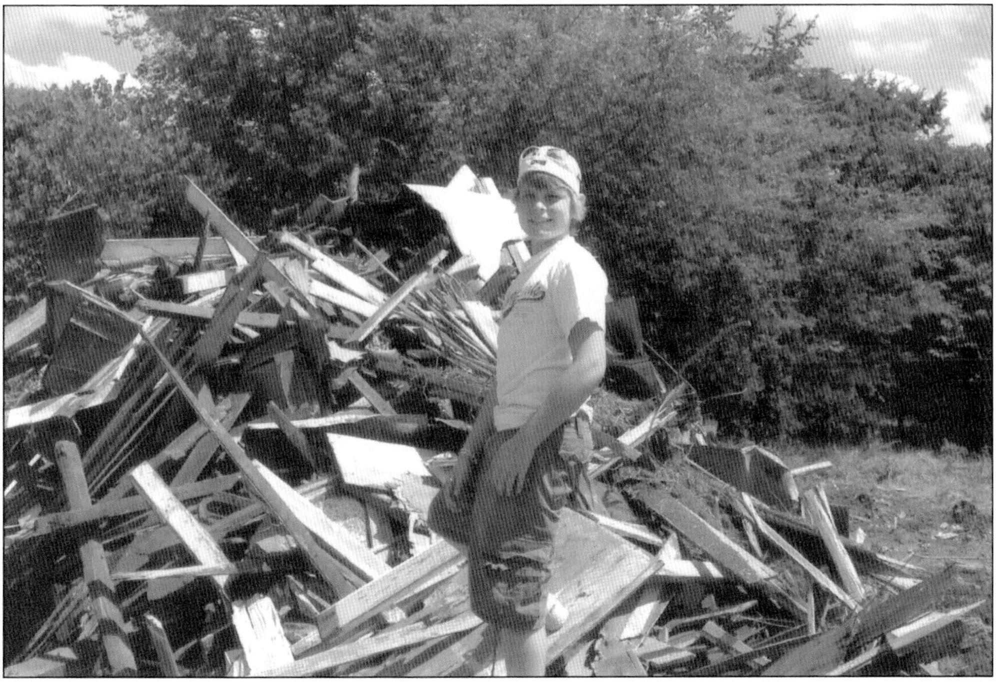

NEXT GENERATION. Brandon Polk stands on the remains of his grandfather's home in 2006.

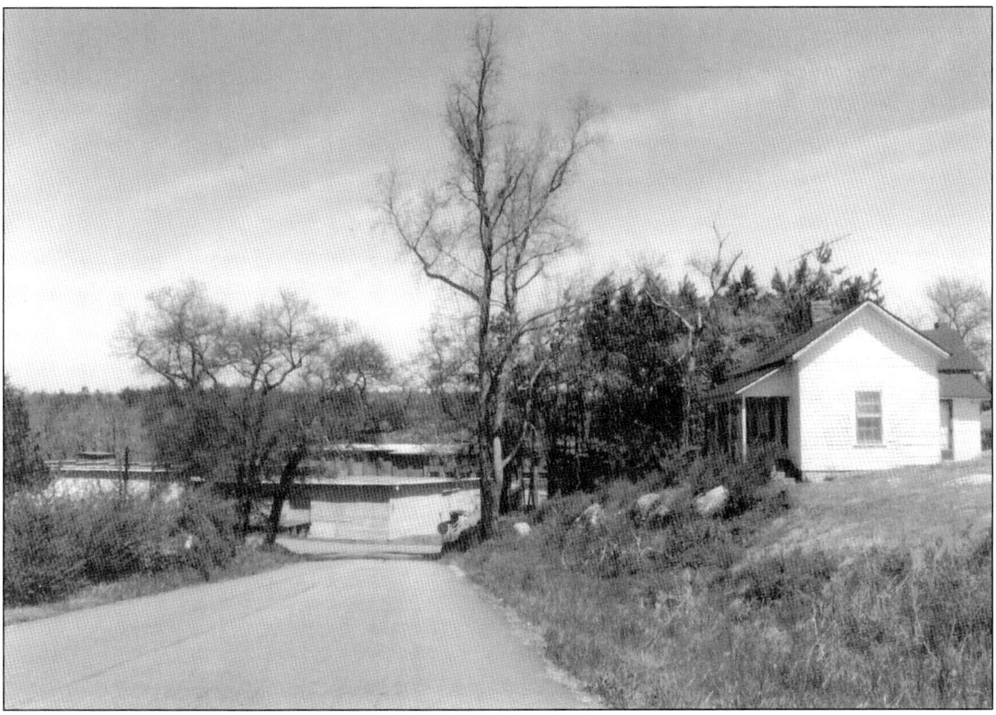

THE PAST AND PRESENT. The view down Lando Street towards Manetta Mills, once the path for workers and children, awaits new development in the 1990s.

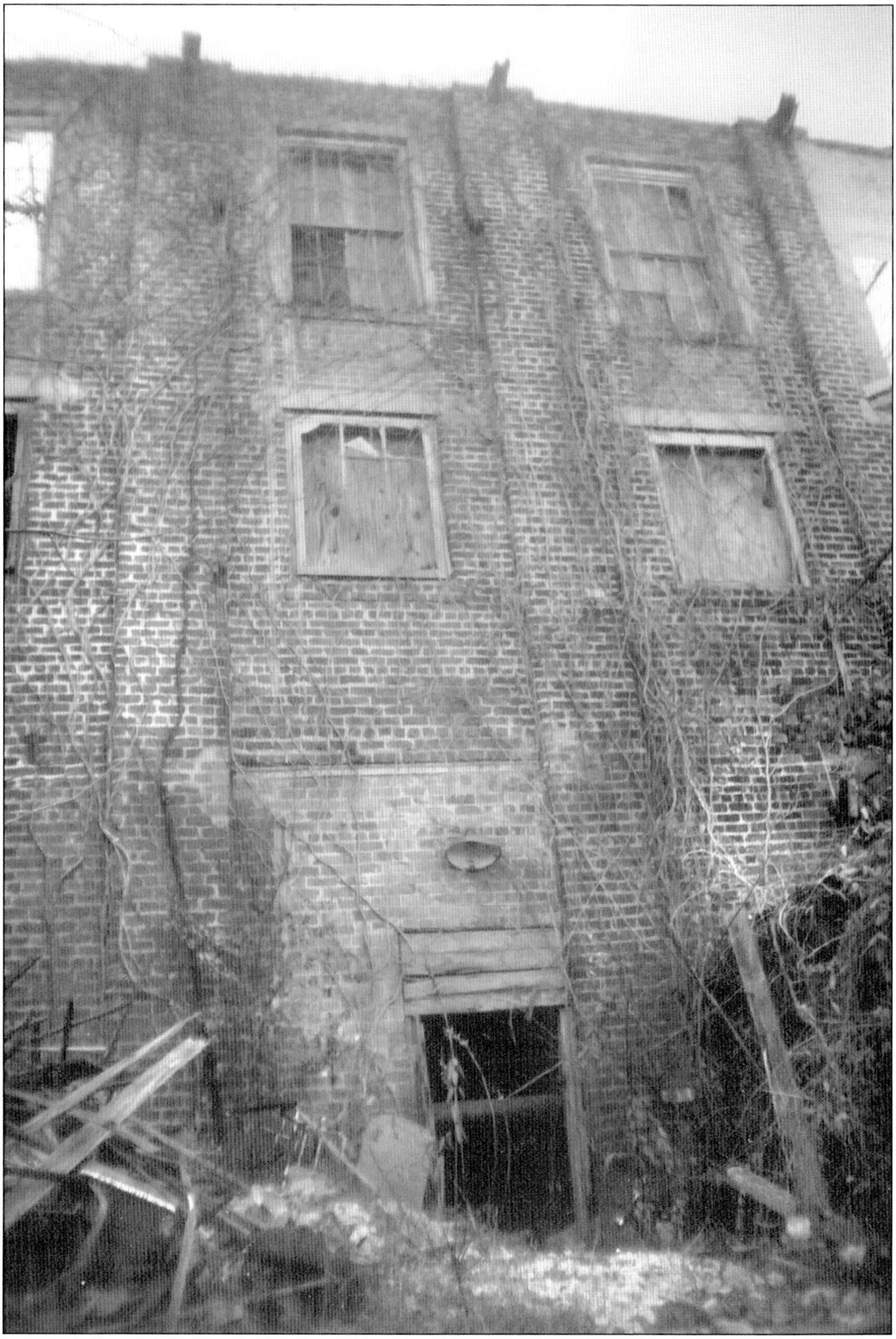

A Light That Shines No More. Seen here is Manetta Mills in 2005, after being deserted for 10 years. A light over a doorway that shined for more then 85 years shines no more.

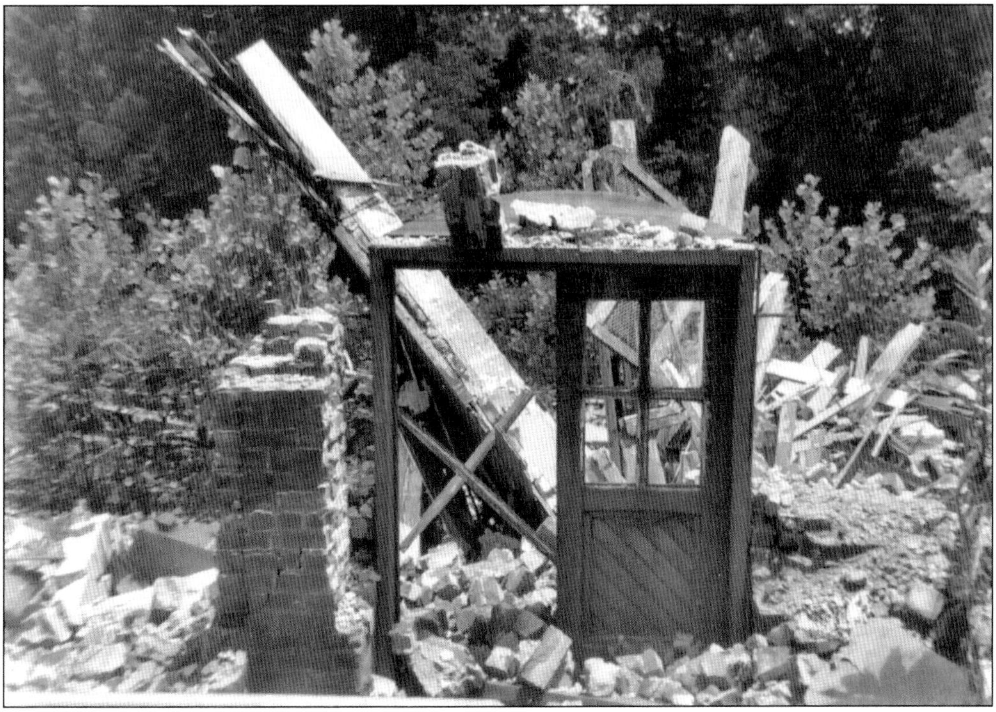

LAST REMAINS. The door to the supervisor's tower from the original Fishing Creek Manufacturing Company still stands among the rubble of the cleanup efforts in 2005.

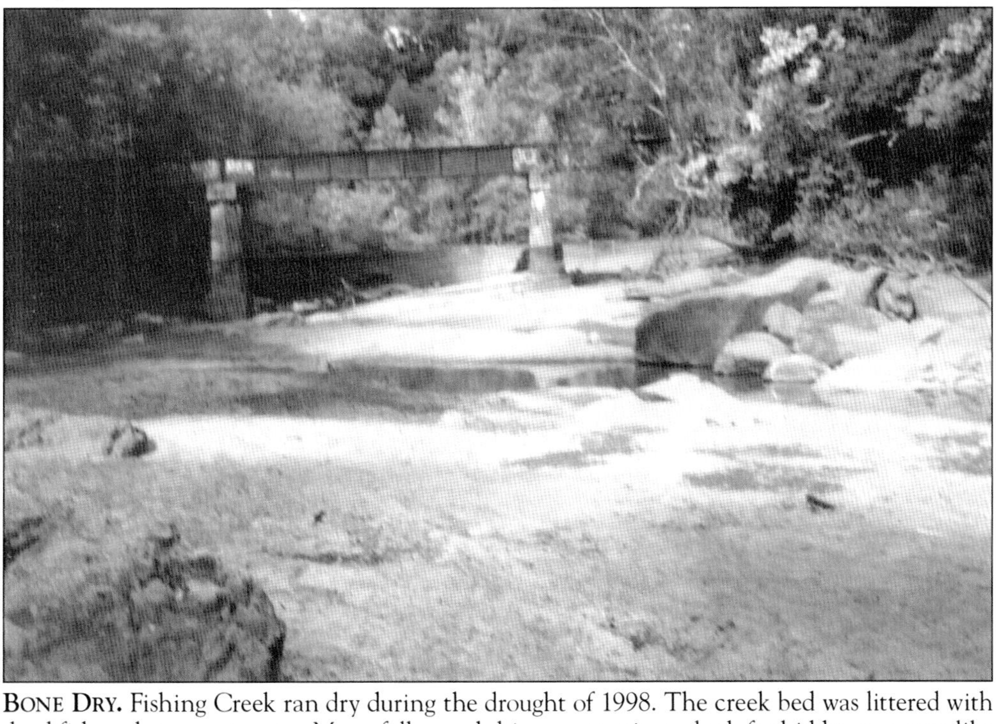

BONE DRY. Fishing Creek ran dry during the drought of 1998. The creek bed was littered with dead fish and stagnant water. Many folks used this opportunity to look for hidden treasures like old coins, bottles, and relics from the mill that were exposed on the dry creek bed.

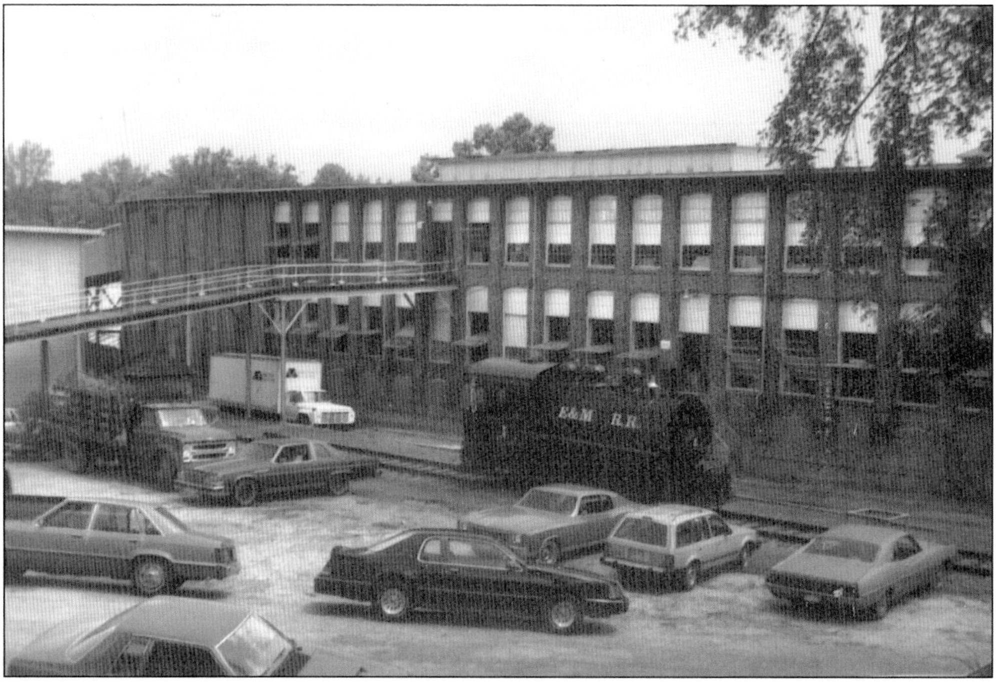

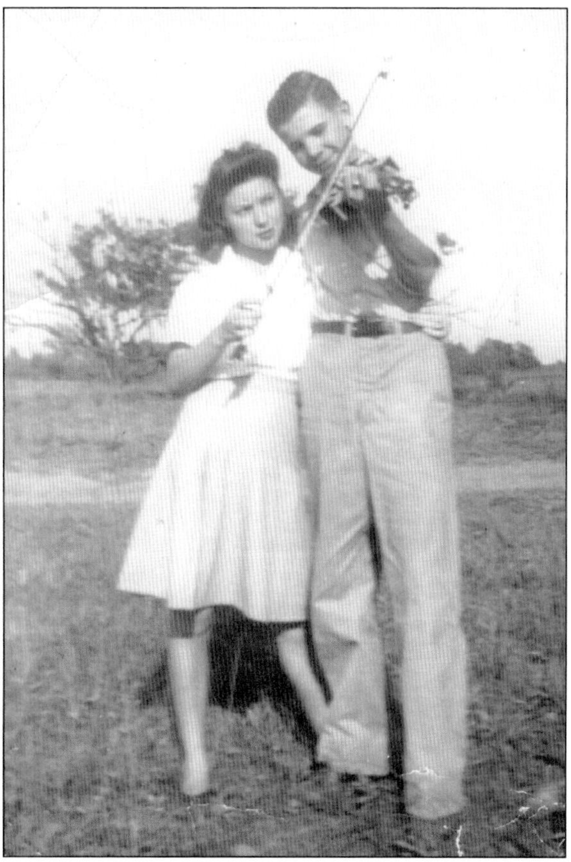

Final Days. Management moved operations to the Monroe, North Carolina, plant when the Lando plant closed in 1991. Manetta Mills provided transportation from Lando to Monroe for employees who wanted to continue to work for Manetta Mills. When Pillowtex purchased Manetta Mills, Lando residents had to provide their own transportation to Monroe if they wanted to keep their job.

One Last Song. As much as the folks from Lando loved their community and work, time goes on. It is sad to say goodbye to friends and family, but as the demand for low-price textiles forced change in many Southern textile communities, the people of Lando had to bid farewell to the place where they worked for many years. Tommy and Doris Scott play the swan song in Lando in the 1940s.

Nine

LANDMARKS

It was the dream of many folks from Lando and Manetta Mills to preserve the history and memories of life in Lando. After Manetta Mills closed, many folks left Lando, taking with them the stories and pictures of their family and experiences in the mill. Fortunately for Lando, in 1976, Charles Inabinet obtained a grant from Kodak and Springs Industries and complied a two-edition publication titled *The Old Mill Stream*, which was a collection of oral histories of Lando residents.

The Inabinets were able to collect hundreds of pictures to use in their publications. *The Old Mill Stream* has first-hand accounts of folks whose parents were part of Fishing Creek Manufacturing. *The Old Mill Stream* has stories of daily life in Lando and Manetta Mills and how people came to live in Lando. There are stories and pictures of almost every part of Lando's history.

The Old Mill Stream is just the beginning. Many people have the dream of preserving the history of Lando and Manetta Mills, but it was the action of two men that got it started. Good friends Allen Heath and Joe Polk were able to salvage many items from the company store and mill office. These items remained in storage until Lando Properties, LLC, allowed Joe Polk to use the old Manetta Mills office building to display the items.

Roxann Yarborough James, Susan Murphy, Bruce Coggins, and Sylvia Jennings also had a "Lando Dream" and offered support and help to preserve and display the items. So, in 2005, a nonprofit organization called the Lando–Manetta Mills History Center was formed. It is due to the efforts of board members and volunteers like Charles Black, Wayne Alley, Arthur Stewart, Ollie and Bud Hefner, and Crawford Whitaker that the deserted mill office and company store were cleaned up and have become the Lando–Manetta Mills History Center.

Board members and volunteers continue to work daily on keeping the Lando Dream alive. On December 3, 2006, the Lando–Manetta Mills History Center dedicated a memorial marker to seven military servicemen who died fighting for the country they loved and also rededicated the memorial marker for Dr. John Gaston Sr. Over 110 people who share the Lando Dream attended the ceremony.

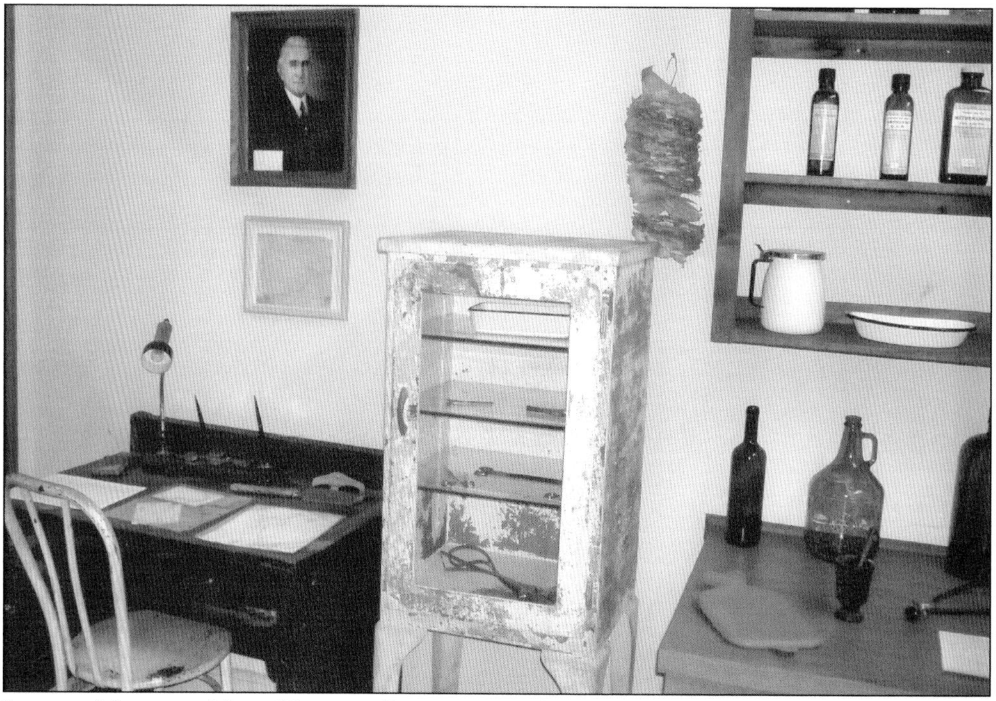

LANDO–MANETTA MILLS HISTORY CENTER. Dr. John Gaston's office has been recreated in the Lando–Manetta Mills History Center. Many of the original items from Dr. Gaston's basement office have been moved upstairs in the history center. Medicine bottles, prescription pads, and medical tools are on display. Dr. Gaston's desk, examining table, and wooden wheelchair are several items preserved to show the office conditions of a mill doctor.

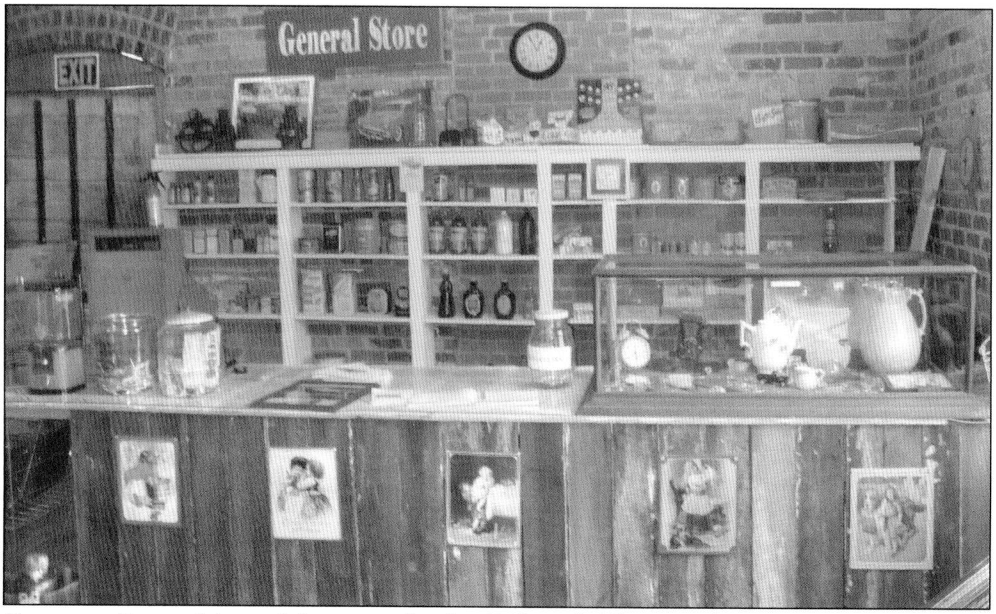

COMPANY STORE. Many of the items that Joe Polk and Allen Heath saved from the company have now been returned to the store and are on display at the history center. All the items in the store were actual items that people from Lando could purchase in years past.

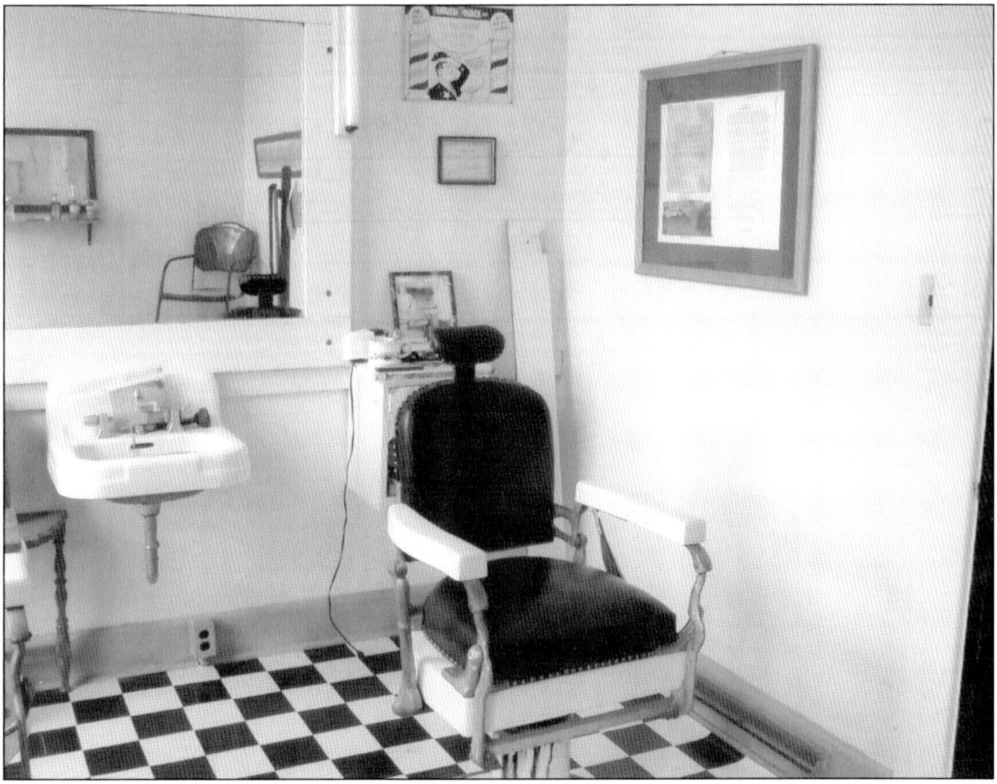

BARBERSHOP CHAIR. The original Lando barbershop chair and mirror are well preserved and on display in Lando. The room has been re-created as closely as possible to the actual barbershop in the Manetta Mills office building. The shoe-shining stand used by Cecil Polk in the 1940s is visible in the mirror.

TOOLS OF THE TRADE. Relics from Manetta Mills are preserved in the Mill Room at the history center. A thread meter for quality control, watchman punch clock, cotton samples, tools, and pictures are just some of the items on display.

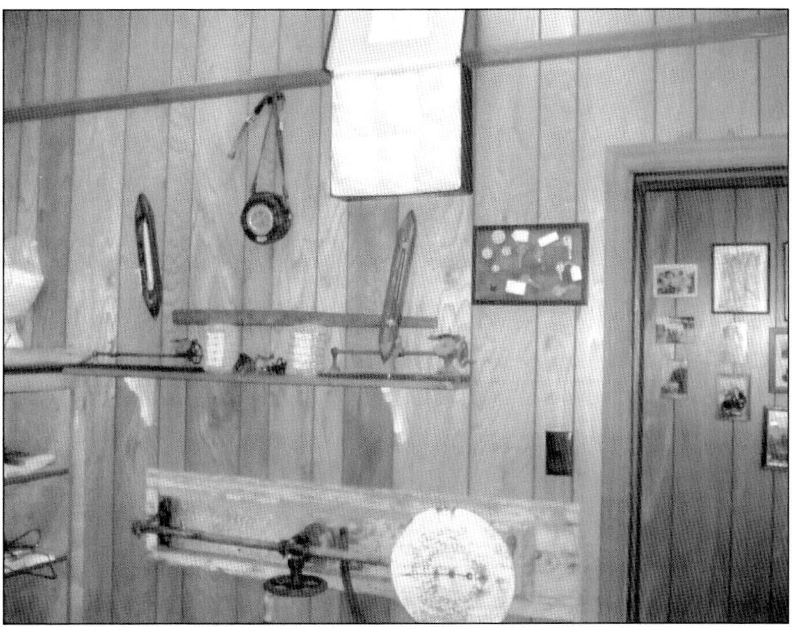

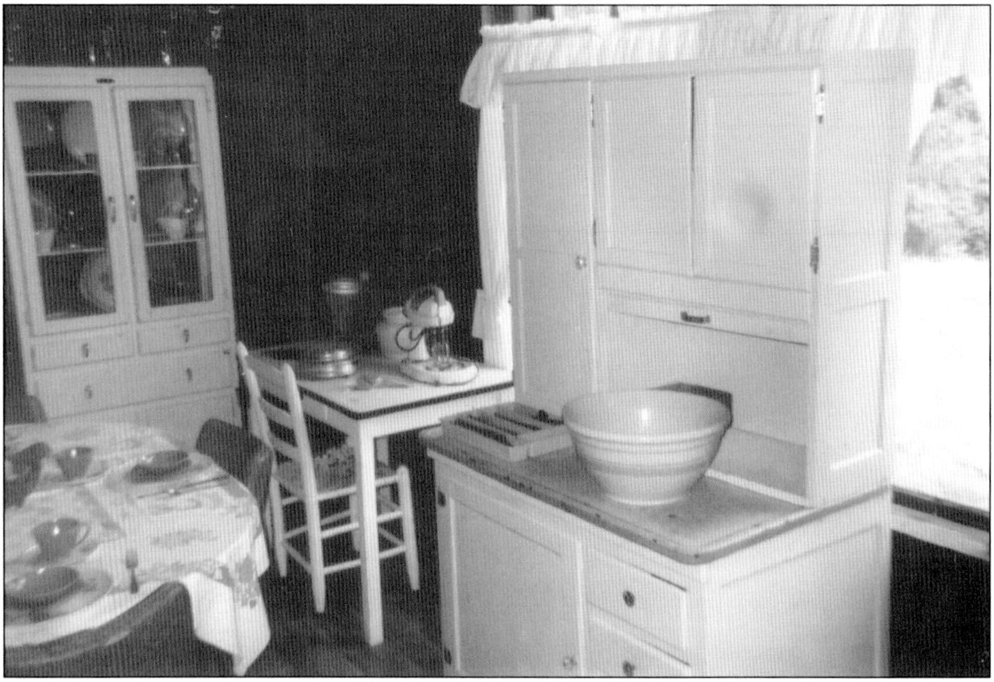

COUNTRY KITCHEN. Pictured is a mill village kitchen recreated from items salvaged and donated from the Manetta Mills village.

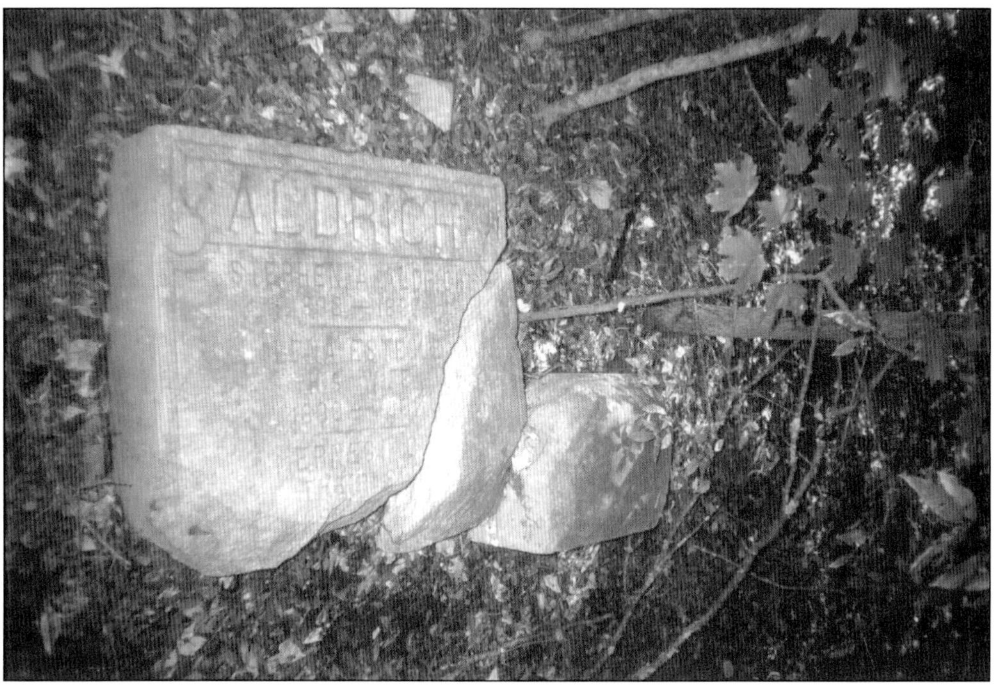

ALDRICH STONE. Fishing Creek Manufacturing allowed residents to create a cemetery. Samuel Harriet Ramsey, Jane Ramsey, Fanny Ramsey, Amanda Irby, along with Stephen, Lena, and Ernest Aldrich are the only known names of people buried at the old cemetery. The Heaths created a new cemetery in 1904. The Aldrich stone is the last remaining marker in the old cemetery.

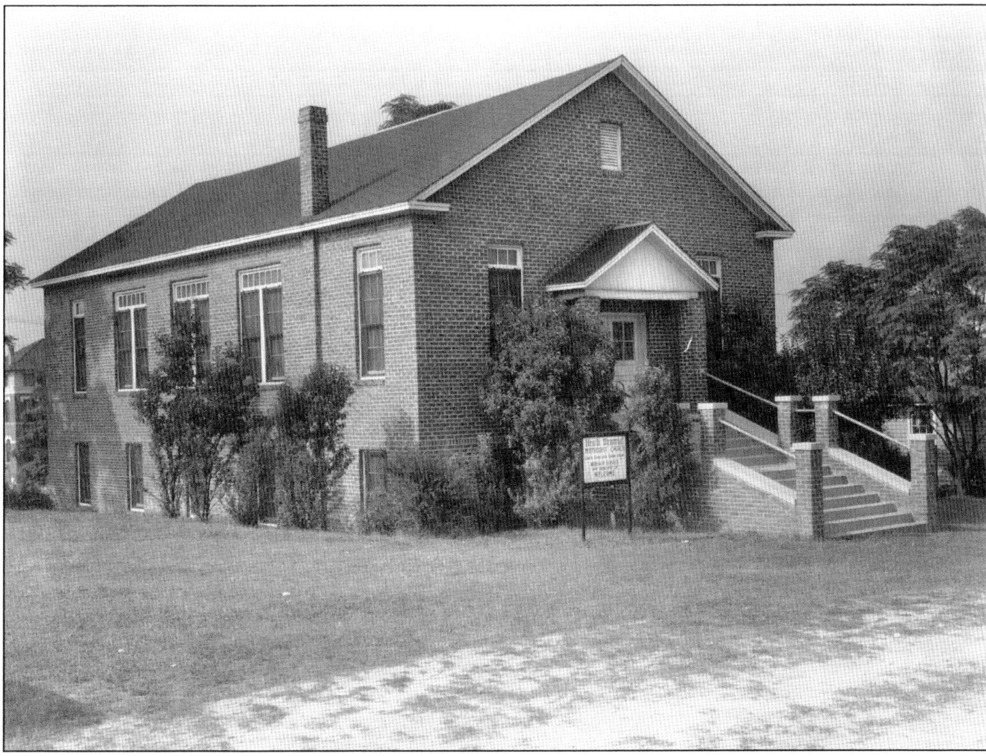

HEATH MEMORIAL METHODIST CHURCH, 1940S. The Heath Memorial Methodist Church is still an active part of the Lando community.

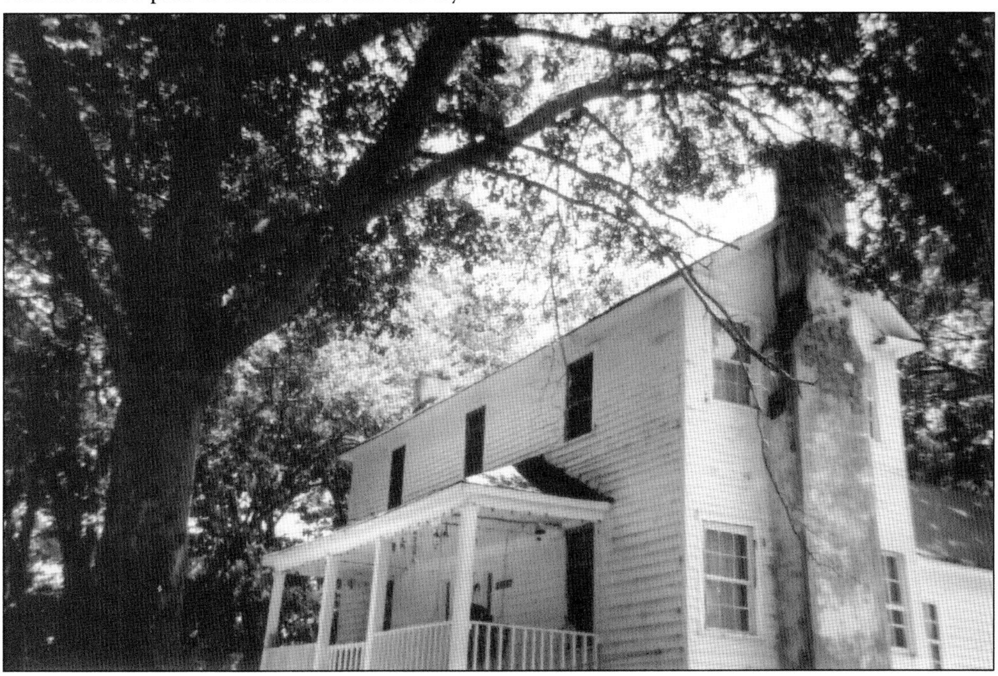

BARBER HOUSE. The last remaining home built by Ferguson Barber c. 1884, known as a "Barber House," still has folks living in it.

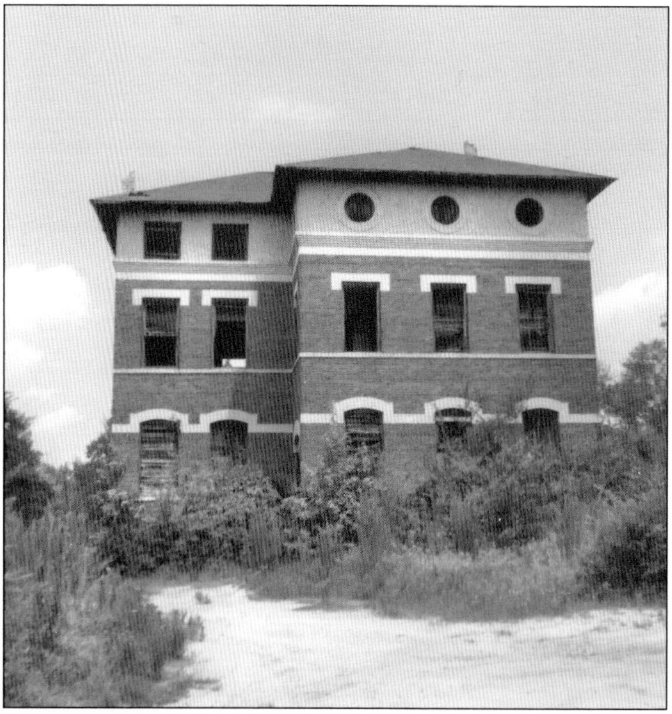

LANDO SCHOOL. The Lando School still stands—colorful and majestic—in the Lando countryside.

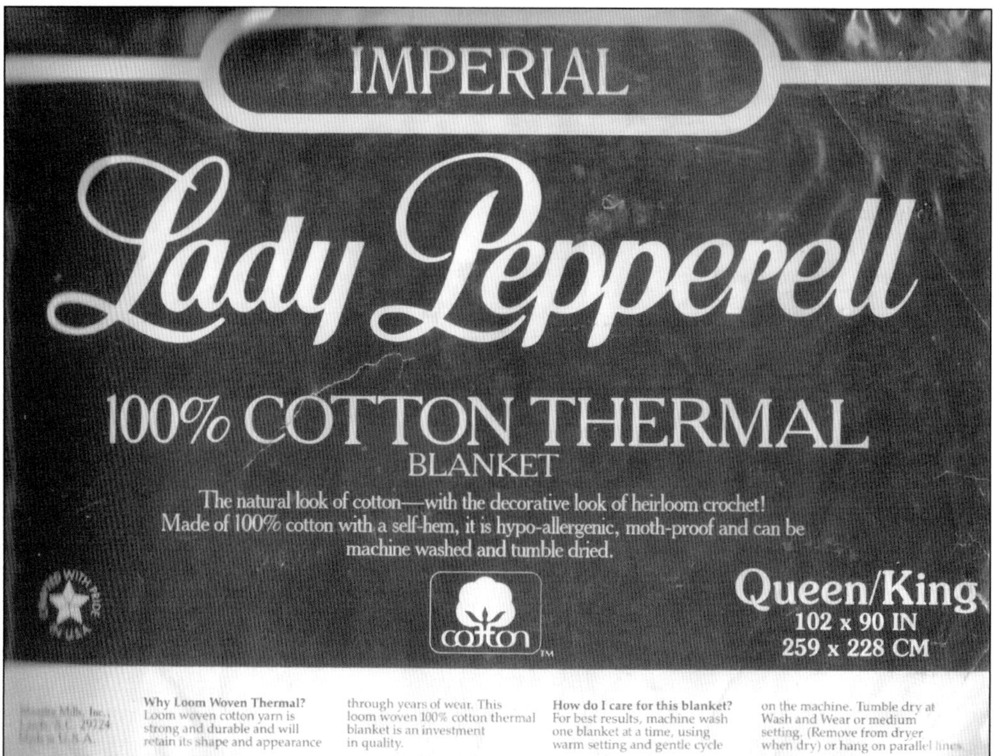

LADY PEPPERELL BLANKET. Manetta Mills manufactured blankets for West Point Pepperell. This Lady Pepperell blanket was the last blanket packaged at Manetta Mills.

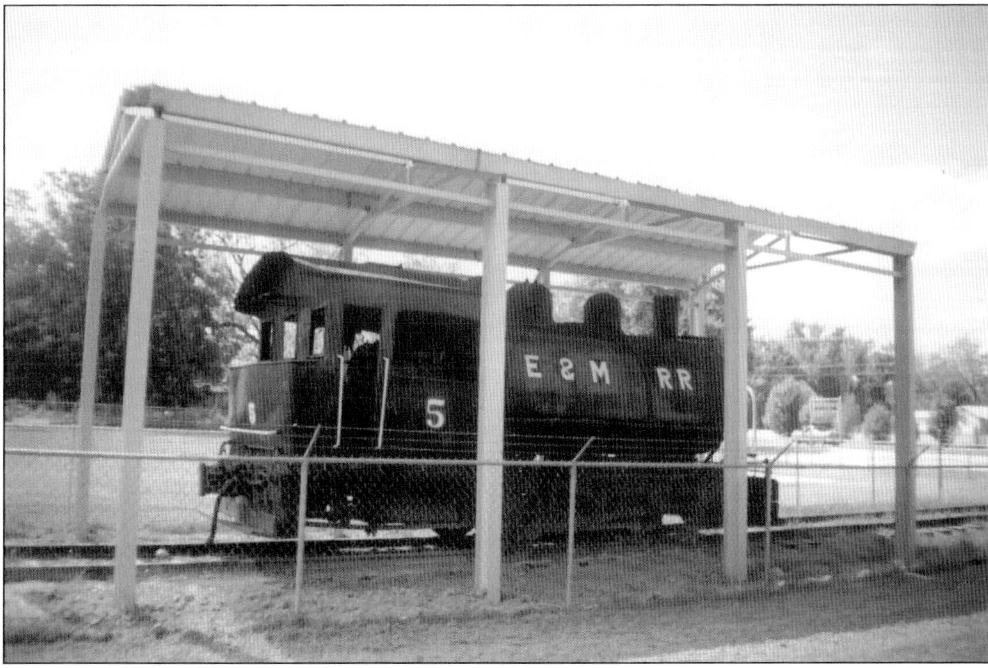

A Proud Reminder. The Dummy sits at the Richburg Community Park in 2007.

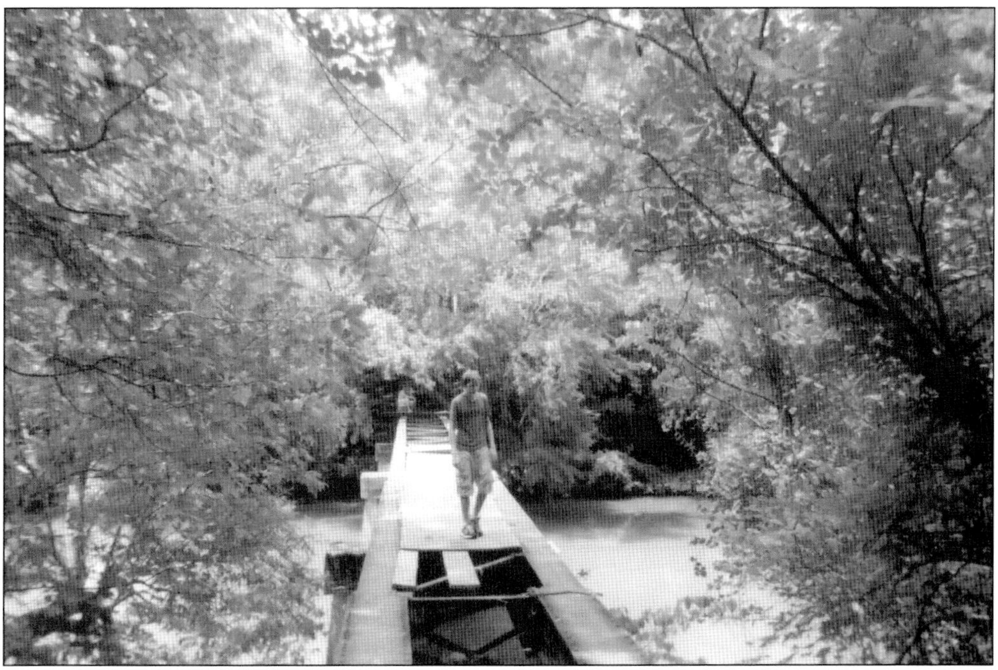
The Old Train Bridge. The nearly still waters and hardwood trees provide a beautiful environment that Lando residents continue to visit. Folks returning to visit Lando love to make the short hike down to the trestle to reminisce about days gone by. Zachary Williams crosses the train bridge in 2006. The area is a favorite swimming hole for locals.

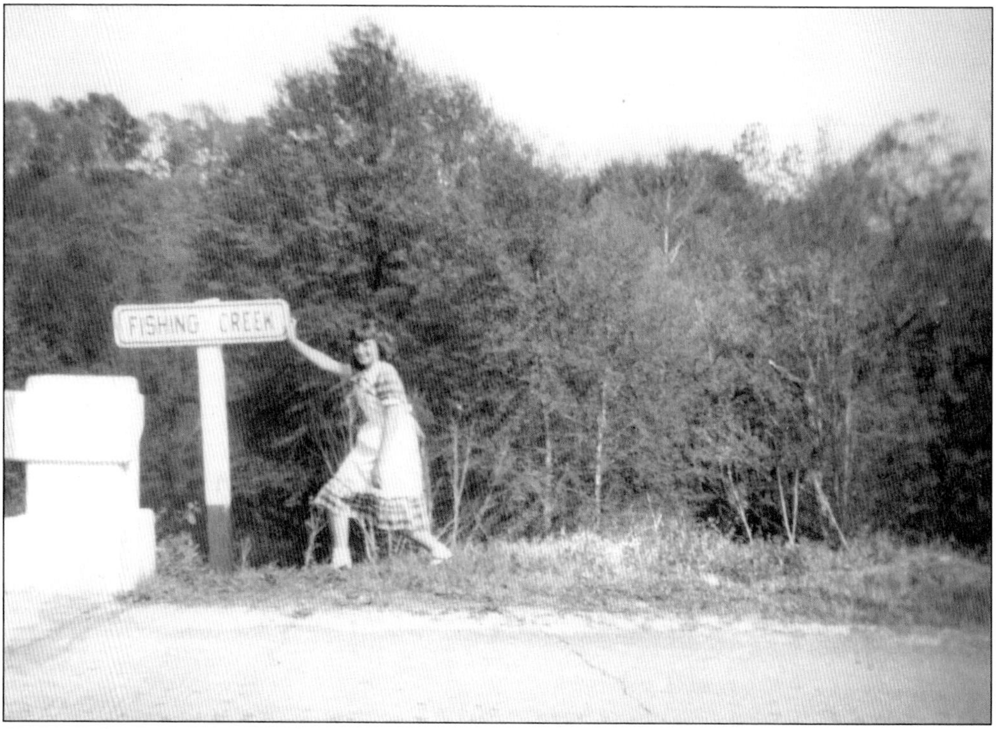

FISHING CREEK. Myra Overby stands next to the Fishing Creek sign on the bridge on Highway 901 in the 1950s. The bridge is 40 feet above the creek bed below. The valley formed over millions of years of flooding, and erosion has created the beautiful landscape in Lando.

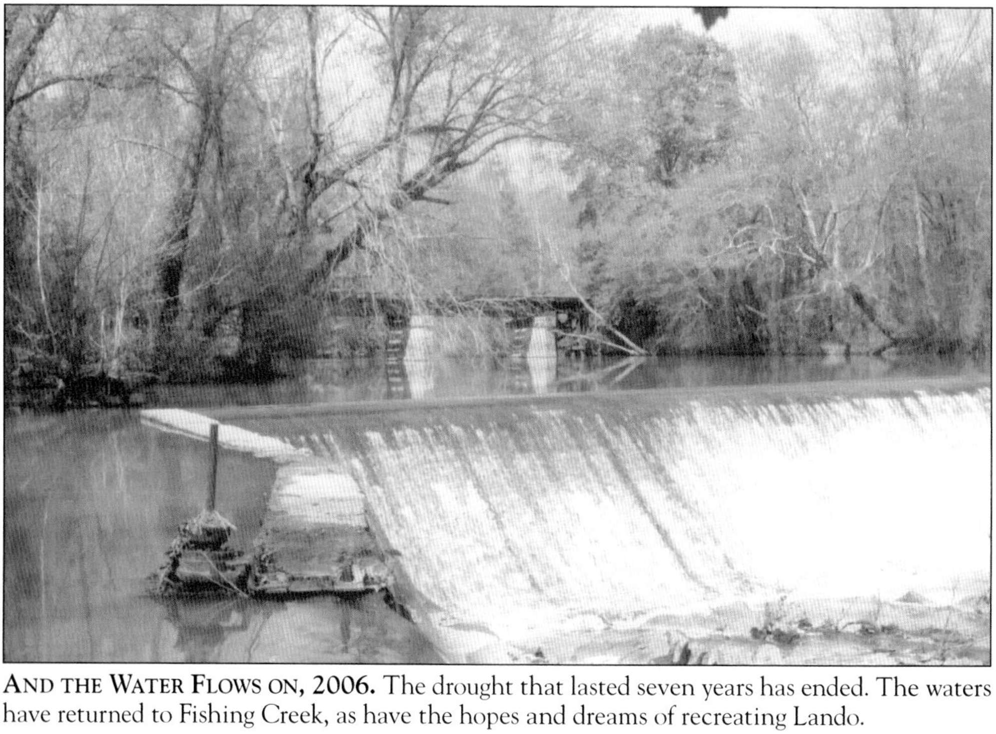

AND THE WATER FLOWS ON, 2006. The drought that lasted seven years has ended. The waters have returned to Fishing Creek, as have the hopes and dreams of recreating Lando.

Ten

21st-Century Revolution

With the efforts of the Lando–Manetta Mills History Center and the Inabinet family, much of Lando's history is being preserved. But where are the people? The skills of manufacturing blankets are no longer needed, so the children of mill workers had to seek work outside of Lando. Textile manufacturing is no longer the main industry in the Carolina Piedmont region. Many mills have been converted into commercial offices and retail space, while others are residential apartments and condominiums. Manetta Mills in Lando is no longer standing, but the memories and dreams of the people of Lando still remain.

Many folks from Lando have gone on to successful careers in Chester County, while other folks have gone all across the United States, taking the memory of Lando with them. Some people have chosen military service, and others have gone off to college or pursued other opportunities to make a living. Now, the great-great-grandchildren of the first workers at Fishing Creek Manufacturing can return to Lando and see the revolution taking place along Fishing Creek.

Joe and Gayle Lanford, along with a group of investors, have created Lando Properties, LLC, and have cleaned up the abandoned mill site. Plans are in place to rebuild Lando as a 21st-century mill village. With architects, engineers, and community input, Lando will become a residential community with Manetta Mills and Fishing Creek as a theme to the community. The company store and Lando School will be focal points of the community, and walking trails and greenways will line the flood plains of Fishing Creek. Lando will soon become a community where children can play and grow up, and families again can call Lando home.

From the American Revolution until today, Lando has experienced change. Lando has embraced its own "revolutions" during the past 240 years.

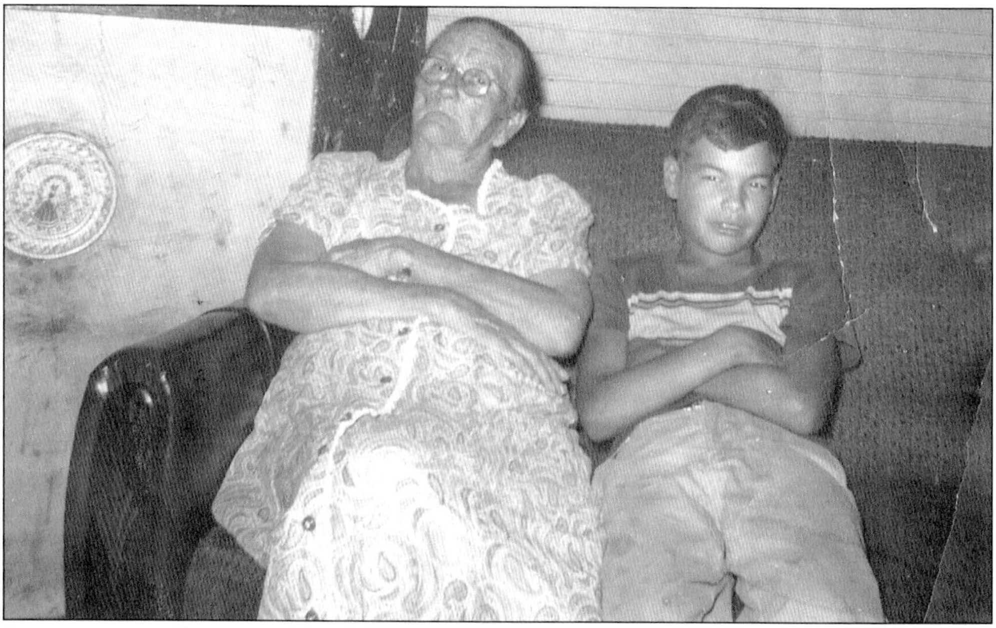

SAVING FOR THE FUTURE, 1950S. Manetta Mills and the Heath family encouraged their employees to be active in a savings program to help plan for the future. Rene Aldridge, grandmother to Walter Aldridge, bought her grandson Lando Savings Bonds from the Savings Bank of Lando.

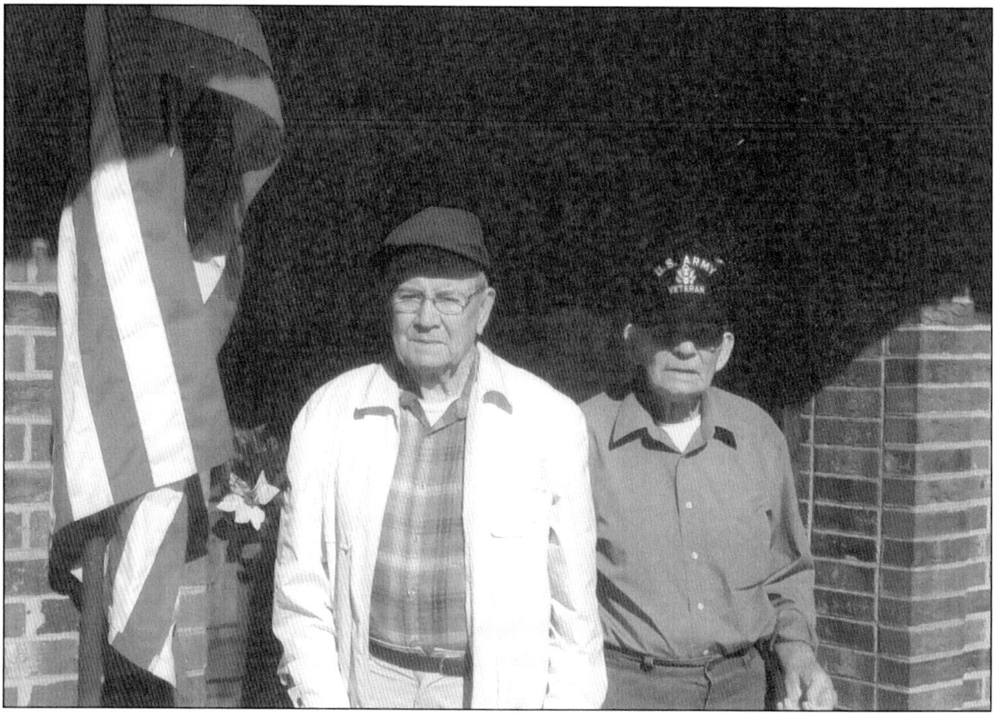

PRESERVING HISTORY. Brothers James (left) and John Coker (right) are working together to preserve the history of Manetta Mills in 2006. John Coker worked in the napping room at Manetta Mills for over 50 years and was working there when the mill closed. James worked in many departments of the mill but remembers the spinning rooms as his favorite place to work.

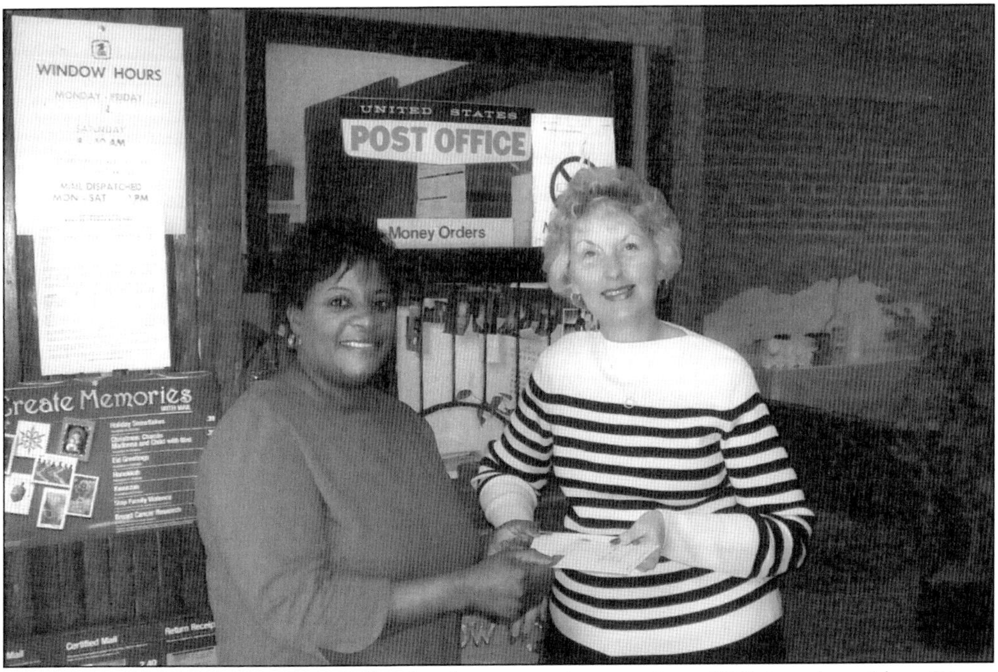

POST OFFICE. The Lando Post Office has been in existence since 1870. Lando resident Diane Crockett (left) collects her mail from postmaster relief Susan Murphy in 2006.

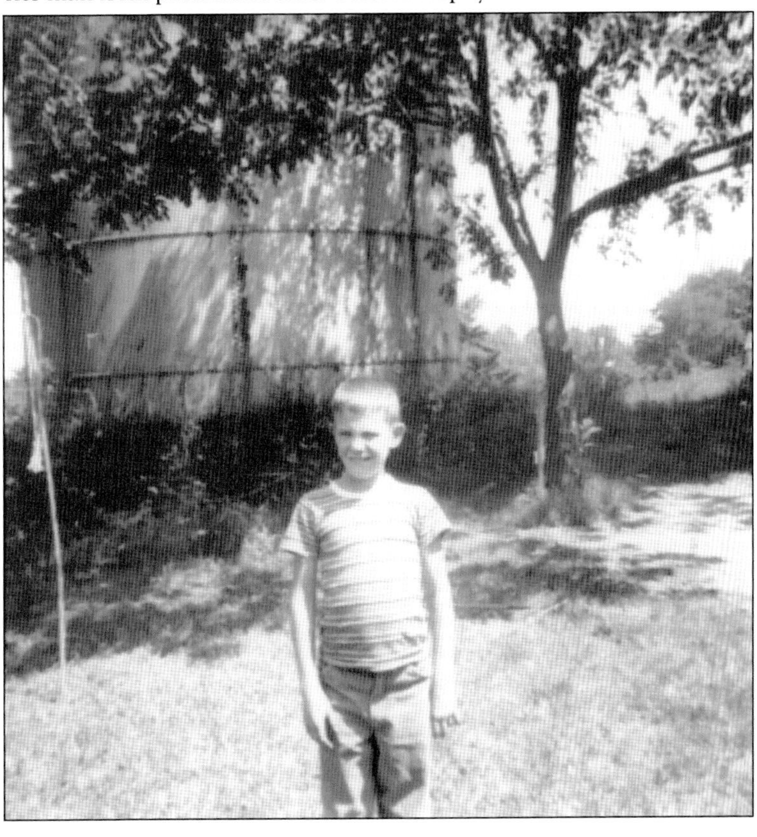

WEASEL. Edward "Weasel" Harris stands in front of the Lando Water Tower in 1962. Now pastor of Lando Church of God, Reverend Harris is loved by his congregation because he can relate to them. It is because of his life in Lando that Rev. Harris is a humble servant to the people of the community and his church.

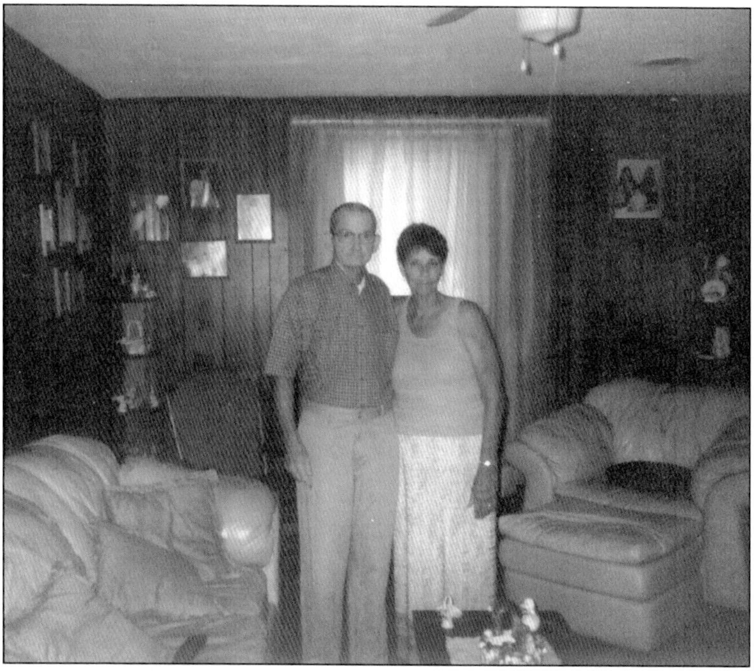

SERVING OUR COUNTRY, 1990S. Bob and Barbara Langley are part of a military family. Bob and his two brothers, Sonny and Billy Ray, retired from the military. Bob and Barbara have three grandchildren: S.Sgt. Scott Langley (marines), Cpl. Nikki Bryant Moore (army), and S.Sgt. Beth Bryant James (air force) are all currently on active duty.

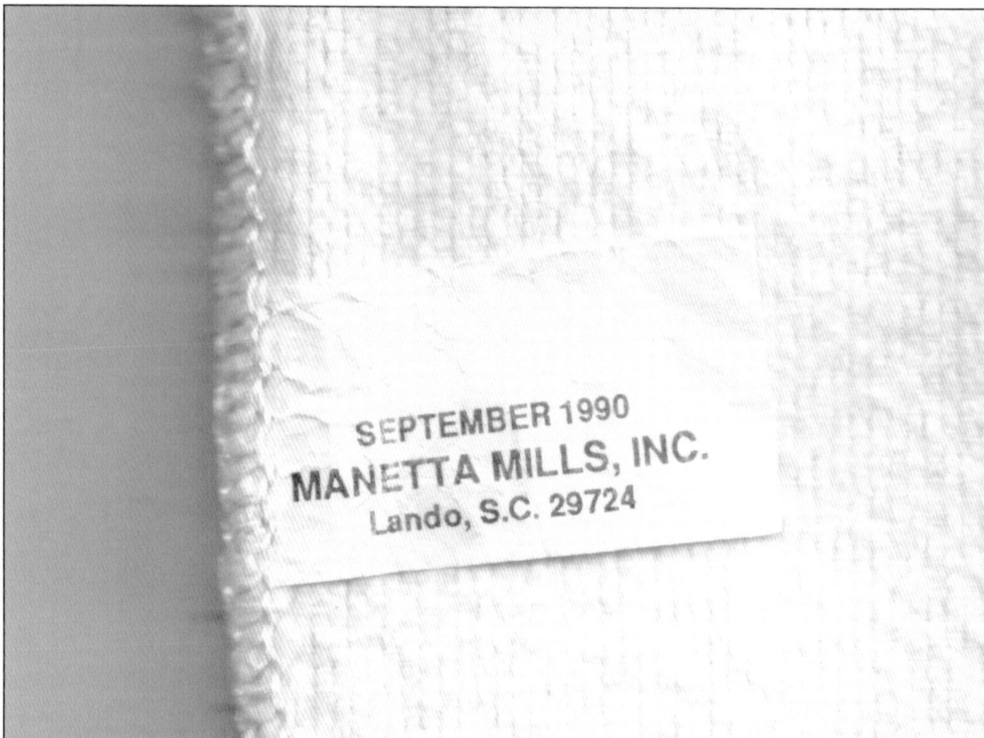

BABY BLANKET. Cindy Langley Jimenez, who was raised in Lando, moved to California with her husband. When Cindy gave birth to her first child in a California hospital, a nurse brought her baby wrapped in a blanket, and after kissing her newborn baby, Cindy noticed that the blanket had a label that read, "Manetta Mills, Lando, South Carolina."

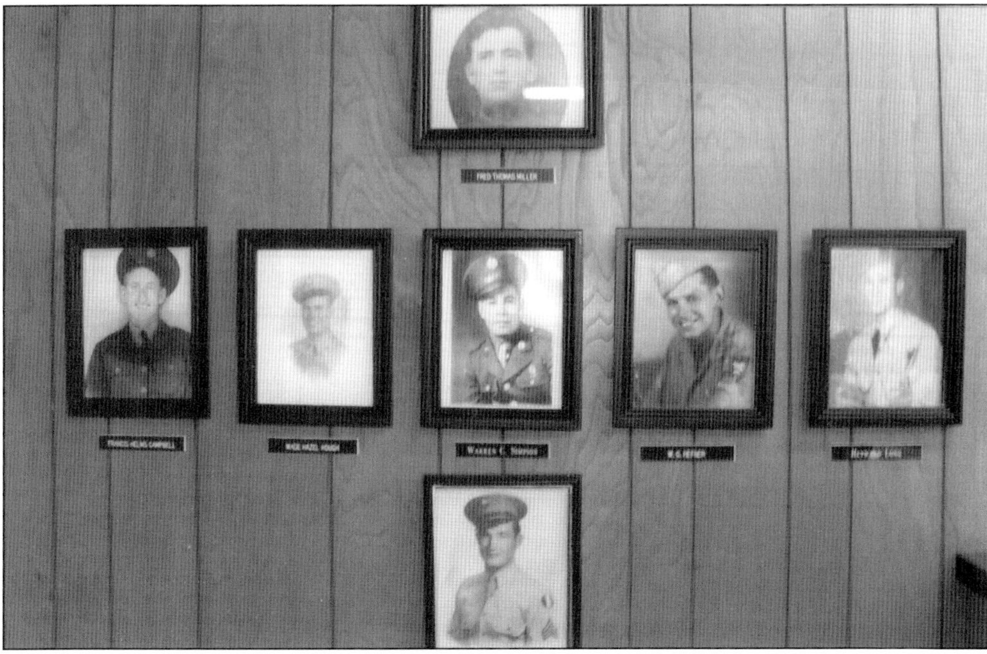

LANDO VETERANS MEMORIAL WALL, 2006. This wall contains pictures of the seven Lando men that were killed in battle: Fred Thomas Miller, World War I; Francis Helms Campbell, World War II; Wade Hazel Hough, World War II; Warren C. Simpson, World War II; William C. Hefner, World War II; Heyward Long, World War II; and Henry Nunnery, Korea.

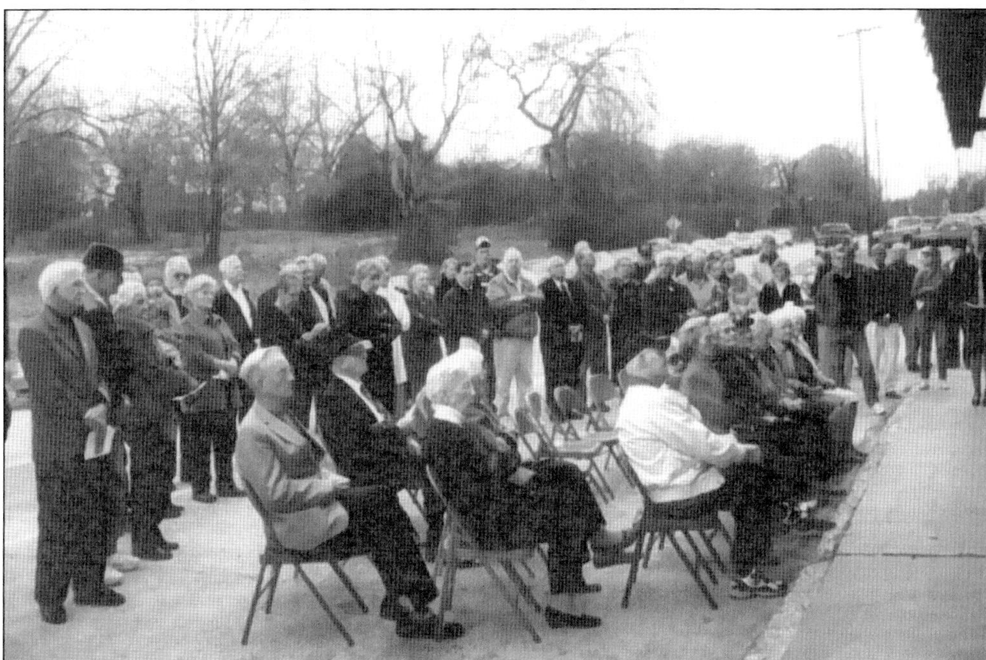

COMMUNITY TIES. On December 3, 2006, over 110 people attended a dedication ceremony for the seven Lando men who were killed in combat. There is still a strong tie to Lando for many people.

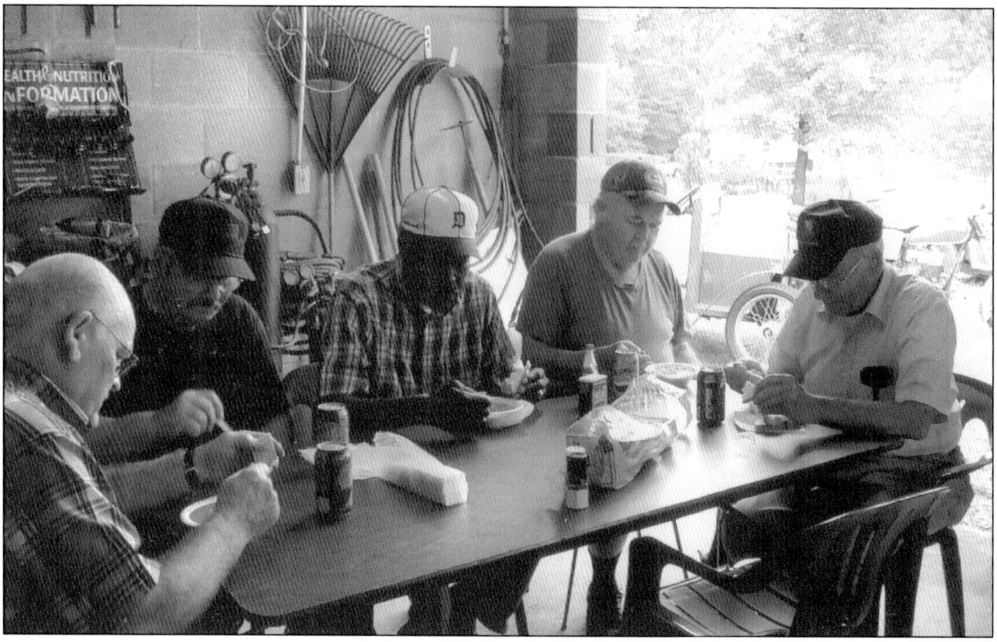

MAKING THE DREAM COME TRUE. Pictured from left to right, Charles Black, Crawford Whitaker, Arthur Stewart, Chubby Long, and Harold Tadlock take a dinner break from preparing for a community event in 2005. People such as these gentlemen continue to give back to the community of Lando with their time, talents, and stories.

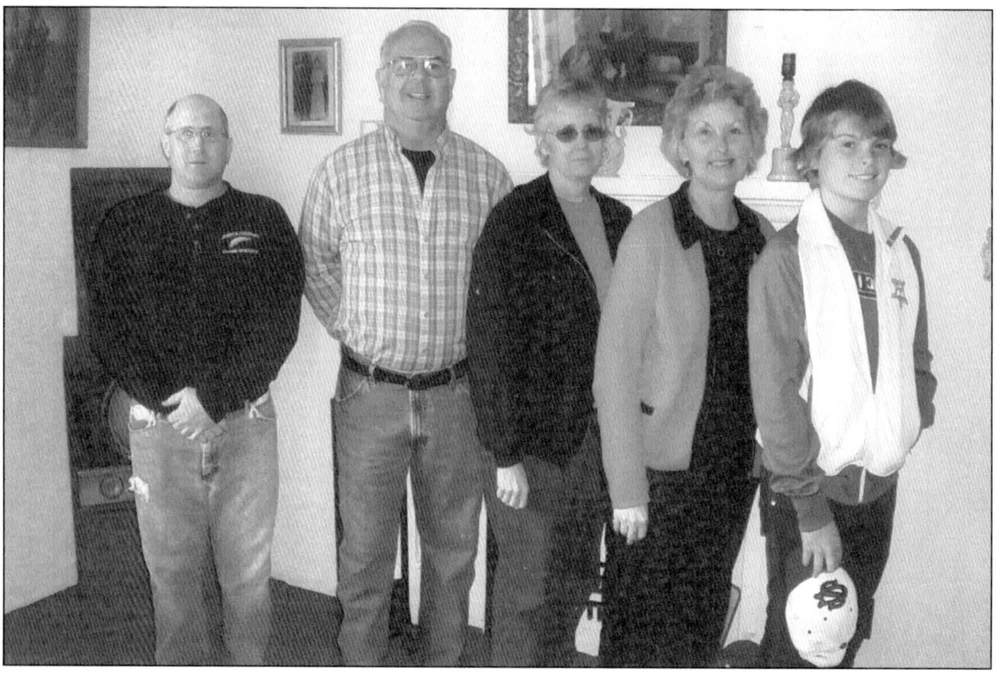

BOARD MEMBERS, 2007. Seen here from left to right, Bruce Coggins, Joe Polk, Roxann Yarborough James, Susan Murphy, and Brandon Polk are the current officers and board members of the Lando–Manetta Mills History Center. Together with a group of advisers, they continue to work on preserving the history of Lando and Manetta Mills.

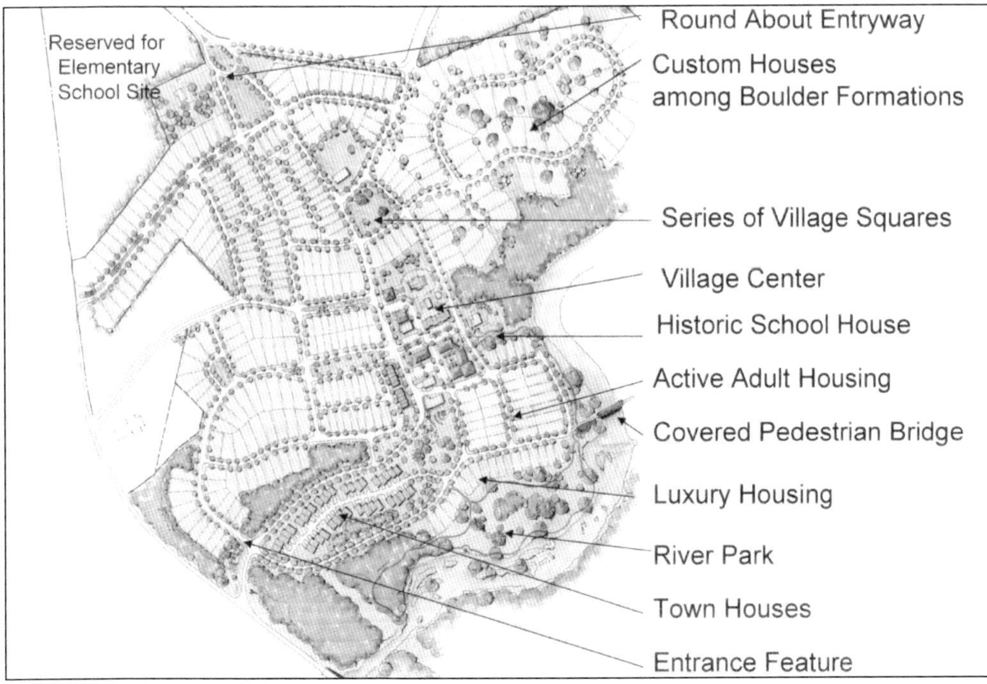

LANDO VILLAGE. In April 2006, Lando Properties, LLC, and a group of developers unveiled preliminary plans for Lando Village. The Lando schoolhouse and Manetta Mills company store will be remodeled, and walking trails will tell the history of Lando.

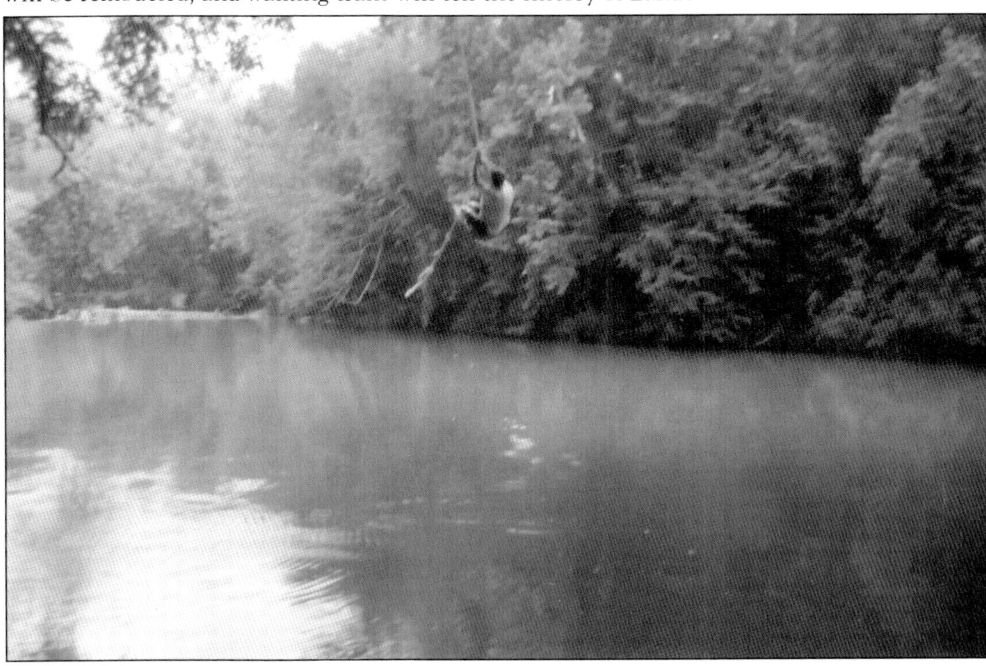

TAKING THE PLUNGE. It takes great courage to join a revolution. The Heath family, Joe and Gayle Lanford, Lando Properties, and the Lando–Manetta Mills History Center have done what it takes to make a dream a reality. A Lando resident enjoys the rope swing at the swimming hole on the millpond above the dam in Lando in 2006.